TO THE LIMITS OF ENDURANCE

First published in 2007 by
Liberties Press
Guinness Enterprise Centre | Taylor's Lane | Dublin 8 | Ireland
www.LibertiesPress.com
General and sales enquiries: +353 (1) 415 1224 | peter@libertiespress.com
Editorial: +353 (1) 415 1287 | sean@libertiespress.com

Trade enquiries to CMD Distribution
55A Spruce Avenue | Stillorgan Industrial Park | Blackrock | County Dublin
Tel: +353 (1) 294 2560 | Fax: +353 (1) 294 2564

Distributed in the United States by
Dufour Editions
PO Box 7 | Chester Springs | Pennsylvania | 19425

and in Australia by
James Bennett Pty Limited | InBooks
3 Narabang Way | Belrose NSW 2085

Liberties Press is a member of Clé,
the Irish Book Publishers' Association.

ISBN: 978–1–905483–27–3

2 4 6 8 10 9 7 5 3 1

A CIP record for this title is available from the British Library.

Set in Garamond
Printed in Ireland by Colour Books
Unit 105 | Baldoyle Industrial Estate | Dublin 13

TO THE LIMITS OF ENDURANCE

ONE IRISHMAN'S WAR

JACK HARTE

AND SANDRA MARA

To fallen friends and comrades, in all the Services.
Their bravery and sacrifices have not been in vain.
Lest we ever forget.

CONTENTS

ACKNOWLEDGEMENTS   7

1	TAKING THE KING'S SHILLING: DUBLIN, 1937	9
2	MY FIRST POSTING AND I ALMOST DIED!	15
3	STRADA STREET AND THE TWO-BOB TARTS	19
4	THE MOVE TO PALESTINE: SCIMITARS AND STRANGERS IN THE NIGHT	23
5	THE SIEGE OF MALTA	38
6	HIGH JINKS AT THE PALACE	43
7	MALTESE TAKEAWAY: FARSON'S BREWERY BANDITS	46
8	DOGFIGHTS AND BAR-ROOM BRAWLS	50
9	BOXING CLEVER	57
10	FLORENCE NIGHTINGALE IS A MAN!	64
11	'GET OUT OF JAIL' CARD	70
12	THE TIPTOE BOYS: THE SAS AND THE SBS	77
13	FROM THE MIDDLE EAST TO GREECE	97
14	DESTINATION LEROS	102
15	STOLEN DRINK, DRUGS AND MORE BOOZE: THE PADRE TURNS A BLIND EYE	106
16	THE BATTLE FOR LEROS	111
17	BRAVERY BEYOND BELIEF	114
18	THE GERMANS ARE COMING!	121
19	BRAVE DESERTERS AND DECENT MEN	124
20	FRIENDLY FIRE AND LOUSY LEADERS COST US LIVES AND LIBERTY	131

21	DYING FOR A DRINK	138
22	THE FINAL PUSH	144
23	TAKING THE CASTLE: THE STENCH OF DEATH AND DESTRUCTION	155
24	ON THE HIGH SEAS AGAIN – CATTLE CLASS	160
25	THE MARCH TO ATHENS	164
26	THE GREAT DRACHMA HEIST	167
27	COFFIN TRAINS, AS PRISONERS HIT A NEW LOW	173
28	RANDY GUARDS, STOLEN SALAMI AND THREATS OF A FIRING SQUAD	177
29	POW NO. 141686: THE MOVE TO STALAG XIA	186
30	ALL CHIEFS AND NO INDIANS	195
31	STARVATION MAKES S—TS OF US ALL	200
32	THE RUSSIAN CHOCOLATE CON	206
33	DOG DAYS	210
34	KITLESS AND WITLESS	214
35	NO ESCAPE FROM STALAG 357	217
36	FREE AT LAST, AND I CAN'T REMEMBER A THING!	227
37	THE BOYS ARE BACK IN TOWN	232
38	ORDERS FROM THE CAPTAIN	236
39	THE GREAT ESCAPE	239
40	WEDDING BELLS AND ARMY BRIDES	242
41	END GAME: A NEW BEGINNING	245

Acknowledgements

Jack (Johnny) Harte is a remarkable man with an incredible recall of events, despite his eighty-seven years. The events of those harrowing times as recalled in this book are indelibly etched in his memory. I owe a debt of gratitude for the assistance of the Imperial War Museum, to the archivist George Malcolmson at the Royal Navy Museum, who has shown tremendous interest in the story, and to the Wartime Memories Project, who kindly allowed us to use photographs from the collection of Windsor Williams, submitted by his son Peter, of Stalag 7A in Mooseburg, one of the POW camps in which Jack spent time.

A special word of thanks to Johnny's old comrades and veterans of Palestine and World War Two, such as Walter Pancott, Gordon Wright, Victor Kenchington, Ted Johnson and Ray Williams, and not forgetting the families of many old pals: Andy Roy and Wee Davy Thompson, along with the lads from *Trooper*, such as Pete Adam, Len Williams and David Grant, half-brother of Lieutenant LAS Grant and author of the book *HMS Trooper*, and of course its captain, Lieutenant Johnny Wraith DSO DSC, whose son Richard followed in his footsteps, and was himself Captain Richard Wraith CBE – Royal Navy.

It goes without saying that none of this would have been possible but for the wonderful support of the team at Liberties Press. To Seán, Peter, Orlaith and Aine, our grateful thanks – it has been a pleasure working with you – and to Audrey Kernaghan-Boran and Dolores Harte, who typed up notes of Johnny's early memories, when the idea of a book was just a twinkle in his eye.

Finally, to our families: to Johnny's wife Myra and their wonderful family, and to my long-suffering husband John, and my family – a million thanks for your patience during the long hours spent in the 'garret', burning the midnight oil.

For my part, the story became compulsive. It is hard not to compare the resilience, courage and fortitude of men such as Johnny – men who, despite their tender years, were tested to the very limits of human endurance, and came through with flying colours – to the men of today. Johnny has never been found wanting: it is a pleasure and a privilege to know him.

Sandra Mara, Dublin, August 2007

I would like to acknowledge Raymond Williams and Ted Johnston for giving permission for me to use material from their books on their wartime experiences.

Jack Harte, Dublin, October 2007

1

TAKING THE KING'S SHILLING

DUBLIN, 1937

As a young lad growing up in Dublin, there was little to occupy mischievous young scoundrels like me. Always on the lookout for something challenging to do, I was never out of trouble with my 'Ma'. Being part of the 'gang' was really important, as it is when you're a kid, but my poor mother was convinced the gang were leading her darling son astray. She wasn't far wrong. She rounded up the rest of her brood – there were eleven of us in all – and between the concerted efforts of my siblings and the rubbing of religious relics and holy water on me, I was steered well away from the bad influence of my erstwhile mates. My brother Tom, home on leave from the British army, put the final touches to my redemption. He took me and my brother Archie to the pictures, and as we feasted on ice cream he made it quite clear that, if either of us got into any more trouble, he'd take special leave from the army, come home, and beat the lard out of us. Tom was not a man to say things lightly, and that conversation with him terrified me. It would have left St Paul's Conversion on the road to Damascus in the shade, such was the immediate impact it had on me. I was more terrified of my big brother than of any member of the 'gang', so I gravely gave him my solemn word, and set about mending my ways. The trip to the pictures had been a velvet glove with an iron fist inside. I knew better than to push my luck with him again. Next time, if there *was* a next time, he wouldn't be so easy on me.

It was 1937, and with little to do in a bleak and dreary Dublin, I was still hungry for adventure. In the strangest of circumstances, while

9

playing football, I heard a few of the lads secretly planning to jump aboard a cattle boat to England, to join the British army. With no money around to pay the passage in those days, and little work to be had, that was the only way out, if they were really serious about going. It sounded like just what I wanted: excitement and adventure. All the stories my Da had told us about his time in the First World War, and seeing my brother Tom's picture, in full uniform, a Sudanese native standing beside him, seemed glamorous and exciting. I knew then that this was exactly what I wanted to do.

When I confided my plans to join the army to my pals Bill Kavanagh and John 'Spike' McCormack, they let me in on their secret: they had already decided to join up. To keep on the right side of the Da, I spoke to him about it – leaving out the bit about my plan to sneak on board ship. I was just sixteen, and I knew there was no way he'd agree to it. Telling me I was much too young, he tried to put me off, promising to help me join up later on, when I was older.

As a gesture of goodwill to prove he was serious, he took me to see a retired Colonel to talk about my plans. The Colonel and my father discussed the matter, and both agreed: I was too young, and that was the end of it. The Colonel chatted to my father about the old days, with no further discussion about me. I was becoming increasingly frustrated, and kept trying to interrupt, to tell them I wanted to sign up, and I wanted to do it *now*, not when I was older.

It was to no avail: I may as well not have been there. The Colonel was of an era when children, as he considered me to be, should be seen and not heard, and he completely ignored me. The meeting was brought to an abrupt end when guests arrived, and the Colonel quickly took his leave of us. With a parting shot, patting me on the head, he told me I had the makings of a good soldier, and said I should join up when I was an appropriate age.

I was absolutely livid. They had discussed my future without even giving me a chance to tell them what I wanted. I'd wanted to speak to the Colonel directly, but instead, I'd been treated like a kid who had no say in the matter. That settled it: I wasn't going to be palmed off that easily, and was more determined then ever. I'd make my own decisions about what I wanted to do with my life, but next time I'd keep my plans to myself.

Meanwhile, I heard that a couple of the older lads, Alfie Brown and Georgie Corrigan, had already joined up, quickly followed by my friends Bill Kavanagh, Davie Davis, 'Spike' McCormack, Billy Reynolds and Mida Clarke, who'd all jumped aboard a cattle boat, bound for Liverpool. Trailing behind them, I was prevented from making my getaway by a ship's hand, who'd realised what I was up to.

There was nothing for it but to return home. Dublin being a small place then, my father soon got to hear about my attempted escape and made sure he kept a close eye on me from then on. On one occasion, not long after that incident, while skylarking with a pal, Charlie Brown, I fell fully clothed into the canal at Broombridge in Dublin. My brother Archie cycled home to get some dry clothes, but my parents, thinking it was just another ploy to get some extra 'clobber', were convinced I was planning to run away again and refused to believe I'd fallen into the canal. Still unconvinced, Da raced down to the canal with a set of dry clothes. He was relieved to see the truth of the matter, and the bond between us was again restored – at least for a while.

Two months later, I made good my escape and sailed away on the *Leinster*, bound for Liverpool, to join up. After a twelve-hour journey, I arrived in Liverpool with not a penny in my pocket, and made my way from Lime Street Station to the army-recruiting office at Seymour Street, on the London Road. Giving a false date of birth, I finally succeeded in my goal, and enlisted in the Corps of the Royal Irish/Royal Enniskillen Fusiliers.

My delight in having managed to get this far undetected was replaced with another emotion, when they told me I'd have to do a medical, and be seen by the doctor. If I didn't pass his examination, I couldn't join the army. I was worried sick. I couldn't begin to think what I'd do then. The thought of not getting in and having to face my father, after running away, didn't bear thinking about. Not being in the habit of visiting doctors, I didn't know what to expect. I was sure he would suspect my real age and send me home. So it was with a heavy heart that I presented myself for the medical. When the doctor declared me to be 'as sound as a bell' for the eighteen-year-old I'd claimed to be, I could have shouted for joy. It took everything I had to keep a straight face and reserve my jubilation for later.

Before I left Dublin, I'd heard a few of the lads speak in glowing terms of 'Blighty', saying it was a land of milk and honey. Given that they hadn't been there long enough to even glimpse Big Ben, and yet could come home with English accents after only a couple of weeks away, I wrote their bragging off as a load of oul' codswallop. If it was that good, why were they back? It was only when I got my first day's allowance from the Recruiting Sergeant that I began to believe there might be some truth in their stories, as I counted and re-counted my first real pay: the princely sum of three shillings. Before this, I'd only earned a few pence as a messenger boy for a Dublin chemist; now I was as rich as Croesus.

I soon met up with a fellow Dubliner, Johnnie Satell, who'd arrived in Liverpool for the same purpose, and we joined forces in search of ways to spend our fortune. We weren't too flash, though. Reluctant to part with our newfound wealth too quickly, we stopped for a free feed at the nearby 'Sally's Army', where the only price to be paid was the singing of a few hymns. We reckoned that the bulk of our fortune would have to be spent on food, and a bed, for however long it took to get our posting to our training camp.

We wanted to find a way to cut down on this 'luxury', and came up with what we thought was a great idea. After the hot food and good cheer in the Sally Army kitchen, we decided to give them all our custom, and returned their goodwill with our enthusiastic renditions of a range of hymns, despite the fact that we'd never heard of them before. Meanwhile, we found other ways to spend our money. Had I held on to my few bob over the next ten days while I waited to be posted, I could have had a suit made to measure at the local thirty-shilling tailors – a luxury I could never have dreamt of before I'd left Dublin (but then, I was only sixteen). Satell and I were posted to different units, he to the Irish Guards and I to the Faugh A Ballaghs, the 87th/89th (The Princess Victoria's) Regiment of Foot, the Royal Irish Fusiliers Faugh-A-Ballaghs, operating out of the same barracks as our 1st Battalion, at Bordon, Hampshire.

I'd made it to the Depot without conditions attached, but some less fortunate recruits, healthy enough but underweight, were sent to the 'muscle factory' in Aldershot before going on to the Depot.

Thanks to the regular meals of bangers, mash and beans dished out by the Sally Army, together with the other goodies my three shillings bought, my weight increased by a few pounds while I was waiting for the posting. I now weighed nine stone four pounds, and was deemed AOK to begin Depot training.

At last I was finally on the road, to what I felt sure would be a life of adventure. Little did I know then what awaited me within a few short years. It was the start of a career that would be rich in comradeship, tough when it came to training, strong on discipline and, in the beginning, boisterously intimidating.

After six weeks' training, the Regimental Sergeant Major (RSM), Sergeant Major, Drill Sergeant and Junior NCO in charge were happy that, finally, we could do justice to the regimental badge. Our training over, we passed out. We were rich, on a whole two bob a day, which was supposed to buy boot polish, Brasso to clean our belt buckles and buttons, shaving gear, a chamois and, if the money stretched that far, maybe even some bangers and mash. The few hours' leave we got was spent on the town doing just that, my only 'treat' being the bangers and mash. I could only barely afford even that, as I had made an allotment of five shillings a week from my pay to go to my mother, or 'Maasie', as I referred to her in affectionate Dublin slang.

We soon found other ways to pass the time that didn't call for money – or at least not much of it. We had the gym, games of cards and, of course, the NAAFI – the Navy, Army and Air Force Institute which sold food, cigarettes and other essentials, as well as providing entertainment – all of which kept us fairly well occupied, before we were sent to Guadeloupe Barracks, at Bordon, for training. Depot training, and the discipline that went with it, was a whole new way of life for me.

There were many times when I found it very hard to hold my tongue and just carry out orders. Following one such incident, I was rewarded with ninety-six hours' detention, for 'making an improper and insulting remark' to my Company Officer. I was a young, strong-minded teenager: I had my own ideas. Luckily for me, I was under the watchful eye of a couple of the older recruits, who kept me in line. On arrival at Bordon, we were marched to a halt, and ordered to stand to attention before the RSM. As he walked around our disorganised bunch, he roared at us to stand to attention when he addressed us, and gave a demonstration as to just how it should be done. As he approached one recruit, Paddy Scannell, he was taken aback as Paddy jumped smartly to attention. The eagle-eyed RSM sharply questioned the so-called 'raw recruit' as to where he had learned his slick drill movements. Paddy, holding back, only admitted to having been in the Boy Scouts. The canny RSM gave a knowing grin, obviously not believing a word of it. Paddy later told us he'd been well trained in drill movements in the Tá Sé's, an Irish-speaking Battalion in the Free State army in Ireland.

Between the almost middle-aged 'Pop' Duncan, who'd also neglected to mention a previous stint in the British army, Paddy Scannell, and the Recruiting Officer, I was well 'minded'. They never let this hot-headed sixteen-year-old lose the run of himself. Whenever I was about to lose my temper, they'd whisper 'whist' in my ear and I knew to go no further – if I wanted to leave the Depot with a clean sheet. In later years, Major Bill Sheppard gave me a reference which included the observation: 'As a young soldier, Corporal John Harte was many times in difficulty with military discipline but later developed into being a very good leader.'

After Borden, in February 1938 I joined the 1st Battalion of the Faughs. The Commanding Officer of the 2nd Battalion, a west Cork man, Colonel 'The O'Donovan', or Red Ned, as he was affectionately known to his squaddies, told us we were being posted abroad, to augment the recently formed 2nd Battalion of the Faughs. All fired up after The O'Donovan's spirited briefing on the importance of our new posting, Malta, its place in the British Empire, and its strategic value, we were eager to get on with the job. Little did I know then that it would be eight long years before I again set foot on Irish soil.

14

2

MY FIRST POSTING AND I ALMOST DIED!

In the middle of March 1938, five months after joining up, with the corners knocked off me, my first posting came through. I was en route to Malta. Full of enthusiasm, never having travelled before, I picked up my kit bags, put on my webbing and side haversack and made a beeline for the army lorries, bound for Southampton, where a troopship was waiting to take us to the strategically important island of Malta, in the central Mediterranean.

All fired up, I couldn't wait to board ship. I was hungry to get a taste of real soldiering abroad. By the time the troopship *Dorsetshire* came into view, I was straining at the leash. In full pack, we made our way up the swaying gangplank, and were led below deck, where a leading seaman showed us how to hang our hammock the right way. A few of the lads didn't bother to watch. This led to much amusement and frustration when they tried to bunk down for the night as, one after the other, they went arse over tip. When the leading seaman returned – rather the worse for wear – he gave them another demonstration, not to mention a large piece of his mind.

The journey out was taken up with various duties, PT, which involved all the usual physical training, life boat drills – in the event of an emergency – and the occasional game of quoits, or a boxing match. Some spent their leisure time playing 'Housey-Housey' or 'Crown and Anchor' with the sailors: their skill and deception would shame a three-card trickster. I tried it once, and it was a case of once bitten, twice shy.

Because of my then-limited knowledge of geography, I didn't recognise the coastlines we passed. En route to Malta, we eventually dropped anchor at Gibraltar for a couple of hours, to allow a battalion of Royal Artillery to disembark. Had this not happened, even the great Rock would have escaped me. Eight days after leaving Southampton, we sailed into Malta's Grand Harbour, dropping anchor alongside a flotilla of British warships, including the battleship *Hood*. I was fascinated to watch the dozens of small boats as they rowed feverishly, all wanting to be the first to reach the newly docked ship. Some were already tied up alongside certain ships, ready to take sailors ashore; others were flogging their wares, from beautiful Maltese lace to ornaments and shirts. Once a sale had been agreed, the item would be hoisted aboard a wicker basket on a rope, with the barter or cash making the return journey.

Once we had disembarked, we had to join up with the 2nd Battalion of the Royal Irish Fusiliers. But first we had to battle our way through the numerous hawkers and dealers, all hell-bent on selling us bric-a-brac from their *dghaisa*s (small, gondola-like boats). We were met by a six foot four hulk of sheer intimidation, in the shape of Sergeant Sam Hatterly, whose thunderous command of 'Quick March' set us off on a six-mile hike to Imtarfa Barracks. We were 'assisted' in keeping up the pace by a few burly Corporals policing the ranks.

After we had settled in and and been given the once-over from the RSM, Bill Sheppard, he welcomed us to the 2nd Battalion. As luck would have it, I was delighted to find that my mates from Depot training, Johnnie King, 'Hookie' Doran, Jimmy Loughlin, Young Pollock, Paddy Scannell and Danny Byrne, were assigned to B Company, a Vickers machine-gun company, commanded by Lieutenant 'Slasher' Doyle. We were issued with our tropical gear of khaki drill shorts, shirts, steel tobies (helmets) and puttees, as well as a holdall with the usual cutlery, a razor and a comb, together with toothbrushes and a buttonstick, used to clean dirt from our buttons and belt and brush, and these came with a lecture, and a severe warning of the perils of not keeping everything in pristine condition, ready for inspection at all times. One other piece of kit was the 'housewife', a small cloth pouch which held cotton wool, buttons and a needle. Much to our surprise, this too was the subject of lightning inspections.

Threats of a visit to the 'glasshouse' at Corredino Detention Centre if we lost any of our kit were heeded by most. But there are always one or two people who are ready and willing to take a risk. We were issued with three blankets, and it was possible to flog two and fold the remaining one in such as way as to deceive the officers who carried out the kit inspections. The one blanket was given three folds, and neatly stuffed with soft paper, and three labels were then sewn on to it. It was amazing how they got away with it for such a long time.

Each infantry regiment took turns at guarding the Governor's Palace. Stationed directly outside the guardroom through twelve hours of searing sunshine, we were exposed to the public gaze as they watched us march up and down with monotonous regularity. We wondered whether this was mainly designed to impress the public rather than to be part of the Defence of the Realm. During my time in Malta, both in peacetime and during the Siege, we carried out guard duties at the Palace for three different Governors: Sir William Bonham Carter, Lieutenant General Sir William Dobbie, and Field Marshall Gort.

Only Dobbie and his wife invited us in for tea and a chat. Their conversation on these occasions went from small talk to advice not to get involved with the local girls. Marriage was a serious business, they warned, and we should be careful not to build up the hopes of the local Maltese girls, as we had a duty to their families in the event of war breaking out. They reminded us that we could be posted abroad, injured, or even killed, leaving a young bride behind. The fact remained, however, that we knew a sizeable number of military personnel who had tied the knot with local girls over the years, and it seemed to be working out well for them, so we weren't put off by the advice. It didn't really apply to me anyway: I was only barely seventeen, and had no intention of getting married for a very long time – or at least that was my plan then.

It was the lull before the storm, as we soaked up the sun. Not least the battles ahead, but for me, I almost met my Waterloo before I ever had a chance to see any action. I was a strong, fit lad and a good swimmer, so to cool down from the hot sun, I went for a long-distance swim with my pal Chesty Hannon. About eight hundred yards from the beach, I suffered a severe cramp in my upper leg and couldn't make it back to the shore unaided. I called out to Chesty, who was an exceptionally powerful swimmer. He lost no time in getting to me, turning me over on my back and dragging me towards the beach. Encouraging me to kick out with my good leg, he talked to me all the way, telling me what great progress we were making. I was completely mortified at being so helpless. About two hundred yards out, the pain eased, and I managed to make it the rest of the way under my own steam. Chesty dismissed my grateful thanks with a wave of his hand. Not bothering to dry off, we collapsed on the beach and got drunk on Farson's Blue Label and Imbid (also known as Ambeet, the local wine) to celebrate my near-miss. (Later, when was broke out, Imbid became known as 'Stuka juice', after the German fighter planes.)

Exhausted and pissed, we fell asleep and missed a very important training session. When we eventually came to, and returned to camp, we were put on a charge of Conduct Prejudicial to Good Order and Military Discipline. We explained my near-death experience to our Company Commander, Slasher Doyle, who benignly accepted our explanation, and the 'nervous exhaustion' that followed, and let us off with seven days' forfeiture of pay and a severe reprimand.

3

STRADA STREET AND THE TWO-BOB TARTS

Our posting to Malta was not without difficulties. The hot sun shines there for around ten months a year, with temperatures often reaching the nineties. This made marching in full kit particularly difficult. By the time we were ready to leave for Palestine, we had acclimatised to the heat and, with little effort, the squad had acquired a healthy tan.

In this pre-war period, discipline and training were tough, but organised so as to allow time for sporting activities. Inter-regimental company, inter-service and even civilian clubs provided plenty of activity. We had hockey, boxing, soccer and tug of war, as well as swimming and diving competitions, held at St George's bay.

Malta is littered with history, but the closest I came to 'culture' in my first six-month posting was a visit to Vernon's Club in Valletta, where I had tea and a game of tombola. Eventually, I graduated to the sleazy bars and cafés of downtown Strada Street, known as 'The Gut', where the worst vices were catered for. The area was full of sailors, air-men, soldiers and pimps, the ladies of easy virtue abounded, and cultural activities were very low on the agenda. Vernon's, a respectable club frequented by clean-living women who'd have made 'respectable' girlfriends, was soon given the cold shoulder as I graduated to more exciting activities.

Being a young, virile lad, and as I thought then, a mature seventeen-year-old, away from home for the first time, the sun, sand and sports came a poor second, to the diversions that were on offer. The promise of going on a taxi tour, accompanied in the back seat by a young lady who was anxious and willing to display her talents, all for two shillings, was too much for an innocent teenager to refuse. Try as you might to avoid it, you were constantly met with the catcall 'Upstairs Irish, your friend upstairs' until you eventually yielded to temptation. Once inside the premises, no business was done before you bought the 'young lady' a few sherries (or at least that's what she called them: they were more likely coloured water), for which you paid dearly. Often too pissed to actually get upstairs, and with the 'two-bob tart' sober as a judge, the lady got her commission on the drink sale *and* her fee, for services unrendered, before leaving you to your own devices.

I'd been courting a young lady for a short while, convinced that I'd met the love of my life. We usually parted company in the town, and she'd walk the short distance home, while I went back to barracks to make the curfew. On one occasion, having spent more than my week's pay on her, I walked her to her door for the first time. As we arrived, a man's voice shouted from upstairs: 'Is that you, love?' I thought, here goes, time to meet her father. Before I could say anything, she got very agitated and urged me to leave quickly, before the man came down. When the realisation that the man was her husband, not her father, hit home, I was stunned. I couldn't get out of there fast enough. Angry, hurt and despondent, I did something stupid, in an effort to relieve my anger and humiliation. I went to a tattoo artist and had 'Mother' tattooed on my arm. It was the first, and last, tattoo I ever had, but the lesson I learned – not to act in haste or anger – remained with me forever.

Before long, even a young teenager like myself grew tired of the attractions of 'The Gut'. Allowing my better taste to come to the fore, I got to know and enjoy the genuine warmth and friendliness of the easy-going Maltese people. Soon afterwards, accompanied by a beautiful young lass, I was fortunate enough to get a guided tour of the island's craggy coastline, including its megalithic temple. Now determined to see the best of Malta, I spent my leisure time wandering the streets, taking in the Maltese way of life. Thursday was always a free day for us in those pre-war days, and I'd head downtown in the hot sun to watch the world go by.

Being a non-smoker with a sweet tooth, I was attracted to the local fruit vendor. Stationed just outside the dining room, he had a novel sales pitch, offering fruit on the 'slate'. When you'd finished your meal, he collected your leftovers and divided them into two separate pails. Returning your empty plate, he'd flog you some fruit, writing your name and regimental number into his notebook as he delivered a selection of figs, grapes and melons.

Overindulging myself on the figs and other fruits brought about two problems for me. As well as having incurred a debt to the fruit vendor that exceeded my weekly army pay, the purgative effect of his fruit meant that I missed out on my first entitlement to a forty-eight-hour pass. With time on my hands between visits to the bog, I found myself rambling towards the boundary of Imtarfa Barracks. Off duty, I decided to take a chance, walking a bit further, still within sprinting distance of the nearest toilet, when I noticed people gathered around a horse-drawn lorry. Making my way towards it, I realised that the fruit vendor was still touting for business, only this time with a different clientele. In return for a penny or two, he'd dip into one of his pails and scoop a handful of the contents onto a piece of greaseproof paper, before handing it over to a delighted recipient, who'd make a quick exit. The question as to why the dining room leftovers were separated was finally answered. The fruit vendor was commandeering them and dividing them up to sell, some for human consumption, the rest as pigswill. Seeing this, while admiring his enterprise, I could only conclude that Malta in 1938 was not far removed from the poverty of Ireland.

I had wised up to the Mecca of Malta and in particular 'The Gut', and gave up the dubious pleasures of Strada Street, concentrating instead on my first love: boxing. I was spotted as being 'handy' by Corporal George Mullett, and he entered me for an inter-company competition. Boxing at welterweight, I won my first four competitions. Sergeant Darkie Finch, Sam Hatterly and Drum Major Tommy Dooley, all members of the regimental team, arranged for me to train with them. Gigs Dineen from Cork and Slabs McKinney from Derry, both seasoned boxers, were the leading welterweights, being winner and runner-up, respectively, in the regimental boxing team. I managed to join up with either Gigs or Slabs in all the inter-regimental tournaments. Even though I was just a kid, and still growing, I did very well, and I soon developed into a middleweight. I had only one outing at this weight before news came that our stay in Malta would be short-lived. I was to be sent to Palestine, where the Arab insurrection was gaining pace. It was to be a considerable time before I could afford the luxury of spending time boxing, or get back to serious training.

By now the military hierarchy, uneasy about events unfolding in Europe, were stepping up the pace of our preparations. Intensive training projects were mounted, and we trained and re-trained in the use of the Vickers and Lewis guns. On most exercises, done in full battle order, respirators were used: we could only assume that the British commanders were still uncertain as to Mussolini's intentions, with regard to Malta, as the Italian dictator had used gas in the conquest of Abyssinia in 1935–36.

Some of our personnel were sent to Ghain Tuffieha camp and were trained to man eighteen-pounder beach guns. Courses in anti-gas and de-contamination duties were intensified, weapons training stepped up, and Lewis magazines and Vickers machine gun belts were filled. Throughout the night, emergency stores were drawn, and black-outs were arranged on the island. Great emphasis was placed on training in the rapid occupation of defensive positions, followed by night withdrawals. After a conference of all commanding officers, presided over by the Governor and Commander in Chief, Lieutenant General Charles Bonham-Carter, we received orders to pack up all our kit and prepare for the immediate manning of Malta's defences.

4

THE MOVE TO PALESTINE

SCIMITARS AND STRANGERS IN THE NIGHT

On 27 September 1938, British prime minister Neville Chamberlain and other international leaders met with Hitler and Mussolini in Munich, and signed an agreement which, Chamberlain claimed, secured peace with honour. The following day, the Nazi jackboot stamped itself all over Czechoslovakia. Mussolini was said to have ambitions to bring Malta – the gateway to both the east and the west – under his control. Like many others, I believed that Britain's top brass did not attach any great importance to Malta, but the British commander there pulled out all the stops to bring the island's defences up to scratch.

At the end of September 1938, we were ordered to leave Imtarfa Barracks and take up temporary residence under canvas on the beautiful beach at Mellehia. We were sent out to firing ranges which could only be accessed by crawling over rough terrain, along goat tracks, carrying full kit, rifle and respirator. Exhausted, we collapsed into the prone position, ready to work on our markmanship, under the beady eye of Corporal George Mullett and Sergeant Clegg. Mullett's mantra was 'DRINK': Designation, Range, Indication of target, Number of rounds and Kind of fire. Slowly squeezing the trigger, you hoped like hell that you hit enough targets to keep Sergeant Clegg's vitriol at bay.

Our orders were to leave for Palestine. On 10 October, all packed up and ready to go, we marched to the dockyard and boarded the troopship *Nueralia*, alongside the Green Howards, to the sound of pipes and drums. After four days at sea, we sailed into the Port of

Haifa. Disembarking the troopship, our B Company was marched to an isolated billet at Kyriat Haim, between Haifa and Acre. As far as I could see, our only purpose in Palestine was to put down the insurrection by the Palestinian Arabs. I knew nothing of the history or geography of the Middle East, or the reasons behind the rebellion, and it seemed that none of my fellow soldiers were any wiser. As a soldier, I didn't need to know: I just had to follow orders.

I soon became familiar with the terrain – the steep rocky areas, the hilly mountain goat tracks, the wadis, and the border regions close to Syria, Lebanon and Transjordan – that we had to patrol and secure. Our base was located in a bleak, isolated area, and it felt even more so when, in the dead of night, posted for guard duty, you found yourself alone, patrolling the ground that stood between the billets and the perimeter wall. The only other sentry was in a high tower, operating a searchlight that had seen better days. In the event of an incident, this 'high security' patrol, operated by two inexperienced kids, was instructed to raise the alarm with a high whistle, to alert the rest of the men.

Rumours abounded of the fate that awaited any man who was caught by the Arab insurgents. On those long, dark, lonely nights, you had plenty of time to consider your position if you were caught by the rebel forces. If the stories were true, a slit throat or castration – just two of the horrors we were warned about – would be a mercy. It mattered little to us that the scaremongers had not actually witnessed such atrocities. While patrolling alone in the almost-total blackness, you were grateful for even a sliver of moonlight to guide your way, as you tried to stay calm and keep your imagination at bay. Thoughts of the swirling robes of local insurgents, armed to the teeth with scimitars and daggers, all ready to slit my throat, never left me, but gradually I learned to 'fancy my chances' should I be set upon in the dark of night, and my fear receded as my courage grew.

Part of the sentry duty involved a changeover with the man in the tower. This was something of a sniper's dream: the temporary lights made us sitting ducks. Fortunately, we never fell victim to this particular opportunity. The only 'good' part of our stay at Kyriat Haim was when a local Jewish trader from a nearby settlement rode his bicycle, stocked with freshly baked cakes and other goodies, into the camp. I can still taste the wonderful treats, and the boost to morale they gave us. Back then, we had no thought as to just how he came and went unchecked, and we never even considered the security risk to ourselves or the trader.

Within a couple of days of arriving in Palestine, I was to get a real taste of adventure. Information came through that some Palestinian rebels were hiding out in a Bedouin settlement in our district. Our job was to pursue, engage and arrest them. We moved out under cover of darkness. Operating in single file, we tracked through a wadi at 2.30 AM. Those of us bringing up the rear were reminded of the fate awaiting those who were caught by the rebels. We moved forward in creepy silence, desperate to keep in touch with the man in front. Every touch of a thistle, or belch of a frog, made us jump. As we approached our target, we concentrated on the task in hand. On high alert, more apprehensive than afraid, we set about working our way through the settlement, searching every nook and cranny for our prey. Nothing incriminating was found: a let-off for the Bedouin living in the settlement.

We were, however, surprised to find two, three or even four lovely young women, sharing a tent with one usually much older man, who was obviously not their father. Our curiosity was sated when the Sergeant filled us in, and told us that such an arrangement was perfectly normal and legal there. Finding one of the young soldiers up close and personal with a young local girl, the Sergeant roared at the squaddie, asking him if he wanted to be 'bitten by a camel' – an army reference to catching venereal disease. The Sergeant's quick action, and the promise to mete out exacting discipline, was sufficient to encourage the young woman and the Arab male, whose 'woman' she was, to back off. I can only imagine the fate of the poor girl after we left: the dishonour of her position probably cost her her life. The culprit soldier got a hard time on the march back, but escaped being charged.

Disappointed not to have seen any action, we left the camp without sighting the suspects. The information given to us by the local CID – the Criminal Investigation Department – had been of little use. As we left the area, five Arab horsemen suddenly bolted in the opposite direction. We let off a volley of shots, to little effect as the horsemen made good their escape. It appeared that they'd been in the camp after all, but had secreted themselves until we packed up and left the area. When we got back to camp, we found out that our colleagues in C Company had come under attack just two hours after disembarking from their ship. They had managed to flush out the gunmen, who, in their haste to escape, had left one of their wounded behind. This encounter ruined our claim to fame: that we, the Company of the Faughs, had been the first to be deployed to pursue the insurrectionists.

This was all very different from Malta. There, we had been trained to be fit and ready to defend the island against Hitler, should he invade, and we had been lectured comprehensively by Major (Monocle) Allen as to the reasons why such action was necessary. In Palestine, by contrast, we had no understanding of the historical, religious or ethnic divides, and the 'fighting' was not what we had expected. We had to go into alleyways and hideouts, right into the heart of the enemy's stronghold: it was guerrilla warfare, something that was then in its infancy. It was a steep learning curve for us, with the language issue being an extra problem.

We had a stroke of luck, though, in that we were assigned a Commanding Officer who had some experience in this field. Lieutenant Colonel Carden Roe told us every aspect of what we could expect when we came into contact with the enemy, and stressed the need for constant alertness, concentration and endurance. Time and again, he demonstrated his concern for our safety and protection. Thinking like the enemy, rather than along the lines of our parade-ground training procedures, would be our only protection in this foreign territory, the Lieutenant Colonel told us.

Roe was also concerned for our safety in other matters, and spared us no blushes in getting our medical officer, Captain Keating, to tell us, in graphic detail, the horrors of catching various sexual diseases from the unregistered brothels in the area. But talk is cheap, and a number of randy soldiers decided to take the risk. There was another risk attached to venturing into these brothels: facing the wrath of the Red Caps, who regularly raided the brothels. Many a man, confronted by a drop of fifteen feet from a brothel balcony or an encounter with the Red Caps, and the ensuing charges, took the easy option and jumped. If they were lucky, they got away without a scratch. Sometimes they left the brothel with more than they'd bargained for: a broken ankle *and* VD.

A trip to the regimental doctor was the only sure way of easing their mind, or confirming the worst. Either way, the doc didn't let them off lightly. Those who were unlucky enough to have picked up more than they'd paid for, had salt rubbed into the wound: the loss of their proficiency pay. Well, they weren't exactly proficient after all, were they?

Just a few days into our posting at Kyriat Haim, law and order broke down in Acre. It all started with an armed robbery of the post office. Joined by C Company, we moved in to quell the disturbances, and were met with opposition from local rebels. In the ensuing exchange of fire, C Company shot three of the gunmen, who made their getaway with the help of their comrades. We were prevented from going in hot pursuit by a large group of belligerent Arabs, bent on helping the gunmen escape. A curfew was imposed on Acre, and we became even more aware of the need for caution. Within thirty-six hours, we were back in our billets.

By 5 AM the following morning, due to the extensive sabotage of the Acre–Safad road, the rest of the 2nd Faughs, backed up by Horse Artillery, and men from the 1st Hants, Royal Ulster Rifles and HMS *Douglas*, together with a field company of the Royal Engineers, put a cordon around the old city and rounded up all the male inhabitants. The discovery of ammunition, uniforms and seditious literature, along with sporadic raids by army units, was designed to unnerve them. According to police information, many of those who were rounded up were believed to be involved with or sympathetic to the rebels forces: they were put to work repairing the Acre–Safad road.

The battalion was never short of work, constantly being moved from one activity to another in an effort to quell the insurrection. Routine searches would often be abruptly halted to deal with a more important task or flare-up, to guard against sabotage on pipelines and the port of Haifa, or to check for illegal Jewish immigrants who were fleeing persecution in Germany and other European countries.

Palestine was a very dangerous, if exciting, place. I was very aware even then of the mindless hurt and destruction to the innocents who found themselves in the wrong place at the wrong time. The guerrillas' relentless mining of roads, railway tracks, bridges and pylons, and their cutting of telephone lines, often hit hard the very people they claimed to represent. Night raids on military billets and police posts, cross-border smuggling of arms and explosives, and the constant search for safe houses, of which there were many, all kept us on our toes twenty-four hours a day.

The guerrilla tactics of hit-and-run – sniping and beating a hasty retreat to fight another day – were very effective. The insurrectionists sought to avoid being caught in a face-to-face; however, when they were forced into such a situation, they proved courageous, tough fighters, and excellent marksmen. They were impeded in their efforts by informers and local civilians, who did not support their cause. This led me to believe that there was not a united front, under one leader, but a mish-mash of different factions, without any cohesive leadership.

Although the insurrectionists were referred to as 'bandits' by our officers, it was stressed that we were not to assume that we were dealing with trigger-happy hooligans. They were determined to destroy anything that stood between them and independence for Palestine. Although I knew little about the background to their fight, to me it felt not unlike the situation back home, where for hundreds of years rebels had been fighting for their independence. I couldn't say I was pursuing a noble cause: orders had to be obeyed, no more, no less. You stood firmly together with your comrades, who would share their last crust with you, and back you up in a tight spot. My respect for the Officers and NCOs reached new heights in Palestine, as I watched them lead their men out front, regardless of the dangers.

And so it went on. The 2nd Faughs, accompanied by a platoon of sailors from HMS *Douglas* and members of the Palestinian police force, cordoned off and searched a number of places in Haifa. The wadi Nymnas and the mosque area of the souq were given special attention. We hit the jackpot when hoards of ammunition, revolvers, uniforms, together with plans and maps of their proposed targets were found, and more than eighty people were arrested and detained. The Arabs sought retribution, and stepped up their attacks on the billets, with HQ Company getting the most attention. A strong military response was unleashed, in which no casualties were suffered on our side.

On one occasion, we were sent out to search the Christian Arab dwellings in Haifa. During the course of the search, one of the men stole a very expensive ring from an Arab woman, who was distraught at her loss. She reported the matter to a senior British officer, who immediately ordered an extensive search of all thirty men in our unit. About halfway through the search, one man, from County Tyrone, stepped forward and owned up to the theft. Turning his Lee Enfield upside down, he opened the butt trap and removed the pull-through and brass oil bottle - used to clean his rifle. He tilted the rifle upside down and the ring fell out of its hiding place in the the empty space beneath the oil bottle: it landed in the palm of his hand. We were all shocked. We had always known the man to be extremely honest and a decent sort. After having been arrested and charged with the crime, he was sentenced to six months in a detention centre in Cairo. As the railway lines were constantly being sabotaged, he had to spent the first three weeks of his sentence in Palestine. There was great speculation – and a lot of well-founded suspicion – that this man had been covering up for the real culprit, and just took it on the chin rather than betray a friend.

From time to time, information came through that we were about to be attacked. Our leaders had one response: get your retaliation in first. The informers, concealed in an armoured car, would be brought into a village prior to a search, to point out the ringleaders. In the course of an early-morning search led by the CID, all males would be marched, five abreast, past the armoured cars, and the informer would identify the person to be detained. Obviously, this was an opportunity for old scores to be settled by certain informers, but we had to investigate every allegation.

The duty would start at around 2.30 AM and finish some forty-eight hours later, when we arrived back at our billets, either on foot, or after being picked up by army transport. We searched two villages in particular – Miar and Sakhnin – over and over again. After persistent heavy attacks by snipers and rebels targeting the military, it was decided to demolish the souq in Haifa, which was a constant source of trouble and a regular escape route for the snipers. The Royal Engineers were supposed to build a street right through it, to ensure that it afforded no cover or escape for the rebels in future. Thankfully, this plan, which would have resulted in the destruction of a historically and culturally irreplaceable location, was scrapped.

Back in the billets, and weary from acting as target practice for the snipers, many men's inclinations bordered on the Lynch Law philosophy – whereby summary justice, without the niceties of a fair trial, is the order of the day. Orders which led to us riding roughshod in the relentless pursuit and punishment of the so-called 'rebels', and those who were giving them shelter, resulted in some homes being demolished or burnt down, with little thought as to where the poor people were to find shelter. There were instances where compensation was paid for these deeds, but no amount of compensation could make up for the destruction of someone's home: to my mind, our actions were high-handed and cruel. From the military point of view, the killing or maiming of military personnel would be met with similar drastic action by the rebels. The wearing of uniforms by the 'rebels' marked them out as an army at war, and in hunting them down, it was inevitable that some civilians could get caught in the cross-fire, not unlike the human shields used in warfare in the Middle East today.

There was never a dull moment during my time in Palestine. Once, when we were just back from a forty-eight hour search, we were called out to another incident, after only a short rest. This time we were despatched to the Tira area to hunt down two men who were believed to have blown up fifteen electricity pylons. Our group was divided in two, with Major Allen commanding the operation and Captain Hill, Major Boyle and Captain French led the columns. At the top of Mount Carmel, we took up our positions in a semicircle, while another column entered the village by motor transport, supported by a single aircraft, flying above the village. HQ Column inflicted several casualties on a number of rebels as they attempted to get away.

30

Eventually, the usual roundup of males took place, with some thirty men being arrested – but not before they had fired off a few rounds at us. A couple of our lads bringing up the rear responded, and wounded one of the gunmen, who was taken prisoner. We continued to come under fire late into the night, but made it back to our billets safely, and even managed to get a couple of days' rest, before being sent back into the fray.

On 1 November 1938, Palestinian workmen declared a general strike, which led to complete military control of all roads and movements by the local population. Just six days later, the strike was broken due to miltary action, which allowed the workers to get on with the job without intimidation by the rebels. In the interim, our duties were to break up the groups of men patrolling the Haifa-to-Acre road throughout the night, and to escort those Arabs who were cleaning the streets. Another clean-sweep-and-search of the Souq was made, and a few hundred Arabs were picked up and brought in for questioning, with some seventy being detained.

With the strike over, intimidation of the workers by rebels anxious to resurrect the strike still had to be dealt with. Our job was to protect the workers and let them get on with their work, particularly at important locations such as the railways and roads. It became too hot to venture close to the Souq during this phase of the situation, and there was no let-up in the guerrilla activity. One night, during a heavy thunderstorm, we had no alternative but to move into this area. As expected, we came under heavy fire, but luckily we suffered no casualties. We detained seven gunmen, one of whom had been wounded. The area was surrounded and cordoned off, while the Royal Engineers moved in and demolished the houses that were being used as cover by our attackers. With the increasing hostility towards the British Protectorate, the attacks against us escalated, and had us running all over Palestine, setting up cordons, searches and roadblocks.

Immediately after Armistice Day, our Battalion was temporarily relieved of all town duties. Pass-outs were given for a trip to Broadway, in Haifa. Each to his own: some took the brothel option, while others went on the beer. One of these boozers, drunk as a skunk and armed with a toy pistol, held up a local shop – for which he paid a heavy penalty: he suffered a loss of pay and spent twenty-eight days in the glasshouse (jail).

The following morning, worse for wear, we were delighted at the prospect of a few days' leave to recover, but we were recalled within hours, due to the substantial increase in the number of murders on the Nazareth road. All available men were needed to block the approaches to this road with barbed-wire entanglements. Assisted by Arab labour, the work was completed ahead of schedule, and HQ Company manned the road to enforce a curfew. We managed to get the job done without any harassment, probably due to the large number of local labourers, who would have been in the same target zone. For three weeks, between mid November and early December 1938, our activity was concentrated around Nazareth. Our duties included the same old routines, but this time our orders were to target the organised gangs that attacked at random. They were forced to leave other targets alone to concentrate on us as we harried them on a daily basis. Communications and transport were their main targets, which suffered the biggest hits. We, on the other hand, had a high success rate in assisting CID in picking up many of the people who were on the wanted list. The terrain posed significant problems, with many outlying villages in which the Palestinian activists were lying low being located on mountain-top goat tracks. In some cases, it took so long to reach these areas that what had been planned as daylight searches ended up being conducted by torchlight. This was not a good plan if you wanted to find the activists on their home ground and get back to camp in one piece.

Despite these conditions, we managed to locate and arrest two Arabs who were wanted for plotting to kill the Assistant District Commissioner. Using torches and lanterns, we pursued and rounded up a further twenty wanted men. They were held in a nearby building and interrogated by the police. Not every sortie was so successful, though: we often came back empty handed, despite having been given good intelligence. The people we were looking for often slipped away under cover of fire as their supporters kept us pinned down before we had even made it to their villages – perhaps the good 'INT' (intelligence) went both ways. All that was left was a few khaki uniforms, spent cartridges from an old Mauser, a few charges, and cordex – a high explosive – but no suspects. Back at our billets, the talk was of what would happen to these prisoners after we had had handed them over to the local police, who transferred them to the medieval prison in Acre.

Although we never had occasion to visit the prison, I later learned something of the horrendous conditions there at the the time. With up to forty men to a cell, there was little room to move – never mind sleep. A bucket served as a communal toilet, which overflowed and stank in the hot fetid jail. Feeding time was like a zoo, when a guard came around with a large steaming cauldron of watery soup, into which each prisoner was 'allowed' to put his bare hand to extract a small piece of meat to supplement his soup. Many were scalded and didn't try it again, preferring to go hungry.

Around this time, led by Corporal Smith and Lance Corporal McCullough to a village on the Affila–Jenin road, to protect a party of workmen who were repairing sabotaged telegraph wires, we came under heavy fire. Moving in closer, we returned fire in the direction of the village of Zirin, when a number of Arab horsemen suddenly bolted for cover in the direction of the village. One of them missed his chance to break away but managed to conceal himself among the rocks. When one of our lads, McCullough came upon him, he thrust himself at the Lance Corporal and, wielding a large knife, lashed out wildly, slashing through his hand. Before the attacker could do any further damage, he was taken out with a couple of shots, sniped rapidly from several locations. This fatality brought about a temporary lull in the attack from the rebels' side. The job of repairing the telegraph completed, we moved out, only to come under further fire yet again. We got off a substantial amount of automatic fire before boarding the transport and moving out, not knowing whether we'd inflicted any more casualties. Although the lorries were hit by some small-arms fire, we suffered no further casualties.

Around the end of November, considerable fire was heard in the vicinity of Umm Ad Daraj, and we went out in response. The platoons encountered a gang of around twenty-five armed Arabs and engaged them in combat. After almost two hours of sustained fighting, all the

Arabs had either escaped or been killed. Sergeant Bill Mitchell was killed in action, while Sergeant Eddie McKerr and Corporal Albert Race died from their wounds. Fusilier John Tripp was seriously wounded in action, and spent the next year recovering from his injuries. British Police Sergeant Otway, who was attached to the regiment, was also wounded in this action. Enemy casualties were estimated to be more than fifty, and we counted twenty-seven bodies on the ground following the engagement.

On 30 November 1938, the bodies of our lost comrades were borne by bearer parties of sergeants, corporals and fusiliers, and placed on three lorries for internment at Sarafand. To muffled drums and pipes playing a lament, an escort of two sections under 2nd Lieutenant Mead preceded in slow time – their arms reversed – as far as the gates of the barracks, before the rest of the convoy proceeded to Sarafand for the burial.

*

From time to time, on guard duty at Haifa Port, I'd be redirected to provide cover for the Royal Army Service Corp supply lorries, which carried general supplies to Safad, Jenis, Jarafad, Nablus and Ramallah. Moving in convoys of up to thirty lorries, we were accompanied by an armoured car, occasionally backed up by a small lorry with a mounted Bren or Lewis gun. On these trips, I had to sit on a bale of hay immediately behind the driver's cab, facing forward, my Lee Enfield positioned across my lap. This was considered to be a vantage point, but I felt like a sitting duck – a sniper's dream.

Perched high up on the hay, I could pass on my observations to the well-seasoned driver, who had done this run many times before. He concentrated on his driving, ignoring all else except to warn me as we approached an area of high risk to our convoy.

The weather was bright and sunny, and the journey was not without its distractions for me, a seventeen-year-old teenager: I paid great attention to the beautiful, tanned and scantily clad young girls picking oranges along the way. On one occasion, I was so distracted that my mate 'Smudger' was able to put his hand through an opening in the cabin, reach out and remove the magazine from my rifle, without my noticing! Taking full advantage of the situation, he roared that he had spotted some guerrillas ready to attack the convoy and that I should put a round up the 'spout', ready for action. I whipped my rifle upwards, only to discover that the magazine was missing. Terrified at finding myself defenceless, I was speechless for a minute, before yelling to 'Smudger' that my magazine was missing. Seeing my agitation, he coolly handed me the magazine and said: 'That'll teach you to keep a lookout for bandits. Tits and thighs are for other times and places. Keep your eyes peeled. The rebels bastards will pull tricks galore to distract you, and before you know it you'll be caught napping.' Smudger had already saved the life of another Corporal who'd been caught unawares, so I took his words to heart.

About seven or eight miles further on, we came under fire from villages within range of our convoy. The supply lorries stopped briefly, and the armoured car and Bren-gun lorry opened fire, while the rest of us got off a couple of magazines, before resuming our journey. We didn't hang around to find out if the attackers had had any casualties. We eventually made it to Nablus without further incident. Other convoys experienced similar attacks, and on some occasions we were sent back to try to find the attackers. As usual, they were generally long gone by the time we reached the village in question, and had taken their wounded with them.

Some of what we had seen and what had been asked of us was almost beyond our capacity, but despite this we stuck together, and no one dropped out from the strain. I remember that, coming up to my eighteenth birthday, which was on 10 December 1938, the conflict became particularly active, as we operated around the harbour port and residential areas of Haifa, and at the railways works at Kyriat Haim and the area around the Eastern Railway station, where a number of arrests were made. At least we were away from the boulder-strewn goat tracks and deep valleys for a while. In the week leading up to Christmas, on 21 December, we were back on high ground, accompanied by the South Staffordshire Regiment. Our Regiment provided two Columns, A and B, under the 16th Infantry Brigade, led by Captain Weldon and Major Boyle. We travelled on foot towards Sakhnin, where we rendezvoused with the other units. From there, we headed for Tamra but, due to the terrain, we could advance no further, and our company commandeered camels and donkeys from the local village. Eventually, after an ardous journey across very rugged terrain, we reached Kakaub, where we rested for the night. Setting up wireless communications, we made contact with aircraft and were alerted to the fact that a band of insurrectionists had been engaged north of Shaab, where additional ground support had been requested by another unit. We were immediately on the move again. Columns A and B linked up at Shaab, where the wanted men were picked up, and handed over to the Hampshires, who took them to Ar Rama Examination Centre for questioning. After a hot meal at Miar-Shaab junction, we returned to Haifa.

Christmas Day 1938 was excellent. We were visited by our Commanding Officer, who commended us for our achievements and wished us well on the frontier at Iqrit and Al Malakiya, where we were heading the following day, St Stephen's Day. Less than two weeks later, on 6 January 1939, one of our lads, Fusilier Sam McClay, was fatally wounded in action, killed by a sniper while on night patrol. It was a sad blow to us all, and a bad start to our New Year. Just two days later, Corporal Jim Wilson was shot in the groin; he died a short time later from his wounds. Reflecting on our past experiences, we all agreed that we had grown up considerably over the previous few months. We were now seasoned campaigners, we thought, used to danger and less living in fear of what was to come. Our time in Palestine was over, for now. The next time I'd be back in Palestine would be in the middle of World War II.

*

Many years later, when I was a senator, I made the journey to Beirut together with a number of TDs from Dáil Éireann. While we were there, we met with Yassar Arafat, the then Palestinian leader, who was in hiding, wanted by the Israelis. He made us very welcome. As we talked, I told him of the time I had spent in Palestine during the Insurrection, and we chatted about it for a while. Eventually he said to me, with a twinkle in his eye: 'You were probably shooting at my father.' With an even bigger twinkle in my eye, I replied: 'Well, I must have missed, or you wouldn't be here, so look what I've done for Palestine!' Arafat's slow smile quickly turned into a loud belly laugh, as the significance of my remark hit home. (The fact that his father had Egyptian origins was neither here nor there.)

We remained friends and some years later, while we were at a dinner in Jury's Hotel in Dublin, he made a point of telling my friends about the encounter, and didn't miss the opportunity of 'ribbing' me again about how my 'bad aim' had helped the cause of Palestine.

5

THE SIEGE OF MALTA

Our next posting saw us return to Malta, an island I had come to know and love. The situation soon took a turn for the worse, however, and in June 1940 Malta was drawn into the midst of a battle that was to last for years. On 10 January 1941, the aircraft carrier *Illustrious* came under non-stop bombing from enemy aircraft. Six direct hits set the hangars on fire, killing everyone inside. Listing badly, she limped into the Grand Harbour. Berthed alongside the *Illustrious* was an ammunition ship, the *Essex*, which was carrying four thousand tons of ammunition and twelve Hurricanes, still in their crates.

The Maltese dockers had refused to unload this dangerous and unstable cargo, so we were ordered to do the dirty work instead. Working in twelve-hour shifts to expedite matters, we had many close calls, especially when the *Essex* came under attack from the marauding Stukas. More than a dozen of us were trying to get a foothold on a single, swaying rope ladder, and we were in a panic as we tried to get away from the incoming dive bombers.

When the all-clear eventually came, we continued unloading the ship, but word soon went round that a thousand-pound bomb had gone down the funnel, blowing the engine room to smithereens. The bomb killed thirty-eight crew members and injured twenty-three others. It also only narrowly missed the ship's magazine, where the torpedoes and more than four thousand tons of ammunition was stored.

*

The three-year-long siege of Malta has gone down in history as the battle of David and Goliath: the little island refused to fall, and fought to the bitter end. The strain began to lift when, in May 1942, a second batch of Spitfires flew into Malta from HMS *Eagle* and USS *Wasp*. Everything was in place for a speedy engagement. Morale soared, as word spread that we now had sixty aircraft ready to support us. The enemy reconnaissance flew back to do a recce, but nothing more happened for the next twenty-four hours. The next day, however, the sky was littered with enemy and Allied aircraft, with the 'Spits' chasing the Messerschmitts, and the old Hurricanes getting struck into the Junkers 87s and 88s. Ack-ack gunners blazed away from their positions at the docks and elsewhere, and bits of fuselage and other pieces of aircraft rained down from the sky. Hundreds of parachutes floated downwards, heading for the drink, while bombs were jettisoned off target, causing some collateral damage.

The Spits had done their job against the German fighter planes, and the Hurricanes took their revenge on the bombers, catching them as they pulled out of their almost-vertical dives. The combined forces of the fighters, the ack-ack guns and the general military teamwork, proved successful in repelling the invaders. The Germans lost some seventy aircraft, and were left under no illusion that Malta now had the means to dish out punishment as well as take it. The Allied forces had finally gained – and retained – air supremacy over the Mediterranean. Young fighter pilots, drawn from all corners of the British Commonwealth, built their reputations that day, as ace fighter pilots.

Although in the eye of the storm, and endangered by the heavy fallout of shrapnel from the bombs, anti-aircraft fire and downed planes, Malta's civilians, who had taken to living in caves in order to escape the bombardment – their homes having been decimated – ignored the danger, screaming with delight as the enemy aircraft took a mauling. Strong in spirit, they never wavered in their support for the Allies, despite the fact that the Allies were a long time coming. A big price had been paid by many ships, including warships battling to get supplies through to the beseiged and starving people, without any aerial support. Finally, with the appearance of the Allied fighter planes, we had something to fight back with. But for the contribution and sacrifice of the seamen in getting supplies to Malta against all odds, we could never have held out.

Every Allied supply ship that set out for Malta from Alexandria in March 1942 was either sunk or bombed, within twenty-four hours of arriving in Malta's Grand Harbour. Our anti-aircraft gunners made good use of the ammunition supplies brought in by these brave men, putting it to such effect that the barrage that Malta sustained was considered to be the most concentrated, effective artillery work seen in any theatre of war during the entire Second World War. The arrival of allied aircraft helped cut the supply lines of the Axis forces in North Africa, and their eventual collapse. Churchill's leadership on the matter, and Malta's immense strategic importance to the outcome of battles in the North African campaign, sustained the besieged island and encouraged the beleaguered Maltese people and the Maltese Garrison.

When you have been closely engaged with the enemy and living under siege for nearly three years, it is hard to remember every hazardous event you experienced – and there were many, with communications and electricity often being cut off. The situation was made worse by the fact that the island was dependent on supplies from Allied ships coming from outside. Enemy submarines, surface craft and the Italian Air Force, Regia Aeronautica, backed up by the German fighter planes of the Flieger Korp, saw to it that the sea rained death and destruction on the crews of these ships. Even those ships that limped into harbour, bent and broken, were not safe. Their presence marked a stepping up of aerial assaults: the enemy were determined to destroy them and what remained of their badly needed life-saving cargos.

Twice the weight of munitions fell on Malta as was dropped on London during the Blitz, crippling the island. Despite the constant sirens warning of yet another German attack, the brave Maltese dockers, assisted by the military, continued to unload the battered ships.

The British soldiers and the Maltese people alike were faced with injury, illness and shortage of medicines, all aggravated by a severe cut in rations due to the bombing of the supply ships. Battle-weary and hungry, they must have doubted the very survival of the island. Nonetheless, despite their best efforts, the German forces failed to put the harbour out of use completely. Over the next five days, the nerve-shattering screeches of the Luftwaffe's bomber aircraft were endless.

Turning their attention to the airfields, where the combined forces of army, navy and RAF personnel were slogging away repairing the badly blitzed runways, the Germans pounded away with all their aerial might.

By the end of the day, we'd had a bellyful of racing for slit trenches, trying to drag heavy tarpaulin covers overhead to protect ourselves from the shrapnel and the fallout from both the attacking aircraft and our own ack-ack guns. There was no let-up: as soon as we had repaired one crater, they made another. The Germans, having failed to destroy the docklands completely, had switched targets. But they failed to understand the resolve of the local and military population, who were hell-bent on keeping the airfields in action, despite the daily loss of life. From March 1942, there was a dramatic increase in the number of air raids, with almost 6,700 tons dropped, day and night for five months, in an effort to annihilate the tiny island. In March and April, the FliegerKorp flew almost 15,000 sorties against the island, and in a seven-month spell, there was only a single twenty-four hour period that was free from bombing. One pilot, Denis Barnham, is quoted as saying: 'One lives here only to destroy the Hun. Living conditions have gone by the board. It makes the Battle of Britain seem like child's play.'

THE HIDDEN ENEMY

Being stationed around the perimeter of an airfield during wartime carries with it many hazards. It's no picnic living in a camouflaged dugout with only a tarpaulin to protect you from the shrapnel, wind and weather, as you try you to conceal yourself from enemy eyes. The arrival of enemy aircraft is predictable in war, and if you're lucky the sirens give you advanced warning of an attack – and the chance to take cover.

This, given the circumstances, is acceptable. The enemy *within* the walls of our foul-smelling dugout was another matter, however: it gave no warning, made no noise and couldn't be seen. This silent enemy had the advantage of surprise: it tended to strike when we were fatigued and at our most vulnerable. A brigade strenght of lice had declared biological warfare on us, there was nothing we could do about it, except to scratch and scratch, in a futile effort to get some relief. Our faces, armpits, ankles and shoulder blades, not to mention other parts, were overrun with the invaders and became infected with sores. We could only conclude that the bastards were in the pay of the enemy.

The adventurous squaddies amongst us – those who got a mere dose of the crabs – were well versed in this particular disease. A close shave – literally – and a dose of mercurial ointment was a sure cure, they advised. Perhaps the soldiers' problems arose through ignoring the graffiti in the public toilets, which advised: 'Do not stand upon this seat, the crabs in here can jump nine feet' or perhaps they 'got lucky' before getting unlucky! One cynical squaddie, Guthrie Kane, a bosom pal of mine, remarked that he'd never regretted knowingly courting infestation, provided that she didn't push him off the bus before the last stop! Despite the irritable state of some of the lads overrun by the 'licean army', such humour helped to lighten the mood.

6

HIGH JINKS AT THE PALACE

Meantime, we continued with our guard duty, with every regiment taking turns at the Governor's residence in San Antone Gardens. Each tour of duty involved the soldiers staying at the palace for seven days, living in the guardroom. During daylight hours, one sentry paraded up and down outside the guardroom; at night, four sentries covered the perimeters and protected the Governor and his advisors.

On one occasion, while Sergeant Digger Dawson was the Guard Commander, and I, then Lance-corporal Johnny Harte, was the relieving NCO, an incident occurred which stuck in my mind. The Governor, his aide-de-camp and his immediate advisors had quarters at the far end of the palace, which they accessed via a winding stone staircase. At 1 AM, I posted two fusiliers inside the palace to guard that post. When I did my rounds thirty minutes later, I discovered that things were far from being in order: the area was not secured. I walked the length of the palace and back again, with no sight or sign of McGuirk or Mooney. It was like the Marie Celeste.

Doing guard duty at the palace was considered an easy number – a relief from the pressures of filling in craters or digging slit trenches. The last thing I wanted was to have to report the sentries to the Guard Commander, Digger Dawson, who was a strong disciplinarian and would swiftly put them under arrest. For the rest of us, it would have meant complete supervision, to the point where the dangerous dockland work, or navvying on the airfields, would seem an easier option. It crossed my mind that the boyos might have female company in the servants' quarters. How would I sort that one out?

I searched high and low, and was on the point of giving up when, heading for the exit stairs to report the missing sentries, I noticed a faint light coming from a room at the end of the hall. Moving closer to investigate, I heard what sounded like giggling coming from the room. I assumed that I'd been right in thinking that the pair had found some female friends. Edging over to an open doorway, I was taken aback at what I saw. Both sentries were stripped of their webbing, their tunics were off, and their Lee Enfield rifles were lying on the floor. They were alone, it appeared I'd been wrong about the female company – they were too busy getting stuck into the Governor's whiskey. The drunken sods were trying to smother their belly laughs as they regaled each other with stories: hence the muffled giggling I'd heard. They were both seasoned drinkers, but I couldn't believe it when they invited me to join them for a drink. I declined their generous offer, venting my outrage against them, and stormed out of the room in a furious state. I returned minutes later – when I had regained my composure – to inform them I was putting them on a charge of being absent from their posts, and that they would be put under close arrest by the Guard Commander.

As I approached the private-party room, there was a lot of noise and movement. Back in full military dress and moving rapidly, they rushed past me. I did my best to keep up with them and, trying to keep my voice down, enquired what the f—k they were up to! I got my answer when Mooney stopped and took up position outside the Governor's door, and McGuirk did the same outside the aide-de camp's door – the positions they should have been in from the start of their guard duty. Cheekily, they demanded that I get the relieving sentries up as quickly as possible, as they were exhausted. My frustration almost reached breaking point. With the pair showing little signs of having just finished a 'session', the changing of the guard went very smoothly. Entering the guardroom after coming off duty, the cheeky pair had the audacity to exchange pleasantries with Digger, the Guard Commander, before heading straight for their bed boards. At last I could breath easily – or so I thought – until the Guard Commander told me he intended changing the night-duty roster, and would be splitting the pair up. He'd obviously noticed that they were somewhat the worse for wear, but I was happy to let things go at that.

I wondered how they expected to get away with drinking all the wkiskey, without anyone noticing it was missing. The answer came a few weeks later. Soldiers on guard duty at the palace got one day free from sentry duties. On that day, their job would be to collect meals from the nearby army unit, clean up, and generally act as a runner for the Guard Commander. Having been rostered for these duties, Fusilier Mooney was sent to collect the dinner rations at lunchtime, but failed to return. Six hours later, he was spotted in a wine bar near Hamrun, drunk as a skunk on Stuka juice, and regaling the locals. He was arrested by the Red Caps and was placed in the tender care of the most feared Provost Sergeant on the island, Sergeant Lackery Woods. Having got away with the pilfering of the whiskey, I was sorry to be given no option but to give evidence against him. He got fourteen days' field punishment for his trouble.

Ever the spiel-er, he couldn't resist telling me how the missing whiskey had never been reported missing. Apparently, he'd noticed that, after a long day working in the offices in Valletta, the Governor and his advisors would return to the palace and continue to do business in a more relaxed way, over a drink and a cigar. Because of the frequent night air raids, the domestic staff would go to bed early, leaving the Governor and his associates to it. The following morning, the staff would replenish the decanters, in the belief that the Governor and his colleagues had been responsible for depleting the contents. On the night in question, McGuirk and Mooney knew that everyone had gone to bed. Satisfied that they were well settled in, they volunteered to take over the drinking shift on behalf of the Governor and his cronies. The strange thing was, both of these daring friends were among the smartest in appearance on the parade ground, and their courage on the docks and airfield hadn't gone unnoticed: that was why they had got the cushy number at the palace. They seldom took shelter during the air raids, and were known to watch for bombs leaving enemy aircraft, betting on exactly where they would land. Not too many joined in this particular betting school. Mad or bad? Who's to say?

7

MALTESE TAKEAWAY

FARSON'S BREWERY BANDITS

Malta is a small island, and is home to a close-knit community, but everywhere we looked we could see death and destruction. No family was left untouched by the deprivation, disease and disaster that was inflicted on their island homes. Let's make no bones about it: the army is a killing machine when it is deployed in war zones. Using a Bren or twin Lewis machine-gun, mounted on a tripod, to try and hit a low-flying aircraft, as it climbs swiftly out of your range, is akin to trying to hit the moon with a slingshot. Hearing the screaming engines of the Junkers as they dive towards your position on the gun is a terrifying experience. You have nowhere to go, as he attempts to jettison his bombs and lighten his load, with the Hurricanes chasing his tail.

You have the chance to do something, to hit back. The sense of euphoria and relief when you let go a few bursts is terrific, even if you actually inflict little or no damage. As he scurries away, you have a momentary sense of being more than a match for him. Firing away from a light machine-gun until it warps from the heat leaves you even more vulnerable, as you then have nothing to fight back with. In the heat of the action, there's no time to think of your safety or the risks you're taking. All that matters is that you make a stand, and try to get off a couple of direct hits on the target. Succeed, and you feel like a million dollars!

When everything settles down, and you see the ever-present craters, trample the debris, and dodge the red-flagged delayed-action bombs, you can't help but think of the deaths of the brave young

Hurricane pilots and ack-ack gunners, and your sense of duty, and the urgency of getting on with the job of defeating the enemy comes to the fore.

After my first brief encounter with the Italian air force, still quite young, I was shaken by the experience. A fellow squaddie, Jimmy 'Bollocks' Thompson, from the Shankill Road in Belfast, offered me a swig from his bottle of Stuka juice to steady my nerves. I later realised that the German aircraft, manned by Italian pilots, did not have enough fuel left to risk slowing down his getaway to take me on. I'd had a lucky escape.

Our scattered B Company sections were brought together in the commandeered Villa Remigio near Naxxar – which was a vast improvement on our recent cave dwelling at Ta'Qali. Mosta was a short distance from Ta'Qali, and the night before our move to the villa, Eddie Thompson, Danny Doyle and myself took off and head-ed for a local wine shop which was a haven for the Stuka drinkers. The Maltese people were delighted to be of help to us: which was just as well, as, before the night was out, we were going to need it.

Totally paralytic, we were oblivious to the tripwire hazards close to the airfield. Eddie and I tried to stop Danny from singing 'Mexicali Rose' at the top of his voice. The last thing we wanted was to be charged with breaking barracks – or in our case, breaking from a cave. As luck would have it, Franco's friend – or perhaps opponent – we were never sure which side he'd been on – from the Spanish Civil War, Bill Twomey, was on duty patrolling the perimeter of the airport. Our luck would only hold if we could manage to avoid the tripwires, as Twomey was not the type to take prisoners – although in our case, that was probably exactly what he'd do!

It was a lovely clear night, and he'd already picked us out from a good distance, and was just waiting to scare the daylights out of us. I fell on to a camouflaged embankment, as Twomey roared: 'Show your-self before I pin you to that f—king camouflage!' Recognising Twomey's strong Limerick accent, Eddie, sober-minded even while drunk, quickly replied: 'If you fire that peashooter, you'll lose a good audience for your yarns.' The 'good Christian' that this so-called communist was, he saw us safely back to what was to be our last kip in our tunnel quarters.

By Christmas 1940, I'd been twenty for all of two weeks, and already had three years of tough service behind me and to prove it, I was now wearing the Palestine medal and bar for active service. It was my fourth Christmas away from home, and although I was not exactly nostalgic, being too busy fighting the war, my thoughts did turn to home and my Ma and Da fussing about, as the entire family gathered at the family home for Christmas. My thoughts were interrupted by the Sergeant Major Mickey Davidson, calling us to parade for church. Being wise to the fact that most squaddies only assembled for church to avoid other duties, he would first call all Catholics, Protestants and Dissenters to assemble and, at the least sign of hesitation, would shout: 'Outside RCs, C of Es, Chinese, Siamese, Portuguese and noted malingerers.'

Davidson was a rogue, but behind it all he was a fatherly figure who turned a blind eye to serious breaches of discipline. He had a peculiar sense of justice, though. For example, when a person had been charged with some breach of discipline, it was the Sergeant Major's job to march you in to the Company Commander. He would stand behind your back, and when he was asked what kind of a person you were, he's say 'He's a good soldier, sir', while silently using an old army trick of hand signals, to indicate a suitable punishment – the number of fingers held up indicating the term of confinement. The Company Commander would then sentence you to seven or fourteen days, depending on the number of fingers Sergeant Major Davidson held up. After a spell in the glasshouse – a military prison – most offenders became more cautious, but for me, the danger of getting caught made it all the more exciting, and the risks worth taking.

After one such episode, I got the full fourteen days, thanks to Mickey. Just three days later, now free from detention, I was heading towards Villa Remigio with four of my buddies when an air-raid warning sounded. A lorry from the local Farson's Brewery was travelling in the same direction. It stopped when the driver and his helper heard the sirens, and they then ran to an air-raid shelter. Sensing that the Axis aircraft were heading for the airfield, we decided that the open-backed lorry – which was laden down with cigarettes and Blue Label beer – was a heaven-sent gift that was in need of liberation.

Ably assisted by my four drinking buddies – Guthrie Kane, Danny Brush, Bollocks Thompson and Foggy French – we used blankets and ropes to haul the booty back to camp, where a hooley was arranged for later. We were a bit worried that the driver and his mate would notice some of their cargo missing when they came back but, as luck would have it, they were in too much of a hurry to get away. Two hours later, after the beer and cigarettes had been divided up, we spotted the Maltese driver and his helper going into the Company Commander's office. Within minutes, an extensive search, supervised by CSM Mickey Davidson, was carried out, but it failed to find anything. The kindly Sergeant Major made it clear from his subtle remarks that he could finger the culprits, and he wasn't off the mark! He went on in general terms to say how stupid it would have been for any soldier to take such a risk during an air raid, particularly because, if they were found out, they could face both civil and military consequences. We felt guilty – not about the brewery's loss, but about the two workers and the trouble they might get into.

Three weeks after our escapade, I spotted the same lorry and crew making deliveries in the village, and my guilt disappeared: I knew that the men hadn't lost their jobs. Within a matter of weeks, the Germans demolished the brewery and a bonded warehouse, leaving the local wine, Ambet, as the only booze to be had anywhere on the island. This was not the first case of high jinks that we five – Dub, Protestant, Catholic and Dissenter, all reprobates together – had engaged in. When the cards were stacked against us, we stood up for each other, regardless of the level of danger involved.

8

DOGFIGHTS AND BAR-ROOM BRAWLS

The Italian aircraft changed their focus to other airfields at Luqa and Hal-far, giving us a temporary respite. During this time, however, three of our number went sick. Bill Twomey, a veteran of the Spanish Civil War, was hospitalised with impetigo, while Tapper Brown and I had a severe dose of scabies, and spent a brief spell in hospital. The rest of the section were given the task of scrubbing the bed boards and fumigating the area. I slept in a real bed for the first time in more than two months, had a decent bit to eat, and enjoyed the luxury of a flush toilet. Even the daily bath in scalding water, scrubbing my body with a hard brush until it almost bled, and being liberally covered with sulphur ointment, all seemed worth it, for the pleasure of feeling clean again.

Returning to the Ta-Qali, which had been taken over by the RAF in October 1940, was not high on my agenda, but a soldier is a soldier, and there is no room for debate on the battlefield. I was back all too soon to my grotty hovel that passed for quarters, with its burst water mains and smelly bombed drainage. I had to queue up to shave in the same cold dirty water as three squaddies before me – unless I could beat them to it. Despite serious water shortages and the stench of blended tobacco, sweaty bodies, dry latrines and the local cheap wine – all added to by the Maltese heat – I had no option but to make the best of it. With five men to each hovel, these were testing times.

Complaints that the pong even penetrated our gas masks abounded, but nothing could be done to eliminate it. The only benefit, during our six-month spell at Ta-Qali was the fact that the enemy air attacks were relatively light, while other airfields were bombarded day and night. The five Italian nuisance bombers, who flew overhead at around twenty-thousand feet to avoid our ack-ack guns, were daily visitors. They travelled so fast that we christened them the 'jilty-five-jilty', 'jilty' being a Hindustani word for 'quick' or 'fast'. At the height and speed at which they were flying, their aim wasn't accurate, but they did occasionally hit some targets. German parachute mines and Italian anti-personnel bombs, disguised as innocuous items, all added to the death and destruction inflicted on the Maltese people, their homes and livelihoods. Many were forced to live in underground tunnels and man-made shelters – where many a Maltese baby was born. With water supplies knocked out and a serious cut in rations, they had to accept communal feeding systems, known as 'victory kitchens'. To add to their woes, in 1942 a major epidemic of polio broke out; this, coupled with eye diseases, dysentery, TB and typhoid, affected civilians and military alike.

For me, the only light relief came when I was lucky enough to get a twenty-four-hour pass. I'd cycle up to the local school in Garguar village, where I'd meet up with a few mates from my boxing days and do a bit of sparring. With virtually no equipment, we'd take turns using the two sets of gloves we had. By the end of the day, I'd have done twenty rounds with everyone, ranging from featherweights to heavyweights. We all headed back to our various camps covered in bruises and with split lips, not having the luxury of a single gum shield between us. Still, it was a welcome break from the other kind of fighting we were doing on a daily basis. After bidding goodbye to my sparring partners – Paddy Ruane from Mayo; Bobby Peden from Ballymoney; Willie Lismore from Dublin; Paudge Wallace, Slabs McKinney and Paddy Campbell from Derry; and Billy Meneice, Rocky Burns, Joe Beatty and 'Polly' McIlwaine from Belfast – I'd cycle contentedly back to my platoon quarters, bruised and battered, but looking forward to the next visit.

On one such visit to Sliema, I was caught up in a brawl with some Maltese civilians. We were outnumbered six-to-one, and in the course of the mêlée I was hit with the starting handle of an old car, while my lifelong friend Dave Thompson was stabbed in the head. (The scars from this attack could still be seen years later, as Dave walked along the Newtownards Road, heading for his ninetieth year.) Two other buddies got a bad mauling. As we headed for a RAP –'regimental aid post' (a forces first-aid station) – we were again accosted by the civilians, who were now mob-handed, having recruited six or seven more friends. In the uneven battle that followed, two of our number, Hookie Connors and Jackie Officer, were brutally lashed with whips, while Davy Thompson and myself were very badly beaten. Davy's head seemed to hold a special attraction for our opponents: it was already flowing with blood when a kick from a heavy steel-capped boot added to his woes.

This was the thanks we got from the Maltese for risking our lives in defending their country. By the time the police arrived, we were in a sorry state, all four of us bleeding and badly cut up. The police took us to a medical centre, where we were treated, stitched and generally checked out. The medics were very concerned about Hookie and Jackie, and insisted on keeping them in overnight. I was pretty bruised and battered, and needed several stitches. My head was still throbbing from the earlier blow with the starting handle. The medics insisted that I, too, stay in hospital, because of the head injury. Davy, tough as nails, refused to stay, despite protests from the doctor. He'd taken a good kicking *and* a stab wound to the head, and still refused to remain in overnight. Eventually, realising that his three pals were being kept in, he reluctantly agreed to an overnight stay. The police took the assailants into custody and wanted us to press charges against them, but we all refused: it wasn't our style.

Released from hospital twenty-four hours later, we decided that a little more recuperation time was needed, so we went AWOL for a further twenty-four hours. In the event, this turned into a seventy-two-hour session of drinking and debauchery, in an effort to ease our pain. This was despite the fact that, between us, we had no serious money to spend.

While we were sitting in the Blue Haven bar licking our wounds, two policemen came in, accompanied by a Maltese civilian, who was in an agitated state. The man pointed me out, and the police asked me to accompany them to the station at Sliema, saying that I was wanted for questioning. It transpired that one of our attackers was dangerously ill in hospital as a result of the fracas. The civilian claimed that we had used army webbing belts to inflict serious head injuries on his friend, who was in intensive care. We had no idea what he was talking about. Thankfully, the police felt that the evidence was not strong enough, but the possibility of being charged at a later date was still very much on the cards. On hearing about the mêlée, a good friend of mine from Dublin, Sergeant Andy Lennon, made his way to the police station and gave a guarantee that I would be made available, should the police want to speak to me again. I was then released, and Andy, with me in tow, went scouring the streets for my three battered buddies. As we were broke, and the worse for wear, he hired a horse and garry (horse and carriage) to ferry us back to our billets.

Seeing the mess we were in – we were covered in cuts and bruises, and were unshaven, and our khaki drill was in a terrible state – Andy decided to conceal us until we had had time to clean ourselves up. Aware that we'd be thrown in the clink for being AWOL, Andy got offside to his own company area, leaving us to it. In his hurry, however, he forgot to tell me that Lance Sergeant Darkie Finch and Sergeant Sam Hatterly, the boxing coaches, had left word that I'd been selected to box against the Devonshire Regiment and was to report for training.

When I didn't turn up, Drum Major Tommy Dooley, a fellow Dubliner and member of the boxing team, called to the clink, where I was serving fourteen days for being absent without leave, as I failed to sign back in after my twenty-four-hour pass. His intention was to arrange for my temporary release so that I could get in some sparring practice for the contest, but he took one look at my face and told me to restrict my training to skipping and roadwork. The skipping was no problem, but the roadwork consisted of a sixteen-mile walk under guard, stopping along the way to dig slit trenches on the coast road. My hands were badly blistered from using the pickaxe on the hard rock. On the night of the contest, I was released under escort to do battle for the regiment. I was just three pounds over the welterweight limit and had to move up a weight and box at middleweight. Needless to say, I was not used to fighting at this weight and I was well beaten.

Consolation came when my mates Slab McKinney and Paddy Ruane boxed at welterweight and won their bouts easily. We managed to get a few snacks and a bottle of Blue Label beer to celebrate before I was marched back to the glasshouse, without seeing the other fights. My escort, Corporal Phillips, was very apologetic about the fact that I'd missed out on the rest of the night, particularly as the Devons were laying on some treats after the bouts. I couldn't complain, though. Philips, a veteran of Malaya and the Far East, was a tough but very fair man. Provided that you took your punishment, he found ways of showing his respect for you. In my case, he had done everything in his power to ensure that I got to box that night.

A few days later, I learned that no charges were to be brought against me for the assault on the civilian. The police doubted that his injuries had been inflicted as alleged. Given that the man had made a full recovery, and the Maltese mob had used weapons against us, the matter was dropped. This was music to my ears, as having this thing hanging over my head had been getting to me. Andy Lennon later learned through his police contacts that, after his encounter with us, the civilian in question had gone back into town looking for more trouble – and had found it, suffering serious injuries that resulted in him being hospitalised.

Meanwhile, the war was still going on all around us. We continued to take cover from the dive bombers in our slit trenches. The trenches generally provided reasonable cover, provided that you made sure that your entire body was in the trench. If you didn't manage to find a tarpaulin top cover to conceal you and give some protection from the flak, even the top of a head sticking out would attract the attention of a rear gunner of the sniping Junkers 88s. The odds of a direct hit on a trench were long, but when it did happen, all the unfortunate occupants were wiped out. Steel splinters and shrapnel regularly found their way into our sanctuary, and these did their own damage. Our only respite came when driving rain and gales grounded both Axis and Allied aircraft alike. Within the space of a few days, my boozing pal from my Ta-Qali days, Belfast's Eddie Thompson and three others from our regiment – Captain Gough, Fusilier Haunce and Adjutant Lowe – were killed in a heavy onslaught by the Luftwaffe. During

April, 5,800 bomber aircraft dropped almost 6,700 tons of bombs on Malta – more than half of this in a single week – making it the most-bombed place on earth at the time, and probably since.

The arrival of the new Spitfires, which were more than a match for the German Messerschmitts, was a welcome sight, and a great boost to morale. The young pilots, drawn from Allied forces around the world, soon became air aces, engaging the Messerschmitts in daily dogfights. Unfortunately, many of these young men paid the ultimate price for their daring.

*

War duties permitting, at every opportunity the regimental bands would march through the streets of Valletta, playing all the well-known songs. On occasion, I watched as they marched in complete harmony, filling the air with the strains of 'Killaloe' or some other Irish tune. Moving along to the rhythm of the beat, seeing the sun reflecting on their highly polished regimental badges, I almost felt like joining in, as I watched with pride the swirling strides of the six-foot-five frame of Sligo's own Larry O'Dowd.

Sometimes they would resurrect the 'pre-war' dance bands to play at the United Services Club, or do radio broadcasts – something which brought great joy and entertainment to soldiers and civilians alike. The light relief of dancing the foxtrot or jiving away on our own 'senti-mental journey' was a great morale-booster in those troubled times.

Comedy came by way of two of the island's drag artists, Bobby and Sugar, who were regular attendees at our boxing bouts. Both of these gay men were very handy with their fists, especially when deal-ing with any servicemen who dared to heckle them during their stage performance. They thought nothing of sorting out the offenders, even to the point of going into the town afterwards and having a go at them. They certainly lightened our spirits – and God knows we need-ed them lifted, after listening to radio broadcasts of Lord Haw-Haw, who described our garrison as being 'trapped like rats' and made explicit remarks to 'Irishmen doing Britain's dirty work'. He listed all the Allied setbacks, saying that we were earmarked for even more pun-ishment. This was met with a defiant roar from the garrison, but nonetheless we all felt like putting a pickaxe through the Rediffusion wireless that was belting out his nasty messages.

Lord Haw-Haw was right about more punishment to follow, though, as the bombing was stepped up yet again. At the height of one particular raid, an enemy Dornier bomber spun wildly out of control. It crashed and burned close to Ray Williams and some others lads from the Faughs. By the time they got to the aircraft, scrambling over unexploded bombs and rough terrain, in the hope of finding some survivors, the plane was a smouldering wreck. All of the crew were dead. The pilot, still in the cockpit, was sitting erect, almost completely naked, with the shreds of his flying suit scattered around him. As they looked at the lifeless figures, all their anger and hatred quickly dissipated, to be replaced by pity and sorrow for the loss of life. They didn't see the dreaded Hun – their enemy – lying there, just ordinary men like themselves, with families back home in Germany.

9

BOXING CLEVER

Despite all the mayhem around us, garrison fight promotions were given special importance, to encourage morale, and attendances were always high. Kept busy between my duties and my beloved boxing, by June 1942 I'd fought and won three contests in seven weeks, and eagerly awaited my next bout.

My buddies – Davy Thompson, Gutrie Kane, Walter Pancott, Jimmy Loughlin, Tom McGee, Johnny King, Ray Williams, Willie Lismore, Andy Roy and Ned Fitzsimons – all made sure to get a twenty-four-hour pass to coincide with the fight. The others rounded up support in the arena, and with their help my support in the arena was guaranteed, as a healthy crowd of their mates turned up, boosting the night's takings. By the time my fight came around, they had my supporters so fired up that I thought my opponents had turned up alone.

I looked forward to these extra pay days: I got two pounds ten shillings for four three-minute rounds. Although the fight money was small, it was a godsend. As a non-smoker, I was always hungry, while my smoker pals were content with their cigarettes, which helped to kill their hunger pangs. The problem was that most of the bars and cafés in Malta were closed: they were either bombed out or had no food. For those in the know, there was always something to be had on the black market. If the price was right, someone would come up with an omelette, chips and bread – usually paid for with my fight money, hence my incentive to win. When I later heard that another man had been arrested for skinning cats, which he then sold as fresh meat, I was glad that I could only afford omelette and chips.

The boxing bouts were proving very popular, and due to demand, a Sunday bill was added to the usual Saturday bill, giving an opportunity for more contestants to join in. Now, with two days of fights, there was no problem getting a bout, and I could always get a fight on either day. With buildings being destroyed on a daily basis, it was easier to stage the bouts in the Command Fair, and soldiers, sailors and airmen, with little else to do outside the daily grind of war, all began to take a keen interest in boxing.

Despite the ever-increasing audiences, the purse was never more than three pounds. The bill was worked out in a mysterious way. If your record was consistent, you got to pick which day you wanted to fight. The problem was that the only available opponent might not be in your weight category, so an alternative opponent would have to be found, and agreed upon, at the last minute. This often meant that you signed up for a fight two weeks in advance, and knew nothing of your opponent's strengths or weaknesses until you stepped into the ring. You found out soon enough when the fight started.

I signed up for my fifth bout, on a bill arranged for the first week in August. I was helped in my training regime by my sparring partners Polly McIlwaine, Paudge Wallace, Paddy Ruane and Billy Meniece. Meniece noticed that I wasn't as sharp as usual, and seemed to be tiring very quickly. Whereas before I could do ten rounds with Ruane alone, now I had trouble lasting even three. Within a couple of days, I wasn't up to sparring at all. Paudge insisted that I report sick, and wouldn't take no for an answer. The army medic, Dr Berber, diagnosed debilitation and was worried that I was passing blood. Given the recent outbreak of typhoid and dysentery in the area, I feared the worst.

He sent me to Imtarfa Hospital, where I was checked out for these afflictions, inoculated, and injected for haemorrhoids. On questioning me further, the doctor asked whether I'd come into contact with any grape vines. I realised that he was on the right track, if the wrong fruit, and had to admit to having 'boxed the fox' – stripping a well-laden fig tree. Cycling down to port to unload a ship, Sean McCaughey had spotted the branches of a fig tree overhanging a wall. We propped the bikes against it and, standing on the saddle, supported by McCaughey's firm grip, I managed to fill our helmets with the unripe figs. Talk about crime not paying.

Thankfully, my problems were not serious, and after four days of being put through the mill, I was released just days before my next bout – which, perhaps surprisingly, I won. My opponent from the Royal Armoured Corp performed well, and I was the most surprised man in the stadium when the referee raised my hand as the victor on points. Being undefeated, I was immediately offered a bout on the Saturday billing in two weeks' time. Sergeant Digger Dawson trained with me for fight number six, and suggested that I enter an 'open' boxing competition that was being organised by the officers at Nexxar the following week.

It was to be an informal match, with no regard for the Queensbury Rules, and despite the short notice, I agreed to enter. The word 'open' turned out to be exactly what it meant. Though still a welterweight, over two days I had three fights; against a middleweight, Harry Freeney from Dublin, and two light-heavyweights, Scotsman Shug Darrock and a chap named Bailey from Durham. In the second round, Bailey, a heavy hitter, caught me flush on the chin with a right cross. From that point on, even his lightest punches sent a ricochet of pain from my jaw to my temple. Despite this, I managed to go the distance without being put on the deck, and came out a clear winner on points. I won all three bouts, and was awarded the prize for best boxer in the competition.

A week later, I won my sixth paid fight at the Command Fair and committed myself to a seventh. Throughout the following week, the pain never left me as I continued to train; by now, even the slightest touch sent the pain shuddering through my jaw. Sparring with Polly McIlwaine – who would have been a world-class fighter but for the war – Polly tested my chin, knowing that I was having some trouble. Light though his punches were, it had a decided effect on me, but I said nothing: I wanted to fight on the Command Fair bill. With my seventh bout looming, I gave any more sparring a miss, and concentrated on putting my energy into the arduous duties the army found for me, as we were called out to one back-breaking job after another.

So much for our belief that the 4.30 AM calls, when we lined up to collect our army-issue bike and a packed lunch, were over. No such luck: it seemed that we still had to haul around those cumbersome f—ing bikes that weighed a ton, and played havoc with your manhood. No matter how hard you pedalled, you never seemed to get up any speed, as you struggled for miles through the potholed, bombed-out wilderness. Still, by the end of an eleven-hour shift unloading the lorries and piling up heavy crates of bully beef, the bike ride was the easy part.

To a bystander, looking at us manhandling the cases of bully beef, it must have seemed as though there was a plentiful food supply, but by that time it was the only food the garrison had. We had it hot, cold and camouflaged as God knows what, but no matter how it came, it couldn't be mistaken for food. Rumour had it that the army cooks took their recipes from a pet-food manufacturer: I pitied the poor pets. Try as they might to disguise it, the chorus rang out from the men: 'More f—ing bully beef and biscuit duff.'

I convinced myself that stockpiling the bully beef was part of my workout, as I continued to prepare for my seventh outing. Billy Meniece took me in hand, organising a twenty-four-hour pass to which I was not entitled. Concerned about the pain in my jaw, he ruled out any sparring and concentrated instead on what he called the four-ring practice. Paddy Ruane, Slabs McKinney and Meniece himself joined me in the ring for mock sparring. No one wore gloves, as I practised the different moves on my three opponents, who came at me from all angles, boxing on the retreat for three minutes, blocking, counter-punching and jabbing like it was the real thing. Meniece had very quick hands and would 'score' by tapping at my jaw. I could feel the soreness as he shouted at me not to drop my guard. He wasn't too happy for me to go ahead with the fight, but as I picked up the pace, showing more speed and reflex action, he was satisfied that I would at least be able to stay out of trouble.

The only problem was the fact that things were getting hot and heavy in Malta, and it was becoming increasingly hard to organise sufficient support for the boxing bouts. These bouts now had no place on the military agenda: the army's concern was to keep the defences intact, and to make sure we had supplies.

Luckily, Davy Thompson wasn't one to let a little thing like the war interfere with a bit of entertainment, especially if it was boxing. He organised all the boys from the Belfast's Shankill and Sandy Row, Republican Derry, Dublin, and Kerry, to turn out and support the lad from their own regiment. Whatever your politics, there was no divide between us. The day of the fight came around, and I was drawn against a chap named 'Guy'. I hadn't come across him before, but I quickly found out that he was a hardened brawler who made me fight his type of fight. Early in the first round, I succeeded in keeping things at long distance, and I frustrated his efforts to land a solid punch to my head or jaw. Just before the end of the round, he was landing punches very close to my kidneys.

When I complained to my corner man, Rocky Burns, about the kidney punches, he said that I'd been aiding and abetting him, turning my kidney area towards his punches, to minimise the power of his body blows. He advised me to keep the fight at long distance and not to get trapped on the ropes. In the second round, things were going well and I felt I was ahead, scoring freely with my left hand – although he managed to catch me with a couple of short hits to the body.

I was growing in confidence and scoring well with both hands, and felt that I could finish him off. Responding to the tumultuous roars of my supporters, as they shouted out our regimental war cry 'Faugh a Ballagh', I hit him with every punch in the book, when suddenly a vicious right hook exploded on my chin. The impact of the punch was so fierce that I staggered into the ropes and almost went down. I was in terrible agony from the pain in my jaw, but my natural tendency to fight back took over, and for the rest of the round, and the two that followed, I was fighting from instinct, oblivious to the pain.

I could hear the crowd roaring encouragement, but I didn't know whether it was for me or my opponent, until I heard the voice of one of my buddies from the Liberties, Tom Magee, and then Hookie Doran, Exxie Leach and a few other Faughs coming through the fog. Loudest of all, I could hear Magee's voice screaming at me to 'Finish him off!' This drowned out every other sound in the packed arena. It was as if I was being programmed, as his words repeatedly broke through the haze. For many years afterwards, the words 'Keep punching, Johnny' sprang to mind whenever I met up with Tom Magee – or Big Maggie, as he was affectionately known.

Though I have no memory of it, I found out that after the fight my corner man, Rocky Burns, brought me back to the dressing room, while Joe Beatty went for the doctor. I had a constant buzzing in my head and kept asking Joe when I was due to go on. I had no recollection of the fight, or of the referee raising my hand as the winner. The pain in my jaw was now intense, and this was added to Rocky's ranting, as he laid into me for not following his game plan. The fact was that I didn't remember getting advice, nor did I recall shaking the hand of my opponent before leaving the ring.

The doctor insisted that I be taken straight to hospital, but his urgent warning was not about to get in the way of a good old celebration with my pals and supporters as we went in search of a few drinks and a 'bit' to eat on the black market. It was the least I could do to thank them. But try as I might, I couldn't open my jaw to take a bite of the stale, greasy chips: it was like trying to prise open a rusty hinge. Beer being scarce, I convinced myself that the by-now-excruciating pain could only be alleviated by spilling a few drops of the local wine – Stuka juice – through my clamped jaws.

Trying to cheer me up, the gang embarked on a series of funny stories, including one about the time we raided a farmer's hen house. Piling it on thick, they recalled that, when it came to wringing a chicken's neck, I was a disaster. They gave a graphic account of the raucous cackling that emanated from every single hen in the coop, as I tried to strangle their mate. The irate farmer, woken by his egg-laying burglar alarms, let loose with a hail of buckshot, causing us to drop our prey somewhere between a grapevine and a ridge of potatoes. All the way back to the barracks, we salivated about the wonderful roast chicken that had escaped our clutches. My attempts not to laugh only added to my pain. Despite the piercing agony, I was happy to be in the company of good, reliable friends.

Noticing my plate of cold, untouched chips, Davy launched into the story of the night we stole potatoes and boiled them up in a bucket. On the advice of a Cavan friend, a former farmhand, we added a guinea pig to give our stew some flavour. When it was cooked, we dived into the stew – only to find out our stomachs couldn't stand the disgusting dish.

I found it hard not to laugh as I recalled the disgruntled farmer arriving at our company sergeant major's office excitedly waving a few green stalks – all that remained of the great potato heist. We'd shoved the stalks back into the ground as we made good our escape. The farmer had the last laugh, though: we each got fourteen days confined to our billets – as if attempting to eat that disgusting guinea pig was not punishment enough!

With plenty of the Maltese 'Stuka juice' on board, we staggered through the bombed-out streets, stumbling on the debris as we weighed up the merits of the various doss-houses. Someone mentioned the 'Haven of Rest', and dissent arose: one of our number reminded us that it was in this kip that he'd got his last dose of crabs. Andy Roy told us that, on his last visit there, someone had pissed in his Glengarry – his uniform hat. He had wrongly accused a sailor of the foul deed; this led to what he dramatically described as 'the entire navy' having a go at him. Too exhausted to haul my drunken body any further, I opted for the Haven of Rest as somewhere where I could at least get my throbbing head down.

If the Germans bombed Valletta that night, they missed our louse house. No blinding flashes or shrieking bombs penetrated my brain that night: I was dead to the world.

When daylight came, I got up automatically, still in a stupor, and made my escape from the haven of rickety beds and the wingless parasites residing there. With the searing pain in my jaw, and complete deafness in one ear, I didn't know where I was, but despite the confusion I quickly realised that something was missing. I raced back up the narrow stairs two at a time, happy that the few bob I'd left under the pillow was still there – and had been neither stolen nor eaten by the parasites that lived all year round in the Haven. My second task was to ensure that the parasites didn't join me in making an exit. I was pleasantly surprised that, although they had left their trademark – bites – they had feasted elsewhere that night. I made good my escape before they changed their mind. By the time I left, Guthrie and the boys still hadn't surfaced. Outside, with the last of my few bob I caught a horse and garry back to barracks, to report to the regimental medical officer.

Captain Barber talked to me for a while, gradually bringing to my mind some of the events of the previous night, before deciding that I was a hospital case. Nothing new there, then!

10

FLORENCE NIGHTINGALE IS A MAN!

After a lengthy examination, I was transferred to the 45th General Hospital with a broken jaw. Anaesthetised, I had my teeth wired up and a barrel bandage put in place. I was now a patient on the surgical landing, or so I thought.

Two days after my jaw had been wired up, Matron told me to report to the senior nurse in charge of the surgical wards. I was looking forward to a bit of female company as I went in search of her. I knew that, as I had been categorised as an 'up patient', they had some kind of manual labour in mind for me. I wondered if I'd end up digging trenches with the 'bomb happies' around the hospital area, or perhaps I'd find myself in the cookhouse, scouring dixies – large pots – mopping floors or doing other menial tasks. I kept telling myself that, whatever it was, it had to be better than the dangerous operations being run outside the hospital gates.

My hopes of female company were dashed when the senior nurse turned out to be a big male sergeant, who asked about my family and my military background. He was a decent sort, who spoke to me man to man, as opposed to the many NCOs I'd met, who generally used abusive language when talking at me.

Sensing my restlessness, he quickly told me what my duties were, working in the surgical ward kitchen. I could hardly believe my luck: I had the freedom to move around the hospital, and a special diet. It was a cushy number, and more than I could have hoped for. Sleeping in a real bed with clean sheets and pleasant people around was, at that time, the high point of my life, in all my twenty-one years.

The spirit of camaraderie and the commitment of the nursing staff encouraged me to put great effort into my work, and I took it upon myself to help out wherever I could, assisting badly wounded patients to make the trip to the loo or in other similar tasks. These small deeds came to the attention of the matron, and I was called into her inner sanctum. I was hoping that she wasn't annoyed with my actions, seeing it as interference.

Out of character, and with some trepidation, I knocked gently on her door, expecting to be on the receiving end of her tongue – which I imagined would be akin to the sting of a dying wasp. Smiling benignly, she invited me to take a seat, just as an air-raid warning sounded. She asked how much longer I thought the island could hold out, but before I could answer, the building shook with the vibration of explosions and the cannon fire from the Spitfires and Messerschmitt, and the rat-tat-tat of the Hurricanes, as they pursued their various quarries. Soon the screech of ambulance sirens was heard approaching the hospital, bringing in the dead and wounded.

Matron, concerned at my silent staring out the window, gently touched my arm and asked if I wanted to take shelter. I declined. In reply to her earlier question, I told her that I was confident we could hold out, provided the supply ships got through. If they didn't, the collapse would come in two or three weeks.

In hindsight, Matron probably didn't need my opinion on the situation but more likely was assessing me. She thanked me for helping her nursing staff, and expressed her concern at the low standard of cleanliness in the ward kitchens, saying that the nurses were overworked. I was way ahead of her, and saw how I could extend my stay in these comfortable surroundings, if I went the right way about it.

Mumbling through my wired-up teeth, I assured her that I'd be happy to sort out the situation for her. As I left her office, I'd made up my mind that this nice-looking middle-aged matron was not the dragon she'd been made out to be by those third-rate barrack-room lawyers.

It's amazing what a couple of days' nourishment will do for a flagging libido. As I was about to leave her office, Matron made a swift movement past me and opened the door. As she did, I got the very pleasant smell of her perfume. Becoming temporarily dispossessed of my senses, despite the difference in our ages, I was suddenly filled with lust for her. I struggled to control my emotions, and thanked her for giving me the chance to improve the standard of hygiene in the ward kitchens.

Thanking my lucky stars that I'd held back from making advances, I winced at how close I'd come to getting turfed out and thrown back to the soul-destroying grind of daily life in Malta. Measured against the soup and minced chicken on offer here, bully beef and hard biscuits – which I couldn't eat anyway through a wired-up mouth – were no match.

I did all I could to help out, and it was an eye-opener seeing the people with missing limbs, eye damage, lost toes, shrapnel wounds and worse. Despite their injuries, their morale remained intact. I built up a good relationship with the patients, including a number of German pilots who had been shot down.

One of these pilots had horrific multiple injuries, though the surgeons did tremendous work in patching him up. One of his legs was badly shattered, and the medics were battling day and night to try to avoid amputation. In a drastic move to save his leg, they resorted to the old method of putting maggots on the wound to clean it up. At the time I couldn't believe what I was hearing, but I subsequently learned of the effectiveness of using worms to clean the infection – something which is again in use today, despite the use of antibiotics.

As further proof of the effectiveness of this treatment, I learned of a good friend, medic Victor Kenchington, who, while moving under fire over difficult terrain for more than two hours, had finally reached Corporal Mickey Pearson, who had lain, wounded, for three days. Victor gave the corporal a shot of morphine and dressed his wounds, which were covered in maggots. Pearson was evacuated to Portolago Hospital in Leros, while Victor was praised for leaving the maggots in the wounds, thereby preventing gangrene from setting in.

As the days went by, my hospital duties were expanded. I still felt that I needed to do something extra in order to impress Matron enough to extend my stay. I noticed her dismay at the state of the aluminium bucket which was used to fetch tea from the main kitchen. It had taken on a filthy dull colour and was badly tea-stained. It was way past its best, but in those hard times we were grateful for any utensils.

Despite it being an uneven contest, I was determined that the badly corroded bucket would not withstand my attack, experienced as I was in the detention cells of Lackery Woods, who made sure that we cleaned rusty dixies until they looked like polished glass. Under attack from a bath brick, soap, water and rags, and after hours of elbow grease, the bucket yielded to the superior force and persistent torture I was inflicting upon it. It shone like a new pin.

Placing it in a conspicuous spot where it was sure to attract Matron's attention, I waited for her reaction. The plan worked well: she spent a full five minutes singing its praises – but with no mention of my efforts. On the contrary, she hinted that perhaps it wasn't the same bucket she had complained about, and suggested that I'd acquired a new one by vicarious means. I was livid, and found it difficult to hold my tongue. The beautiful, angelic Florence Nightingale who'd first interviewed me had turned into a interfering oul' Jinnet who dared to insult my efforts, and bruise my ego. Now, in my anger, I saw her as a scrawny-necked, snub-nosed, oul' wretch who couldn't tell the difference between a bucket and a donkey. I couldn't help noticing her ill-fitting uniform, and thought that I'd seen better clothes on a tailor's dummy. By now, my thoughts were far removed from flowers and candlelight.

I was so angry that I never saw her leave the kitchen, nor heard her congratulate me on my efforts. It was only when the sergeant mentioned her intention of writing a favourable report on my contribution to the running of the hospital that I realised my mistake. If ever a man felt guilty or embarrassed, I did that day. I wanted to apologise but, since Matron hadn't seemed to realise how I felt, I let sleeping dogs lie, and reverted to declaring her worthy of my reverence. I resolved to find new and even better ways of keeping on the right side of the Lady of the Lamp.

Hearing about my toadying to Matron, my buddies came to see me at the hospital and gave me a hard time. My boyhood friend Bill Kavanagh brought me a bag of walnuts, knowing full well that I wouldn't be able to eat them because my jaw was wired up.

Things seemed to be going well for me, and I got the seal of approval when the sergeant said he'd managed to get permission for me to have a bottle of Guinness a day – for health reasons. The fact that I had to drink it from a feeding cup, pushed through the gap in the wire, did nothing to diminish the taste of the wonderful 'Black Champagne'.

The spin-off from a diet of Guinness, minced chicken and soup meant that my weight increased rapidly. I decided to get in some physical training and mentioned this to the sergeant. To my astonishment, he told me that the toilet in the hall was usually free for an hour in the afternoon but that if I was discovered using it, I was on my own.

The next day, I checked out my proposed training ground, and found it anything but free. As I hung around waiting for the occupant to vacate the loo, all I could hear was a series of bangs, clangs and bumps. Eventually, a patient on crutches emerged, but he refused my offer of assistance. Delighted at last to have a vacant training spot, my plans were cut short when I entered the loo and was assailed by such a foul smell that I threw up. Hopefully the medics were prescribing enemas laced with anti-pollutants in his medication. I made my escape to the sanctuary of the ward kitchen.

The following day I ventured back, in the hope that the skunk-swallowing patient was no longer in occupation of my training ground. My luck held out, and for the following six days, I did routine training, including shadow-boxing and skipping, which brought about a new problem. Due to my excessive movement, the wire on my teeth came loose, and I was back to the ward for a further stay, having impressions taken and a vulcanised splint – to lock the top and bottom teeth together – put in place. The barrel bandage was replaced with a head harness – which didn't last long, as the bottom part of the splint came loose. I decided to say nothing. Instead, I became an expert at making it look intact, particularly when the doctor was around. With the bottom part of the splint free, I could loosen the head harness and open my mouth enough to drink from a glass. From small beginnings, I moved on to the temptation of the ever-present bread and marmalade. Close to bedtime, alone in the kitchen, I cut a couple of slices of bread, plastered it with marmalade and cut it into tiny slices, which I pushed through the gap, onto my tongue. Unable to chew, I washed it down with a cup of soup, and went to bed content.

I awoke a few hours later, feeling as though I was choking to death. I had chest pains, and found it difficult to breathe. I managed to alert the night nurse, and gasped out what I'd done. She lost no time in getting the doctor, and both gave me immediate first aid. When I recovered, I apologised for not reporting the loose splint, and readied myself for a reprimand. The doc thought this was hilarious and, between gasps of laughter, told me that I had no chance of getting away with it. He promised to make the splint so tight that I'd hardly be able to suck liquids through a straw. Just as well I didn't tell him that I'd broken barracks and left the hospital, via the mortuary, on more than one occasion, to slip down to a local wine shop – much to the amazement of the local Maltese customers.

After almost three months in hospital, waiting for my jaw to heal, it was time to return to my unit, and I was released, with strict instructions not to box for at least a year.

11

'GET OUT OF JAIL' CARD

Out of hospital, I was ordered to report back to my unit – A Company of the Faughs – to await further instructions. During my time in hospital, my weight had increased to twelve stone nine, thanks to the regular food. Arriving back at Company HQ in the village of Gargur, I was met by Corporal Bobby Peden, who was in charge of my section and was a fellow member of the boxing team. It wasn't exactly a warm welcome, as he slagged me for being a flabby, out-of-condition slob. I ignored his remarks, teasing him that I'd been unable to resist all the goodies that had been foisted on me by the beautiful nurses.

He was not impressed with my sarcasm and, realising that he was about to flip his lid, I adopted a more conciliatory tone, sympathising with his having to work in demanding conditions while surviving on meagre rations. The vision of Bobby's vicious left hook sinking into my newly recovered jaw didn't excite me. I assured him that, once I was back on a diet of bully beef and biscuit duff, I'd soon be back to skin and bone. This seemed to satisfy him. Thinking about it later, I could understand his resentment. Starvation puts a different complexion on things: this six-foot-three man, once a fine athlete, was a shadow of his former self. I realised that none of my buddies at Gargur could be described as robust, but they concealed their situation with good humour and craic. It was back to business for us all.

September brought a temporary lull in the dawn-to-dusk bombings, and though people were still being killed, the attacks were not as widespread, as Allied and Axis forces switched the focus of their efforts to North Africa. Four days after my arrival back in Gargur, I received confirmation of my new posting to the Manoel Island submarine base in Marsaxlokk Bay. Until I moved out, I was detailed to work with my platoon, piling foodstuffs in an isolated storage dump. Back on the old rations, I was already missing the hospital diet; the other lads were starving.

Still brawny from my hospital stay, I volunteered to climb to the top of the stockpile and prise open one of the seven-pound tins of bully beef. The NCO and the other lads all agreed that it would be foolish not to. I managed to prise open one of the cases, and extracted a seven-pound tin of bully beef. Jacking it open with my army penknife, I tasted a knife-full before passing it down to my fellow squaddies. The plan was to put the tin back in the case and reseal it, to allow for further pickings later. Corporal Peden and the five other lads got about four or five ounces each.

Just as I'd finished the resealing job, a young officer suddenly came on the scene. Seeing me about to descend from the pile with a lever in my hand, he took possession of the lever and climbed up to investigate matters. Finding the case had been tampered with, he charged me with pilfering and placed me under close arrest. As the only one who had been caught on the pile, I was accused of having gorged myself on the bully beef. Ironically, Corporal Peden and the lads were to become witnesses for the Crown.

Although I felt annoyed, not to mention ashamed, my annoyance was due to the sneaky tactics of the young officer. I was outwardly calm, but felt like kicking the s—t out of the bastard. The fact that my partners in crime were to be called as witnesses didn't bother me. The army's unspoken rule of 'you don't tell' was rarely departed from, and when it was, the retribution that followed would seriously upset the offender's happiness.

When under siege, a charge of stealing food is not a matter to be dealt with by your CO. Going before him is merely military routine, before being placed under close arrest, to await court martial. Once again, I was to be a guest of the hard man, Provost Sergeant Lackery Woods. While I was awaiting trial, Lackery was constrained from putting me through his imaginative courses, designed for those who were already serving a sentence. The main military detention centre, at Corredino, was overcrowded, hence the use of regimental centres. Soldiers sentenced to 'field punishment' endured severe hardship.

Wearing full winter kit, helmet, webbing and a respirator, carrying a fifty-six-pound pack on their shoulders and a Lee Enfield rifle, they drilled at the double in temperatures into the nineties. The 'punishment area' consisted of a field of a hundred yards square, with small man-made hills and inclines spaced out in a circle around the field. The hills had a gradual rise of about two feet and a sharp decline. Anyone losing their stride while negotiating these obstacles would be bawled out. After half an hour of this, the prisoners would strip off their gear and, following a few minutes' break, would have to build bunkers – known as Sangers – from the heaps of large stones lying around the field. Once these had been completed, they had to dismantle the Sangers, and put the stones back where they'd found them, before getting back into full kit, minus the respirators, and marching for ten minutes.

As a wind-down, they stripped down to their trousers for fifteen minutes of physical jerks. Due to a water shortage, when they returned to their cells they had to share a couple of basinfuls of water to wash and cool down. After a quick rub of a hard towel and a change into light khaki drill uniforms, they'd be off again, ready for other duties digging slit trenches, scouring rusted dixies and shoring up local air-raid shelters. It was tough going on meagre rations.

During my time awaiting court martial, two good friends, Bob Harris and Walter Pancott, did twenty-eight days' field punishment. Both had served time in Corredino Detention Centre and had been hardened up by very tough Marine sergeants and instructors. Lackery Woods, himself a hard man, had great respect for them: try as he might, he couldn't break them.

Beaver Elliott, yet another hard man, served time with these boys at Corredino. He asked Walter and Bob to drop a boulder on his hand so that he could be hospitalised. Each time the boys were about to let it go, he'd pull his hand away, claiming that he wasn't ready. Eventually they gave up, but Beaver found another way to blag his way into hospital. Nicking the front of his tongue, he claimed to have swallowed all the nails in his cell. He spat enough blood on the floor to make it look realistic, and the nails – used for hanging up his gear – were disposed of through the small cell window. Lackery took no chances and transferred him to Imtarfa Hospital. After two days, his scam backfired and he was returned to the loving care of Provost Sergeant Lackery Woods. I lost track of Beaver until later on, on Leros, when he again came into my life, in an unexpected way.

*

'Conduct prejudicial to military discipline' can range from insubordination, adultery and desertion to looting, cowardice and homicide, and many other crimes in between. The charges against me stated that 'the accused is guilty of conduct prejudicial to the good order and military discipline, in that he pillaged a seven-pound tin of corned beef, government or war department property, or the misapplication of the people's property at a time when the island was being blockaded by the deeds of the enemy'.

To my mind, this was over the top. I wasn't into looting, pillaging or black-marketeering. To steal bully beef in order to ease the hunger pangs of my mates hardly translates into using a war situation for profit. The prosecuting King's Counsel made the most of the fact that the civilian population were under constant threat; weren't we all. He demanded severe penalties for a crime 'of this nature, where foodstuffs are taken for the selfish means of ensuring personal robust health and comfort for the culprit'.

Some f—ing comfort and robust health, from the consumption of five ounces of bully beef. He should have been writing fiction. The nearest this boy got to firing a shot was at a partridge shoot. To hear him, any innocent bystander could have been forgiven for thinking that I'd been looting from dead bodies. That said, I was well aware that he had been specifically instructed to ensure that any black-marketeering was hit hard, and not allowed to take hold.

Such a situation did develop in Malta in 1941 and early 1942, to the extent that coloured dockets were issued to military and civilian lorries being loaded from the docks. The dockets were colour-coded, to identify which depot the goods should go to. However, some drivers ran a racket printing their own dockets: when they were stopped at a checkpoint, they could produce a docket appropriate to the area. Once he had been waved through, the driver could safely move on, to link up with his accomplices. In 1942, this scam was knocked on the head, with the introduction of colour-coded lorries, each accompanied by a Maltese policeman. Each lorry were painted in accordance with the food dump it was going to.

While I was waiting to appear before the special court martial, although I was not subject to the 'field punishment' as yet, like every other soldier I was put to work under escort, digging into the hard rock to cut out slit trenches. Regulations allowed me to choose my defence counsel, and I picked Lieutenant Paddy Slaney as my defending officer. Paddy, with a lengthy service in the ranks behind him, had just become a commissioned officer. My past experiences of soldiering with him had demonstrated how bright he was, not to mention his compassion and generosity to young soldiers, who had yet to learn army discipline.

He interviewed me as to my defence, but I had no excuse to offer, other than hunger. On the day of the court martial, which was presided over by three officers, a colonel and two majors, I thought of asking Paddy to go for a plea of leniency, given the limited mitigating circumstances I had to offer.

The arguments of the British civilian King's Counsel were heavy and persuasive, designed to secure both a conviction and a severe penalty. To hear him, you'd imagine that I'd plundered the island and set up a major enterprise racketeering.

Given the slimness of my contribution to the case, Paddy Slaney's performance was a master class. Dismissing the prosecution counsel's argument as not only misleading but inaccurate, he added, almost as an afterthought, that the arrest itself was illegal. I wondered how he expected to get away with this argument, until he told the court that, at the time of the arrest, I had made an admission statement, as the result of a direct order given by a superior officer, the arresting NCO, who had suggested to the accused (me) that he was in breach of military discipline and would pay the price. Quoting the relevant military law, Paddy claimed that the arresting officer was wrong in suggesting guilt, and assuming punishment, at that point, and was thereby intimidating the accused into making an admission of guilt. Because the right of the accused to remain silent had not been afforded to him, he was put at a disadvantage, claimed Paddy.

The court martial sentenced me to one hundred and fifty days' detention, loss of pay, and a reduction in the ranks. The sentence did not take account of the two weeks I had been detained while awaiting trial. In accordance with custom and practice, the findings of the ad hoc tribunal could only be put into effect by the general officer commanding the garrison, so Lackery Woods could not dole out his special brand of punishment just yet.

I was still condemned to dig slit trenches in the middle of nowhere; the walk there and back got longer every day, as they sent me further afield. After four weeks of this, Paddy Slaney brought me the good news that the general officer commanding had refused to ratify the decision. After six weeks as a guest of Lackery, I was released and returned to normal duties. Two weeks later, my stripe reinstated, I joined the Special Boat Section: the SBS Commando Unit.

*

Wartime conditions never got in the way of our 'spit and polish' inspections. Discipline was important, and there was usually some element of inspection on a daily basis. We were regularly lined up, and the sergeant in charge of the guard would decide who was the smartest in drill movements and best turned out. The best candidate would be instructed to fall out and was rewarded by being excused a night's guard duty. This prize was known as 'the stick'. Many of the men felt that they had done enough to win, but what they didn't realise was that some of us – no names, no pack drill – regularly borrowed the best heel-balled boots, well-blancoed webbing, and the cleanest rifle in the platoon. I walked away with the accolade. The reality was that the owner of the borrowed kit, Wilkie Ward, was never picked out when he wore it for inspection. Although he was immaculate, his posture never seemed erect. During inspection his arse stuck out, bringing to mind the old Dublin saying: 'Here's me head, me arse is following.'

His unfortunate posture made his drill movements look awkward, and inevitably he was passed over for the prize. I considered it a shame to let his hard work 'bulling up' his uniform go to waste, especially when it fitted me so well. Wilkie was not too bothered: I gave him my ration of fags for hiring out his spotless clobber to me.

*

By May 1943, the battle for survival had been won. Malta had been saved by the combined sea and air power of the Allies, its garrison of defenders, and the resolution of the Maltese people. Testimony of friend and foe alike agrees that Malta played a major role in the defeat of the Axis powers, and in the ultimate restoration of peace in Europe.

12

THE TIPTOE BOYS

THE SAS AND THE SBS

Before going into hospital, I'd been selected for secondment to the commando training unit at Manoel Island in Malta. In September 1942, twenty of us were sent for training, under Major Jock Larraik of the Special Boat Service. Lining up with personnel who had been selected from various regiments, we were billeted close to Marsaxlokk submarine base. The plan was to knock us into shape as an effective raiding unit that would be ready at short notice to undertake undercover missions into enemy territory. Our introduction to this world of undercover operations came by way of a talk where it was made clear that the purpose of our training was to develop our ruthless single-mindedness, raw courage and determination of purpose. There was no room for shirkers or anyone lagging behind: we had to be fully committed to whatever was demanded of us, with no quarter given or expected. This was not a million miles from the current SAS or Special Forces training of today – though not as sophisticated.

To my delight, Lieutenant Charlie Clyne, my former platoon commander in the Faughs, was once again my immediate superior officer. A New Zealander I believe was called Stud Stellin was a training officer. Johnnie King, a close pal I'd soldiered with from the depot days of 1937, was on the training course too. The course was tough, but it dramatically increased our fitness and agility. The idea of penetrating enemy territory in an attacking role, rather than in the defensive role we'd been used to, was an exciting prospect.

We were given extra rations to build our strength and help maintain our stamina. Boy did we need it, as we went on forced marches in full kit, ran eight miles wearing heavy khaki in soaring temperatures, and swam six hundred yards, partly clothed, as part of our training. When you were at your lowest point, hot and exhausted, you still had to crawl through barbed-wire entanglements while marksmen cut loose with live rounds – both ahead and behind your position. Your legs and arms ached as you carried ammunition boxes filled with sand and walked in full gear along the beach until you were waist-deep, twenty yards into the sea. Instinct told you to drop the leaden boxes, or the tommy-gun you were carrying, but you kept going, knowing that anything less would mean an immediate return to your old unit, with no further chance of joining the clandestine 'tiptoe boys'. Lackery Woods would have been proud of us.

I joined forces with Johnnie King, Charlie Lee, Sab McMaster, Victor Kenchington and Gordon Wright, and we all supported each other. No matter how tough the task or the terrain, we encouraged each other to keep going. In between lectures on the handling of explosives, which included practical demonstrations, and lessons on how to get the best effect from the charges that we had laid, we had regular PT exercises aimed at strengthening our legs, arms and stomach.

After lectures, we went into the field to practise handling gelignite charges, exploding gun cotton – often used to derail trains. A piece of gun cotton would be laid inside both sides of the track, causing it to buckle as the train attempted to pass – it literally cut the track in two. Other 'special ops' training tactics included the operation of small sea craft, to be used to get us to and from our landing sites along enemy coastlines. We were given training in the use and utilisation of fishing caiques and sailing boats at sea, but instruction in the art of raiding harbours and island-hopping by night was put on hold, until we had some more experience in the field.

I was now fitter than ever, and the urge to get back to boxing was gaining momentum, despite the doctor's advice that I was not to box for a least a year. It was just two months since I'd left hospital, and Johnnie King urged me to forget about boxing for now.

Bill Kavanagh, my pal from Dublin, came across to Manoel Island to tell me he was transferring to the Parachute Regiment. While there, he told me about a new officer who'd taken charge of the boxing team. Before the night was out, I'd agreed to take part in an inter-service tournament. This was to be my last outing after forty bouts for the Royal Irish Fusiliers. Due to the missions I was to undertake with the SBS, I didn't expect to get a chance to box again. I boxed at middleweight and lost on points.

After the battle of El Alamein, rumours abounded that the SBS would be deployed to make landings along the coast of North Africa. The plan was that fifteen or twenty members of our unit were to be sent to Tobruk, in Libya, North Africa, to help out the British Western Desert Force, but the move was postponed and nothing came of it. Between January and March our training intensified, and we were on standby to take part in an as-yet-undisclosed mission. The training included how to cut railways lines for derailment and sabotage, and how to lay charges using both long and short fuses, so as to make it appear that multiple explosions were going off at once. This tactic was often used to mislead the enemy as to the real target. We were taught how to cut through reinforced perimeter wire and to use 'time pencils' which were filled with acid and designed to eat through the obstacle. Things were always operated on a 'need to know' basis.

In the interim, we had more training with Thompson sub-machine guns and other automatic weapons, hand grenades and explosives, as well as in the use of low-profile vessels, laying multiple charges of .808 and gun cotton, together with escape-and-evasion tactics. Where possible, training took place in the environment that was about to be attacked: if the target was in the Aegean Sea area, we'd train there. We were taught how to recognise 'lying up' places behind enemy lines – where was suitable to take cover and, more importantly, where was not suitable, however inviting it might appear at first glance. Parachute training for clandestine missions into enemy territory was also on the agenda.

We were transported to Tripoli by destroyer on 28 March 1943 and based under canvas in a transit camp, with strict instructions not to discuss with anyone the nature of our unit. With neither drink nor diversions to be had, we had very little to do as we waited for our orders. We were amazed to see some American soldiers queuing outside a brothel that had a warning sign saying 'Keep Out Typhus' painted on the wall. Did they have some inside information that the epidemic had passed?

The only diversion we found led us to the dockland area, where we 'liberated' some long-range desert boots, which were in short supply. We figured they might come in handy on our missions. Not many people would take the risk of falling foul of the Gurkha soldiers protecting His Majesty's goods, but we foolish Paddies did – and very nearly paid the price with our lives. Two of the Gurkhas fired warning shots, and pursued us as we ran. Fortunately, a passing army lorry took us aboard, and we lost them. We learned not to mess with Gurkhas again. With the exception of the boots, our venture into the city was fruitless.

We made our way back to the transit camp, bartered some clothes in exchange for a drink of illegal hooch called Iraq Plus, and staggered back to our bed boards. I was woken by Jock McKay telling me that my brother Arthur, whom I hadn't seen in five years, had been looking for me. Arthur was serving with the 7th Armoured Division, and had driven an officer down from Tunisia on some business. Seeing some of our lads, he'd asked where I was, and was told I'd be back in half an hour. Unfortunately, the officer had to rush back to Tunisia, and Arthur and I never got to see each other.

THE KERKENNAH ISLAND JOB

Around midnight on 9 April 1943, we left camp and were transported to the harbour area in Tripoli, where we waited for the signal to board the vessels for our mission. Some of us boarded motor launches, while others scrambled aboard fishing caiques. Only then were we told that we were heading for the Kerkennah Islands, located west of Sfax in Tunisia. Our job was to take out some Italian troops who were located there. We arrived well before dawn, and found anchorage half a mile from the islands. Major Jock Larraik and Lieutenant Charlie Clyne went ashore in dinghies and eventually gave the agreed signal, by hooded torches, that we were to launch our small landing craft and row in.

Our flat-bottomed boats were designed to be rowed through shallow waters at low tide, without the bottom being ripped. That night, due to a sea swell, a couple of our boats drifted off course and got entangled in fishing nets that were spread across bamboo stakes. The silence being broken by the lads trying to extricate themselves from the nets should have been enough to alert the Italian soldiers, but no gunfire ensued, and twenty of us got ashore at various points. Our group of four agents could see the outline of dark shapes, that looked like manned gun emplacements, as we moved cautiously on the enemy's position.

We edged ever closer, monitoring for sounds or movement, before making our assault with grenades and machine-gun fire. Dawn was just breaking, and we realised that the position we'd advanced on was a decoy, giving the impression of strong fortification – something the Italians were masters at. Our ammo unused, we went in support of our other units, and found the same decoys everywhere. Inside these well-built sangers were two shafts of a horse-drawn cart set on a base of sandbags, camouflaged to give the impression of being a manned anti-aircraft-gun position. It had all the signs of being ready to engage low-flying aircraft or land-based targets. If this ploy was intended to delay intruders, it worked: it cost us forty minutes. Extensive searches by our units found similar decoys, but not one f—ing Italian in sight.

Our senior SBS officer, Charlie Clyne, questioned some of the islanders, who told him that the Italians had been ordered back to Sfax at dawn on 8 April and had left on confiscated fishing caiques. We were bitterly disappointed that our raid had been so unproductive: we'd missed our targets by twenty-four hours. Was it coincidence, or did they have intelligence, we wondered? It seemed that someone had rumbled our purpose during our stay in Tripoli, which was a hotbed for enemy agents.

We flew back to Malta on a Lancaster bomber via Tripoli and Cairo. Back in Malta, we resumed our training with the Special Training Unit on Manoel Island.

I took a break and slipped away from base to visit Bill Kavanagh, and a few other friends who were bounds for Palestine with the Paras. I seriously thought of looking for a transfer to join them, but back at base later that day we got instructions to return to our respective regiments on a temporary basis and await instructions for our next mission.

I was hardly back when Charlie Clyne told me that I was on a shortlist, with five others, to join him for another SBS job. The boys in question were Charlie Lee, Gordon Wright, Jock McKay, Johnnie King, George Seymour and myself – Lance Corporal Johnnie Harte. That put paid to any thoughts of transferring to the Paratroopers.

Within the week, Seymour and I were selected to make a return trip to North Africa. Sent to Sousse in Tunisia, we arrived within hours of the port having been evacuated by the retreating Axis forces. We boarded Motor Torpedo Boat No. 75; our job was to patrol the North African coast and the hostile Sicilian waters. The mouth of the harbour was full of shipwrecks, many boats having been scuttled by the fleeing enemy. Getting through the wrecks required great skill, but despite our caution and careful manoeuvring, MTB75 hit a submerged wreck and needed emergency repairs to a hole in the engine room.

The British and American engineering units did Trojan work, but progress was slow, and it was after dark when we cautiously edged our way out of the harbour. We patrolled the coastlines along Gabes, Sfax, Sousse, Tunis and En Fidaville. When we were close to occupied Sicilian harbours, we moved on silent auxiliary engines. The MTB75 was a Vosper MTB that had been converted to a gun boat, with confiscated 20mm Breda guns mounted on a revolving platform. The Tunisian coast was riddled with sea mines, and it was part of our job to explode them – a tricky job. Our task was to sink, burn or destroy – whatever it took – but to let nothing pass.

After fourteen days on patrol, George and I were called back to Malta, and we parted company with the skipper, who had been good to us while we were on board. Shortly after we left, MTB75 suffered a direct hit from shore batteries in the Messina Straits, killing many on board. Harry Smith was badly injured but survived. We returned to Manoel Island to link up with Major Ian Lapraik and Lieutenant Charlie Clyne on 14 May 1943, the day after the Germans surrendered in North Africa.

Our daily training routine of early-morning swimming, running, weapons training and the handling of explosives became more intense. We assumed that another special-ops job was coming up soon. Before it did, the Malta Command and Garrison Championships were on. I boxed for the Faughs at middleweight in the semi-final, and won. Unfortunately, a few days later, events with the SBS prevented me from competing in the final. Still, the Royal Irish Fusiliers emerged as champions, so I wasn't too disappointed.

On 22 May 1943, we left for another clandestine operation. Ordered to be in the vicinity of the HMS *Talbot* at Manoel Island, a submarine called *Trooper* came into sight, and within a short time we were aboard, carrying our gear with us.

We were welcomed aboard by Lieutenant Johnny Wraith, the commander of *Trooper*, together with two army officers and four other ranks, and were put at our ease. Its crew of sixty-one submariners was supplemented by three extra crew members and our group of tiptoe boys.

There is nothing straightforward about getting gear aboard a sub, but Petty Officer Dickie Sleep and some of the crew, Stoker Petty Officer Pete Adam, Able Seaman F. W. Tripp and Leading Seaman Len Williams, organised the gear, and we managed to get our folbots – small, kayak-like boats – shovels, stones and a suitcase aboard, and to find a place for them.

Petty Officer Sleep, while praising the sturdiness of our little craft, questioned the wisdom of using such boats in choppy seas with strong headwinds. Meanwhile, the crew was busy getting ready to leave harbour, but still found time to show us the ropes: how to sling our hammocks, the torpedo compartment and, most important of all, where the galley was, so that we could make tea and coffee. We could see that life aboard a submarine in wartime was no picnic. Between the constant running of the engine and the machinery, it was very noisy, and hard to sleep, and conditions were cramped and dirty. Despite all this, the submariners seemed to be a happy bunch.

At seventeen hundred hours on 22 May 1943, *Trooper* slipped from alongside HMS *Talbot*, and followed HMS *Rorqual* out along a narrow channel, heading for the west coast of Greece and the Adriatic. About forty minutes out, the submarine dived. We had yet to find out the details of our mission. Crew morale was high, and it rubbed off on us as we settled into the new experience of life on board a submarine. Shortly after diving, one of our lads was taken short, and made a bee-line for the heads. He was astonished to see a large sign blocking his entrance to the loo, which read 'Ask First' in large print. Not knowing what to do, he yelled to a crew member 'What the f—ing hell does this mean?' Amused by his panic, the sailor rang the control room and got permission for our man to get on with his business. We hadn't realised that, before allowing the submarine's toilets to be used, crew members in the control room had to check for surface ships or enemy aircraft, as when the waste was discharged it would float to the top and alert enemy agents to our position. Hence the notice to 'Ask First'.

Unfortunately, when tidying up, our man ran into a setback, as the pressurised water, designed to dispose of his waste, somehow went astray and covered him. Mortified by the backfire, and not smelling too rosy, a couple of willing hands helped him to clean up. It took some time to learn the simple art of discharging the waste but, thankfully, a recurrence didn't befall us again: we'd learnt from his nasty lesson. Providentially, our man managed to clean himself up before we became aware of the water restriction on submarines.

For the rest of the trip, we had an occasional wash but couldn't shave. Killing time on board, the crew gave us a rundown on the radar, gyro compass and hydro planes, and on *Trooper*'s past activities. Under supervision, we were put to work acting as extra lookouts at night, and on duty on the gyro compass.

Submerged for up to eighteen hours a day, with only dull artificial light, these small tasks eased our boredom. We got to know the crew, and heard about *Trooper*'s impressive record in sinking enemy ships and charioteers – two-man 'human torpedoes' made of steel. These vessels were manned by two divers wearing canvas diving suits, heavy breathing apparatus, lead belts and lead-soled boots. One diver controlled the battery-operated 'chariot', while the other fixed the warhead – weighing between two hundred and six hundred pounds – to the bottom of an enemy ship, using magnets. For the most part, these were considered to be 'suicide missions': if they weren't 'taken out' by gunfire, divers often died from hypoxia, commonly known as 'the bends'. Despite the high risks involved, charioteers were also used by the British military.

On 23 May, Charlie Clyne told us to stand by for the first landing job, which would be soon under way, but as yet he could gives no details of time, place or purpose. Two days later, the job, codenamed Operation Entertain, was on. At twenty-one fifty hours the submarine surfaced off the south coast of Zante and the sub commander, Lieutenant Wraith, supervised the launching of the first folbot, to be occupied by Charlie Clyne and another officer for a trip that would take them into hostile enemy territory. We were on standby to take action in the event of any distress signals from the boys.

Luck was on our side: the mission was successful and without incident, and both agents returned safely from enemy territory. On the way back, moving along the enemy coastline, they had succeeded in taking sea depths at various points en route. The rest of the mission was not discussed, but few days later, with *Trooper* up to periscope depth, a congratulatory message was received, the essence of which was that the operation had been comprehensive and flawless. Obviously, the taking of sea depths would facilitate landing points for future clandestine operations. The information sent back from this mission included other useful reconnoitred material, the boys having made contact with collaborators ashore.

On the morning of 26 May, Lieutenant Clyne joined us for breakfast, but despite the small talk, he took care not to reveal the details of Operation Entertain. Everything was on a 'need to know' basis, and all we needed to know was that the operation had been successful. In a matter-of-fact way, he drew our attention to the ship's armoury, in particular the fact that *Trooper* carried two 202 Lewis or Vickers machineguns. In a throwaway remark, he mentioned the possible need for our involvement, should surface action be required. Charlie said that Gordon Wright and I would accompany him and another officer, a New Zealander, on the next mission, Operation Tiger. On our sixth day out, the condition of our flat-bottomed boat became a concern. Petty Officer Sleep reported that the choppy seas and strong headwinds had completely destroyed our assault craft, which had been strapped to the hull of the submarine. There was nothing for it but to dump it at sea, at an opportune time. Despite this little problem, we would have to make it ashore when the time came to put Operation Tiger into effect, and all efforts were made to ensure that the folbots would be ready for the job.

The longer we were at sea, the more difficult conditions became. Fresh food was already a thing of the past – the dank conditions caused it to rot quickly – and eventually we were living on hard bread, tinned fruit and bully beef. (The bread became so mouldy that the cook had to cut away the mould and stick it back into the oven to make it halfway edible. It was also hard to keep the mould from clinging to your clothes.) The sub was so overcrowded that men had to 'time-share' a bed, in a system known as 'hot-bunking'; while one man slept, another worked, and they then swapped not only their work shift but also their bed. The submariners were a special breed to stick these difficult underwater conditions for so long: none of the men on *Trooper* had any desire to return to regular navy ships. To each his own, I suppose.

There was no smoking allowed on the submarine – something that the hardened smokers found particularly difficult. The men suffered from various skin conditions: boils and rashes were commonplace and difficult to treat, as little water was available for washing or keeping clean. What water we had was often contaminated and smelt rank, and we were soon banned from using it.

On 27 May, we dived through the Straits of Otranto, a heavily mined channel leading to the Adriatic. No other British sub had been in these waters since January, as they had become too dangerous to operate in; this fact brought home to us the gravity of our mission. When the submariners became very tense, *we* began to worry. We weren't sure what was wrong, but the eerie silence and the looks on their faces was enough to let us know that it wasn't good. We could hear a loud, dragging noise clattering along the hull: we didn't know what it was, and no one was talking. We later found out that we'd been trailing mine cables that had become entangled in the sub. The boys had expected the worst, but said nothing. There was no point: if our number was up, there was nothing anyone could do about it. Happily, thanks to the good captaincy of Johnny Wraith, we managed to disentangle ourselves and escape from the danger.

We had been at sea for what seemed an eternity, but as yet not a word had been spoken about the job ahead. Eventually, we were brought to the control room, where we took turns looking through the periscope. It was amazing to have clear sightings of enemy territory, the railways and bridges, as we moved the scope along the Italian coastline. The skipper picked out something we might appreciate, and called us to have a quick look. I hurried to take a look, and was pleasantly surprised to see a foal feeding from its mother. For me in wartime, it was an incredible sight of peace and tranquillity, and evoked childhood memories of my father tending his mare and foal, and my desire to befriend them, back in 1928.

We sailed up and down the coast near Vieste, on the eastern side of Promontarios del Gargano, looking for a suitable landing spot for our mission. A few hours later, having been told our target, we got a look at a small bay not far from Bari which was to be the landing point for the next operation. We were given time to study aerial reconnaissance photographs, which had indentation marks and identified certain structures in the area. As we were not allowed to carry anything that might be incriminating, in the event of our being captured, the photographs were collected by our leader before we left. He carried on with the briefing, emphasising the gravity of our mission, the timing, and the need to get back to the sub undetected. We were issued with a map, camouflaged as a handkerchief, which, when held at a particular angle, showed the geography of the general area. We were also given a concealed buttonhole compass, eight large watertight tins of explosives and a wireless transmitter/receiver. Though we had still not been given a departure time, we knew it was closing in and that it was now just a matter of checking our gear.

Our pack of baddies – what we called the detonators and other 'tools of the trade' – consisted of gun cotton, primers, fuses, cordex and some Italian lire, and the all-important wireless transmitter. We also had small shovels for digging, and a few rocks to be used as markers – all items destined for the partisans aiding the Allied cause. All these were supposed to have been carried in the assault craft, now lying beneath the sea. We would now somehow have to fit them on our tiny folbots. The sub was to launch us two miles from our landing point, and we had between two and four hours at the most to get the job done and rendezvous back with the sub.

If we failed to make the deadline, we were in trouble, as *Trooper* could not afford to hang about in deadly enemy waters. If anything went wrong and *Trooper* had to dive, one more attempt to recover us would be made, at the same time the following night. Anything beyond a second attempt would be out of the question. If we were still alive by then, we would be on our own.

It was down to us to make sure that everything went to plan, and we made it back to the pickup point at the agreed rendezvous time. For his part, the submarine skipper would do his utmost to keep to the initial arrangement, while evading enemy mines and avoiding detection. Failure by either our unit or the sub to make the rendezvous would result, where possible, in a signal being passed at a prearranged time, well before first light.

If all failed, and we found ourselves out on a limb, we would just have to deal with it as the situation presented itself, and think on our feet. We were a tight unit and we intended to make it through. If the worst happened, we knew that, somewhere, British Intelligence would be aware of our operation, and would hopefully make contact with the Underground, to assist us in working out an escape route. That, however, would undoubtedly take a long time: in the meantime, we'd have to fend for ourselves in enemy-occupied territory.

The contingency plan in the event of this happening was to keep low and keep moving, regardless of the terrain. If we were captured, the rule was: don't get caught with the map or compass, and do your damnedest to convince your captors you're just infantry soldiers. How we were supposed to do that, while armed with a tommy-gun, and wearing desert boots and a commando-style woollen hat, is anyone's guess. I suppose that we could have tried to abandon our weapons and balaclavas and claimed to have escaped from a POW camp, but then we'd have had to explain what had happened to our POW ID tag.

The possibility of suffering a similar fate to less fortunate tiptoe boys, who had clandestinely dropped in or arrived by canoe, was always there, but we couldn't afford to let this distract us from the job in hand. These men were not considered to be normal invading forces and so were instead summarily executed as spies, as distinct from regular soldiers, who were taken as POWs. This action stemmed from the Hitler Commando Order of 1942, part of which stated: 'All Allied troops deemed to be involved in so-called commando operations should be exterminated to the last man, and no quarter should be given to Allied persons in raiding operations or in assisting indigenous partisans, i.e. anyone who landed from boats or submarines or parachuted down to help indigenous landing forces to carry out sabotage would not be treated as prisoners of war even though they be in uniform. Armed or not, they were to be handed over immediately to the S.D. civilian agency and not to be held in military custody'. The 'S.D. civilian agency' was a misnomer – the Sicherheitsdienst or the S.D. as it was known – was in fact the Nazi security service. In effect, this meant that the Germans were refusing to afford them the protection of the 1929 Geneva Convention governing the treatment of POWs. After Britain initiated intelligence raids on German-occupied territory, there were several executions, many of which took place in Greece, Italy, France and Norway.

Prior to launching Operation Tiger, we had one more reconnaissance of the coastline by periscope. At twenty-one forty hours, on 30 May, we were ready for the off. *Trooper* surfaced four miles from our landing point, and then moved inwards for a further two miles. Meanwhile, we were getting the gear topside, onto the forecasing through the fore hatch. Just as we were about to depart *Trooper*, we had a serious setback. In the process of loading the gear and launching our small craft, ready for take-off, the vibrating of the submarine and the curved, slippery edge of the sub made it difficult to hold a footing. The effort to prevent our canoes from drifting away unoccupied led to a lot of unbalanced movement, with one of our unit precariously perched on the side of the sub. Just as he made his move to get into the folbot, the sub went into a wild vibrating movement, pitching him forward towards either the folbot or the drink. In an effort to avoid hitting the water, he swung his body around, whacking the butt of his machine-gun against the side of the submarine in the process. The crashing metallic sound reverberated for miles around the sea and coastline. The German/Italian searchlight batteries immediately swung into action, criss-crossing the skies and the sea. We could see numerous lights along the coast, possibly from small fishing vessels, and were concerned that their presence would lead to us being detected.

The timing and weather being in our favour, we made the decision to take the risk, as so many underground operators ashore were depending on us and our supplies. The naval ratings helping us took command of the situation and made speedy progress in getting us launched. Within seconds we were out to sea, alone in our canoes. As we reached for our oars, we heard a lone voice coming from the conning tower, wittily offering some unkind views about SBS boys and their problems.

Concerned about the unwanted attention we had attracted,the lads were in no mood to hang around. Frantically rowing towards our landing point, I ventured a backward glance – just in time to see *Trooper* diving. The fact that we were not picked up by the enemy searchlights can only be described as providential. Some of the fishing boats appeared to be getting closer to our line of approach, but we stuck with it. Putting distance between ourselves and the sub, Charlie, the Kiwi, Gordon Wright and myself rowed steadily, and despite the fact that the gear slowed our rate of progress, we reached our landing point in good time.

Once ashore in Vieste, we hid our boats and, working on the memorised aerial-reconnaissance photographs, we moved quietly and stealthily inland. We concealed ourselves at a given point to check out the ground, before moving on to the target area to bury our explosives and other goodies for use by the partisans.

In Bari, we tried to locate a number of structures we'd noted on the photos. We saw a few structures of uncertain nature and, in the distance, what appeared to be a footbridge. Our designated burial point was close to some palm trees, and provided enough cover for us to dig without being spotted. Charlie posted Gordon Wright as lookout at a high strategic point, and although we couldn't see him, this gave us cover to get on with the job. After having buried the sabotage materials in the designated spot, we made sure that we left no traces behind. It was time for Charlie to let Gordon know that the job had been done. Gordon was keeping such intense observation out front, towards the danger area, that he didn't see or hear Charlie approach from the rear. In an effort to get Gordon's attention quietly, Charlie reached up and gripped his ankle. Gordon was normally a cool character, but the unexpected touch threw him, and he just managed to stop himself letting fly with a burst from his tommy-gun. The thought of the consequences, had this happened, doesn't bear thinking about.

When we had completed our mission, I was instructed by Lieutenant Clyne to make the twenty-minute solo trip back to where the folbots were hidden. Moving silently and cautiously through the palm trees, my mind went back to Palestine, and the ever-present snipers. This location was likely to present direct confrontation, with machine-gun fire. The rule was: stay cool, don't act on impulse and stay concealed, to await more favourable circumstances. With this in mind, I took up a concealed position, lying low close to the hidden folbots. This gave me a range-card view of approach positions.

Tommy-gun at the ready, I sat tight and waited anxiously for the return of the three other raiders, who were about twenty minutes behind me. I kept a close eye out for a signal from *Trooper*, in case it showed up earlier than expected. This was a possibility, due to the constantly changing nature of the game. The agreed route back had been out front and to the left of where I was positioned, so I was startled to hear movement coming towards me from two different directions: there was rapid, noisy activity coming from what was definitely the *wrong* direction. Instantly moving from the prone position, I shifted up onto one knee, my machine-gun in the firing position, aimed in the direction of the activity.

There was nothing for it but to let go the full magazine at the first sighting of the enemy. It looked like our unit was in trouble. Unable to find any sightings for my uneasy trigger finger, I tried to stay cool and wait for a clear target to emerge. Seconds seemed like minutes as I felt the tension rise, to the point when I said the first few words of the *Confiteor* – 'I confess to almighty God . . . ' – as by now I was sure I was about to meet Him. Just then, I heard a loud whisper, in the distinct Scottish accent of our unit leader, Charlie Clyne, advising me to hold my fire. As he quickly moved forward to join me, mixed feelings of anger and relief raced through me. Through clenched teeth, I managed to enquire where the rest of the unit were, and what the f—ing hell did he think he was doing, coming back by the wrong route. He told me that the lads were OK, and were out in front, awaiting his signal to return to the canoes.

By way of explanation of the breach of his own instructions, he held up some palm leaves, telling me that he had been specially requested by some of the submarine crew to bring them back, as a souvenir of enemy-occupied territory. Apparently some sailors kept such items in their pay books as a memento, or to get a rise out of less experienced sailors as to what would be expected of them on a trip into enemy waters.

Without another word, he moved cautiously towards the lads' position, and gave the agreed torchlight signal. Within minutes, we were in position by the canoes. Sensing my lingering annoyance, he remarked: 'Corporal, you're still agitated.' I took the opportunity to have a go at him, and let him know just how close we had come to disaster. Not being one to pull rank, he grinned and called me a silly bastard, saying: 'Johnny, you wouldn't have been selected by me if you hadn't measured up to my criteria. I observed your discipline in many contingencies and supervised your special mission training. I'd seen enough to know I could rely on you to always do the right thing.'

Having my ego boosted like that served its purpose, and I cooled down: I knew damn well what he was playing at, but let him get away with it. We were now settled into position, to watch for *Trooper*'s signal for us to return. I was so distracted by the thought that I had been seconds away from pulling the trigger on Charlie that I didn't notice the signal from the submarine calling us home.

A tap on the shoulder from Charlie had only one meaning: launch the canoes. Charlie flashed back our acknowledgement and we were on our way, getting our canoes to the water's edge – and climbing aboard without capsizing them. The situation became worrying when we realised that the sub had surfaced much further from shore than anticipated. Our position was aggravated by a swelling sea, which forced us to row diagonally towards the sub; the hazy mist which began to encompass us became just one more problem. With the distance between us and the sub rapidly increasing, there was nothing for it but to row harder. At least we were putting distance between ourselves and the searchlights, which were constantly scanning the sea. We made it back safely to the submarine, but not before we had a nasty moment. An enemy patrol boat passed too close for comfort. Everything stopped: the sub's engines and all the machinery went into 'silent' mode as we held our breath, hoping that we hadn't been spotted. The enemy patrol was so close that one sweep of its searchlights would have been enough to give us away. As it passed by, everyone on board let out a sigh of relief. The submariners helped us out of the folbots and welcomed us on board. Were we glad to see them!

Safely away, *Trooper* resumed course to patrol the Adriatic and Mediterranean. Shortly after we got under way, the navy boys began scurrying around, heading in all directions, before taking up specific positions. Out of the blue, our unit leader came to us and told us that there was to be no moving about, and that under no circumstances were we to go near the heads – any use of the toilet would have to wait. Trooper was targeting an Italian merchant ship which had been spotted leaving the Port of Bari. They'd fired three torpedoes at it, but the ship had altered course, and the torpedoes missed the target.

Suddenly, our sub fell deadly silent, with no detectable noise from the engines: we'd gone into what the crew called 'silent control'. The concentration on the submariners' faces made the message loud and clear: when you go after a target in wartime, you'd better make bloody sure you get it, or the tables will turn. Now *we* were the prey.

For the next twenty minutes, we were beset by depth charges being dropped by enemy ships. The noise became a long, rumbling roar, getting closer and closer as the charges neared their target. Lieutenant Alick Grant gave us a vivid description of what would befall us if the charges came too close. What he described was an unparalleled disaster, but he quickly reassured us that the enemy charges were probably a couple of miles off-target. The sub was making good time in running from the immediate danger.

The following day, we came up to periscope depth to receive communications. To our delight, we learned that our mission had been successful: the Underground operators had retrieved the goods and had already put their plans into action, with good effect. We were congratulated by the navy lads, some of whom had been sending us up, saying that the added weight of the tiptoe boys had caused *Trooper* to list, making the torpedoes miss their target. Our anxieties behind us, we could afford a laugh over the grog.

Following further reconnaissance of the coastlines, we headed back to Medway in Beirut, twenty-three days after leaving Manoel Island. On the way back, we were on restricted rations of both food and water. We had seven or eight pints of water for all purposes, and one loaf between eight men, per day. After having traversed the Adriatic and Mediterranean back and forth unscathed, between minefields, depth charges and other hazards, it was unfortunate that, en route to Beirut, *Trooper* struck submerged wreckage and was damaged. We limped into harbour in the early hours of 13 June, relieved to be back on terra firma, and to have our first decent wash since we had left Malta. Charlie Clyne, who was suffering from severe jaundice, was hospitalised as soon as we got back to Medway.

We had a ball during our stay at Medway. The sailors made us welcome, and the bucket of lime juice outside the mess helped with the scurvy – the scourge of sailors. We also discovered the local jungle juice, as Dickie Sleep, Pete Adam, Len Williams and a few of the lads took us downtown to try their famous Iraq Plus, which was so potent, it felled us quicker than any Jerry could have done. After some more partying in Medway, Beirut and Syria, our call-back came through. We were to be picked up by Lancaster bomber and taken to Cairo to await instructions for our next assignment. Before we left, Charlie Clyne told us that he'd heard that his extended secondment to the SBS had come through, and he promised to expedite ours. Just a short time after we left *Trooper*, we heard, with great sadness, that she'd been hit by an enemy mine in the eastern Mediterranean. All sixty-three men on board perished.

*

With Medway behind us, we arrived in Cairo on 4 July 1943 – American Independence Day. The plan was that Charlie Clyne, Gordon and myself would stay there until orders came through for our next mission, on our extended secondment to the SBS – the Special Boat Service. Meanwhile, under orders from the senior officer, we bedded down at the transit camp and were given routine duties alongside the other squaddies, in order to keep a low profile. Surprisingly, given the circumstances of war, our pay always arrived on time.

After what we'd been used to in Malta, this was pure luxury. We thought the army food was as good as a four-star hotel: after our miserable nine-ounce ration of bread in Malta, I suppose it was. Charlie's orders came through, which meant that ours weren't far behind. Before leaving for Athlit in Palestine, where he was to pick up his unit, Charlie introduced us to a few lads from the Long Range Desert Group (the LRDG) and arranged some training sessions with them. Unfortunately, the plan was short-lived: three days later, they were called away on a mission. Two weeks went by, with no news of our move to Athlit. On the positive side, my promotion come through, and I got my second stripe, which had been delayed by my time in Manoel Island – not to mention my court martial.

We kept fit and trained, ready for the off. When I'd left Malta, I thought that I'd left behind any chance of boxing again, but the pull was still there. When I found a tough Nigerian middleweight preparing for a contest, I volunteered to be his sparing partner. It suited both our purposes, and he certainly made the most of the situation, training twice a day for the next week. After the four-star food, I was already a full-blown middleweight, but it wasn't long before I began to look forward to his departure: the twice-daily sparring bouts were becoming hard work, as we pounded away at each other. My reward came when the Nigerian won his contest: I felt that our bouts had been instrumental in helping him win.

The guy was tough, and fought me as though I was the only person standing between him and success. He gave no quarter. Not holding back on a single wicked punch, the Nigerian dished out more punishment than was warranted for a purse of a few dollars. There is something about boxers that makes them relish a hard-fought 'touch and go' fight. They find it exhilarating. I was no exception to this, and, while secretly praying that my Nigerian sparring mate would just go away, I knew that, given the same opportunity of fighting again, I'd jump at the chance. (Little did I know then that that's exactly what would happen – this time while I was a prisoner of war – but that's for a later chapter!) Meanwhile, Gordon and I were still waiting for news of our extended secondment to the SBS. Word filtered through that the 2nd Battalion of the Royal Fusiliers – the Faughs – had already left Malta on 11 June, bound for a secret destination. Rumour spread that the target was Alexandria. This seemed plausible, as we were located within striking distance of it, but we were puzzled that our orders to rejoin the SBS still hadn't arrived. We were in no man's land, officially still members of the Royal Irish Fusiliers, but on secondment to the Commando Unit of the Special Boat Services.

Having had a taste of exciting SBS clandestine operations, we were straining at the bit, just waiting to infiltrate enemy territory and get behind their lines. This was real *Boy's Own* stuff, but we were under no illusions: we knew the seriousness of it all. Our mission would be tough: penetrating enemy defences in order to cut railway lines, blow up well-defended installations, airfields or rolling stock. We were scared and exhilarated at the same time, and all the waiting around for orders was making us nervous. Anything would be better than the daily boredom of routine and parade-ground discipline. Word filtered through that our call-up to the SBS base at Athlit, south of Haifa in Palestine, had been delayed by a clerical error – something to do with the disruption and logistical nightmare of moving No. 234 Brigade from Malta to Egypt.

Someone in the 2nd Battalion of the Faughs, tasked with expediting our continued secondment to the SBS, had lost the file. We were left kicking our heels back in Cairo, just waiting for the call. After almost five weeks of hanging around, with the war seeming to be passing us by, we finally got the call – but not quite the one we'd been expecting.

13

From the Middle East to Greece

On 10 August, two officers from the Royal Irish Fusiliers showed up in the camp with orders from our commanding officer, Lieutenant Colonel Maurice French, for us to return to our regular battalion, which was under-strength and was now stationed at Wetshod Training Centre at Kabrit, near the Suez Canal. Our orders for another clandestine mission had not come through in time. Gordon and I had proven our physical and mental capacity as part of a raiding party, and were bitterly disappointed to be assigned to invasion training. Dejected or not, we had no option but to follow orders: no more undercover operations for us, it seemed. I couldn't believe that our SBS ops had been abruptly brought to an end because of a clerical error! On arrival at Kabrit, being greeted by my old buddies, with the usual reminiscences, craic and exchange of news, helped me settle back in, and I soon got over my frustration at missing out on the 'special-ops tasking'.

Training with the Faughs involved scaling the high mountains of Syria, with mules in tow, rock-climbing, jumping off invasion barges into chest-deep water, and intensive assault training in the Sinai Desert. It was great to see my comrades in high spirits, especially after leaving behind the tensions of Malta. From now on, I was part of this team, training to take our place in any operation. It was tough going, but a welcome relief from the siege environment of Malta.

Neither decent food nor leisure time had been on the menu in Malta; now, in our new environment, we had both. In my case, I saw this as just reward for having survived three years of hardship on Malta. Soldiers are no different from civilians when it comes to appreciating their leisure hours, and, like civilians, they spent it in various ways. Some chose to make excursions to Biblical sites, others sought out the charms of the ladies of the night, while many indulged in the luxury of a few drinks – for luxury it was, with both draught and bottled beer available, something we hadn't had in Malta. By now I was well settled back in with my boozing buddies, so no prizes for guessing which route I took.

I was happy as a pig in s—t, and in good company, with Guthrie Kane, Jimmy Loughlin, Wee Davy Thompson, Sean McCaughen, Danny Brush, Johnnie King, Jock McBride, Andy Roy and Walter Pancott, as we navigated our way to the nearest bar, close to the beach, and made it our HQ for the next three days, only taking time out now and again for a quick swim. Training over, and back in Syria, we earmarked a local boozer that was worthy of our custom. It didn't take long for the boys to notice that the bar owner never shut up shop. He slept on the counter top, trusting that we would pay him later for any beer we'd had while he was asleep. It was an extraordinary sight to see the lads go behind the counter and pass crates of beer out over the body of the sleeping owner. I thought to myself: 'Does he not realise that, in a war situation, looting is almost obligatory for a soldier?' Since no one present was overburdened by a conscience in such life-and-death times, I wondered whether the bar owner was trusting or just stupid. Normally, booty like watches, cameras, or even guns were the currency of the day, but somehow we felt honour-bound to pay in cash for the gargle we'd drunk. We left the money on the counter, beside the sleeping owner.

After our three days of R&R and much self-indulgence, we were back to military discipline. Lieutenant McCarton Mooney came into our tent to speak to us, and on his way out he took me to one side. I was surprised when he passed on a message from the beach-bar owner to thank us for the money we'd left behind to cover our bar bill. The mystery about his trusting ways was soon solved: prior to our three days' R&R, all the local bar owners had been summoned to the camp HQ by the company commander, who had told them that any soldier misbehaving or not paying their bills would be disciplined. If found guilty, they would have their army pay stopped indefinitely. A very good incentive for the local bar owners to put their trust in their customers!

Many a night was passed discussing what our future might be. Speculation abounded as to whether we had we been trained for Italy, Rhodes or Greece. On 15 September, orders were issued for an early move – but we had no idea where we were going. The problem was what to take. No Bren-gun carriers, anti-tank guns or motor transport were allowed. Our new gear was all to be left behind, and everyone had to take anti-malaria precautions.

The next day, we were dispatched to Haifa, to a sand-fly-infested camp at Mount Carmel. For those of us who'd been there in 1938, during the Palestinian insurrection, the memories came surging back. It was at this very spot, shortly after our arrival on 9 October 1938, that the Palestinians had shot up my section of B Company. This time, our biggest threat was the sand fly – at least for now. Fortunately, before they could inflict much damage, we were on our way. Just as we reached the port of Haifa, Lieutenant Colonel French left with A and B Company, boarding destroyers bound for a secret location. We were followed by the other companies. While at sea, we were told our destination and the dangerous waters we'd have to navigate, through enemy lines. Laden down with battened-down Bofors guns, motorbikes, cases of supplies, food and other gear, there was little room left for the men. More than two hundred men in the advance guard were packed in like sardines, with just a few lifeboats between us.

The Mediterranean heaved, tossing its cargo to and fro. Between the swell of the sea and the zigzagging of the ship – designed to throw any submarines that might be around off our track – we were past caring what our destination, or even our destiny, was. No one felt much like talking, except for one soldier, who, despite the groans of protest, insisted on giving a graphic account of the battalion's ordeal on board the troopship *Nueralia* as it sailed from Malta to Egypt. He told how part of the convoy had been hit by a torpedo, and had taken twenty minutes to go down. Soon the silent majority entered into the mood, and one by one told their own stories. Each had a different version of how the torpedo had missed the *Nueralia* by inches.

One man had had enough, and brought the conversation to an abrupt halt. He announced that, given that we were struggling to battle the high winds, sea spray, sea-sickness and his desire to throw up, he would be sorely tempted to aim directly at the s—t-stirrers if the stories didn't stop. This had the desired effect, and a silence came over the motley crew. The conversation took a turn for the better when the ship's captain told us that we were bound for the Dodecanese Islands. He told us that Rhodes, and its two airfields, were under German control. After Italy had surrendered on the Greek mainland, the German garrison of 6,000 men had seized power from the 36,000-strong Italian military.

Churchill believed that the capitulation by the Italians presented an opportunity for the Allies to occupy the Dodecanese. The Americans weren't interested, so he decided to go it alone, but speed was of the essence. The task of convincing Campioni, the Italian commander of Rhodes, to obey the terms of the Armistice and resist the Germans fell to Major the Earl of Jellicoe, Commander of the SBS. The SBS and other units, along with the Greek Sacred Heart Company, had been carrying out daring raids against Italian and German garrisons on various islands, with substantial success. On the night of 9/10 September, Jellicoe, his wireless operator and an interpreter parachuted into Rhodes. Dodging the German patrols, they made contact with Admiral Campioni and got down to business, trying to persuade the admiral to use his force of 36,000 men to disarm the understrength Germans, under the Command of Von Kleemans, leaving the way clear for Allied forces to land.

Italian morale was low, and Campioni procrastinated. Jellicoe could offer little help, beyond a promise that some SBS would arrive within days. In fact, three thousand men from 234 Infantry Brigade arrived only days later, on 15 September, to assist in the capture of Rhodes. The Italians urged Jellicoe to leave the island before his presence was betrayed. With time running out, Jellicoe had no option but to take the advice. As a precaution, lest he be caught by the Germans, Jellicoe disposed of Wilson's letter to Campioni by eating it – not an easy task, given that it was written not on the usual rice paper but on heavy-duty office paper! I'll never understand why he didn't just burn it.

As events unfolded, it transpired that General Von Kleeman had a contingency plan for his understrength force. He lost no time in putting it into action, and took the Italians by surprise, gaining control of Rhodes and the airfields – the prize that we needed so badly to support Leros and the other islands.

These islands became a powerful asset to add to the already dominant air power of the enemy. Nevertheless, the Allied plan of occupation went ahead.

14

DESTINATION LEROS

Still on the high seas, we realised that we were heading for Leros, fifteen miles off the coast of Turkey. The rough seas of the Mediterranean had not prepared us for our latest cruise, as we tossed, pitched and rolled about in what a ship's officer described it a 'placid sea'. We wondered exactly what he was used to. It was certainly no picnic, as we dodged about, under constant threat from the prowling U-boats, aerial torpedo attacks, and mines which had escaped detection by the minesweepers. I was grateful for my experience on the MTB's launches and fishing caiques, which stood to me now. Measured against the destroyer, the MTBs offered more room to manoeuvre, making them better equipped to dodge enemy fire. Slipping past Rhodes, things quietened down on board, so that we didn't attract unwanted attention from enemy ships. As daylight broke, our twenty-four-hour high-speed journey was almost over. It had been a couple of weeks since the Italian capitulation, but we weren't sure whether the Italians, still on the occupied islands, would be hostile to us. We prepared for the trip inland, to Portolago harbour on Leros, and were ready for anything that might come at us.

Our commanding officer, Colonel French, reached the quayside ahead of us. As we got close to the jetty, I was pleasantly surprised to see him being warmly greeted by some Italian officers, especially since my weapon was not loaded at the time. With no Italian troops in sight, it seemed that the garrison intended to co-operate fully with our occupation of the island, leaving us free to take up our respective defensive positions.

Leros's rocky terrain is very difficult to cross, especially in full kit. With no aerial cover and only one so-called road, even the jeeps had trouble getting across the island. The bays afforded easy landing, but on a large part of the coastline it was almost impossible to mount scramble landings, or so we thought. The rest of the island could only be negotiated by lightly equipped troops – provided that the weather remained calm.

The Italians had developed Leros as a naval and seaplane base, but there were no airfields on the island. A detachment of the Long Range Desert Group, the Special Boat Squadron and the Greek Sacred Company, under the command of Major the Earl of Jellicoe, had established its HQ at Alinda, on 18 September, and this paved the way for the arrival of our advanced guard the following day. We concentrated on the narrow strip of land between Alinda and Gurna bays.

Colonel French decided to hold the highest point, in the middle of the island, in order that troops could be deployed on foot to any part of the island, as available troops were understrength. Rifle companies were weak in numbers, and events were to deplete them even further. I was dispersed with Company A to the northern slopes of Merliviglia, covering Gurna and Alinda bays as well as Rachi. As a No. 9 platoon section leader, we headed off, equipped with one anti-tank gun, one Vickers HMG (heavy machine-gun), one Bren light machine-gun, a few Lee Enfield rifles, a couple of hand grenades, and my illegally held 9mm Italian Beretta light machine-gun, which I'd 'acquired' while deployed to Sousse for Special Service action aboard MTB75.

OPEN FOR BUSINESS!

We dug in at a spot where we had a clear vision of Alinda and the coastline leading to Leros harbour. Corporal Jock McCullagh and I were selecting areas to place gun positions and slit trenches, when we noticed a small group of women all excitedly waving at us from below our position.

Through our field glasses, we saw that the women were standing outside a large wooden structure, gesturing for us to join them. McCullagh and I were off the starting blocks in a flash, scrambling down the steep, rocky terrain to check out what was on offer. When we got there, we found that the wooden hut was a local brothel, recently used by the Italian garrison.

The ladies were trying to generate new business, since their Italian customers had surrendered! The women had no English, and we had no Greek or Italian, but with the universally understood expression of 'jiggy jig', accompanied by their body language, we were left in no doubt as to what was on offer – for a price.

Hard cash was the preferred currency, but they kindly offered to keep us warm for some of our grub. We were unable to oblige. As the advance party, travelling light, we'd been given no stores or provisions, so we were forced to face the 350-foot climb back to reality, and our dugout, resolving to get our priorities right next time. This was just as well: if word had gotten out, there was no way we could have stopped eighteen squaddies from scrambling down, in an effort to promote international relations.

In *The Long Road from Leros*, Raymond Williams describes how his platoon moved into an evacuated former brothel to escape torrential rainstorms. It seemed a good idea, especially as their sleeping arrangements were outdoors. Their tenancy was short-lived, however: after two nights of torment, they beat a hasty retreat after being eaten alive by mosquitoes – not to mention their self-inflicted injuries. Raymond and his buddies, searching for the source of their tormentors by torchlight, discovered a legion of bugs ascending and descending the mosquito netting in orderly columns, reminiscent of an army manoeuvre. Despite the heavy rain, they conceded victory to the destructive little parasites and their voracious appetites, and quickly evacuated the building. When a Junker 88 later strafed the hut with a stick of bombs, Raymond swears that he could hear the pests crackling in the inferno.

Who knows what might have happened to our lot had our lads enjoyed the favours of the ladies of Leros? Perhaps our lack of hard currency or food was a blessing in disguise. Someone could have collected a 'full house' – otherwise known as a VD – and in the absence of medical supervision, this would have been no picnic, ensuring ongoing pain, ostracisation and loss of pay. Any thoughts of presenting the 'lurker' for jiggy jig were soon dispelled when the German aerial assaults began to really hurt, forcing all the islanders to take to the caves at Mount Clidi and in smaller, safe neighbouring islands.

After the siege of Malta, we knew the very difficult, if not impossible, task the navy had of trying to sustain our brigade against very heavy odds. As long as the enemy had control of the air, keeping the garrison in reasonable fighting shape would exact a heavy toll on our ships and their crews. As the days and weeks passed, the German air force began to dominate the skies above Leros completely. We were proved right in our assessment: we were not to taste bread, potatoes or fresh meat for the following two months, as we defended the island.

15

STOLEN DRINK, DRUGS AND MORE BOOZE

THE PADRE TURNS A BLIND EYE

On Leros, our diet was frugal. All we had was McConachies tinned stew, bully beef and hard biscuits, and even these were in very short supply. Some supplies got through via submarine, destroyer, minesweeper or fishing caique, under cover of darkness. This was an eerie, unnerving experience for the navy, who had to sail through the perilous waters in the dark. Without these additional supplies, we would never have survived.

It was a strange sight to see jeeps and Bofor guns arriving by the submarine *Severn*. Lashed down with steel wire, they made it to Leros, and the Faughs were allocated one prized jeep. Other supplies were dropped in containers by parachute, and had to be manhandled across difficult, mountainous terrain. Our only contact with the outside world came by way of brief visits from fast-moving naval units, which were anxious to get back to the relative safety of the open seas. Morale was boosted thanks to the brave deeds of the navy, who were to pay a terrible price for bringing us supplies and extra troops.

We were worried that the Germans appeared to have complete aerial domination of the Aegean. And although they turned a blind eye to British naval vessels encroaching on their territorial waters, the Turks, our only hope of aerial support, were not about to risk their neutrality by allowing British forces to use their airfields. Their 'blind eye' policy was also applied to German peripheral activity, as they allowed the Axis ships to take shelter in their harbours at night.

Another problem was illness. Each platoon was well below strength, partly as a result of sand-fly fever, which many soldiers had contracted while we were in Haifa. The work of building defences, laying mines, filling in craters, unloading cargo, arranging dropping zones, struggling in the darkness across rough terrain to find containers, getting them away before daybreak, and finally standing to, all the while under constant bombing attack, contributed to our being dead on our feet the whole time. The only thing keeping us going were the army-issued Benzedrine – better known as 'Bennies' – and they didn't last long. (Hence the wartime song 'Who Put the Benzedrine in Mrs Murphy's Ovaltine'!)

With no place to take cover, or grab a little shut-eye, the nearest large boulder was a heaven-sent refuge to ease a weary body. It was not unusual to find a bloke on guard duty, given a piece of rock face for support, asleep on his feet. Thoughts of Leros ladies or jiggy jig were a long way from his mind: he'd happily have settled for a few hours' decent sleep! Due to the circumstances, this breach of discipline never went further than a long bollocking, usually administered by an NCO, who could have done with some Benzedrine himself to keep his eyes open long enough to dish out the reprimand.

'Sleep parades' were arranged, depending on the German air force's bombing timetable, and of course whether our services were required by the nocturnal visits of our own naval and air force supply teams. Generally, it was a case of two hours on and two hours off. As the bombing tempo increased during the day, it became imperative that those on two-hour 'off' periods should be under cover. It was decided to try to create sleeping shelters in the rock. There was a plentiful supply of mastic gelignite 808. No one knew why we had so much of it, as it wasn't associated with our defence, but all the same we were glad to have it. This, together with the detonators and primers that were available, allowed us to blast into the layers of volcanic rock.

Due to my experience with the SBS in this area, I was given the job. Progress was initially slow, due to the increased bombing, which had been significantly stepped up. This, and the need for some initial pick-work, in order to shape an entrance, significantly slowed progress. To help in creating the entrance, we made good use of the projectile infantry anti-tank rifle. Experience showed that it was better to hit the target full-frontal, rather than a glancing blow, which would cause the shell to ricochet, resulting in collateral damage to anyone in close proximity. Fortunately, I had a steady hand and a good aim, and made the hole where the first small charge was placed. We could then move ahead rapidly.

Our new sleeping arrangements proved a much better place to shelter than the slit trenches. Unless you were manning the mounted Bren gun for anti-aircraft duty, you could usually grab a short kip. Once the Stukas and 88s began an attack, everyone was on high alert doing their job, despite their fatigue. The strategic location of our section allowed us to observe the enemy's flanks on the move. Our most forward slit trenches and gun positions overlooked a very steep, narrow winding road. When the lorries, loaded with supplies, came to a sharp bend beneath our forward position, they would struggle up in a low gear, taking time to negotiate the bend, and continue upwards, for an even steeper climb.

From our front position, there was a straight drop of about nine feet down to the roadway. Once we were down, it was easy enough to catch up with the struggling lorry, in an effort to purloin something to eat. This was not the done thing, especially when the truck was one of your own, but hunger and temptation usually proved too much, and a little buckshee food was always welcome.

Yours truly and Joe Kane did the drop, and returned triumphant with a bottle of whiskey and a tin of streaky bacon. The whiskey was the first bottle to arrive on the island, and was warmly welcomed by one and all. The bacon, however, with its greasy cellophane wrapping, held less attraction.

As we sipped the whiskey, my close friend and fellow marauder Joe Kane warned that the regimental padre had seen us pilfer the whiskey and bacon from the lorry. It was a pity he hadn't mentioned this earlier, before I'd offered the holy man a drop of the 'crateur' from my own mess tin.

Without moralising, he politely refused, and sat amongst us while we enjoyed the jar, then gave us his blessing before departing, with a smile and a caution not to drink too much, to see some other poor reprobates in outlying posts. We smiled. One bottle of Scotch between four drinking men was hardly going to set us raving mad. But perhaps he was right: the whiskey, on top of our punishing schedule, prompted us to fall into a deep sleep. When we were eventually roused, we set to our tasks like robots, the routines implanted in our brains – or what was left of them.

Despite the Germans' shelling with 88mm field guns from the nearby island of Kalimnos, and our daily visits from the Luftwaffe, one heavily sleeping friend defied all efforts to wake him for the 4 AM stand-to. He slept through for the entire dawn shelling, and remained comatose throughout the day, despite wailing air-raid sirens and the sound of our ack-ack Bofor guns pounding away at the Luftwaffe. Eventually he came around. Following a severe reprimand from me, he told me that, before joining my section, he'd been laid up with sand-fly fever. He claimed that he'd also fallen foul of malaria, for which he was still on quinine. For the time being, he was off the hook. Still, I had my doubts – which didn't prove unfounded. I subsequently discovered that the local taverna, which opened at night after the bombings, had become an attraction for our friend, who, it seemed, always managed to down a skinful of cheap banana brandy.

I let the section know that punishment would result from any act that would put the section in jeopardy, or add to our already heavy burden. It was imperative that discipline remained strong, and I laid it on thick and heavy to the offender. I rostered him to depart at 1 AM, get to the parachute drop zone some distance away, locate and collect supplies, and return back to our post for a 4 AM stand-to. As a further disincentive, the chancer, by now already dead on his feet, was placed on the end of turn for sleep parade, making him responsible for rousing us when the platoon commander showed up at 7.15 AM. Having spent three hours dragging the heavy gear over boulder-strewn terrain from the drop zone, he then had to remain on patrol until the platoon commander departed. He would get his sleep from 8 to 11 AM, a grand total of three hours, after a gruelling twenty-one-hour day.

Coincidently, that morning we were called to assist sappers who were erecting barbed wire, laying mines and filling in bomb craters. I had no choice but to pull the sleeping beauty out of the comfort of his slit trench, after just an hour's sleep, to give us a hand. Hardly able to stand up straight, and constantly yawning and rubbing his eyes, he marched with the rest of us at 9.45 AM. Despite his exhaustion, he pulled his weight and was every bit as good as the rest of us. We arrived back at fifteen hundred hours, just in time for the evening meal, to the accompaniment of JU88 and JU87 bombers. During this attack, the 'heavy sleeper' gave a good account of himself, manning the Bren gun. As far as I was concerned, all sanctions were lifted against him, and I rostered him for the last sentry duty of the night, to allow him to get a decent kip.

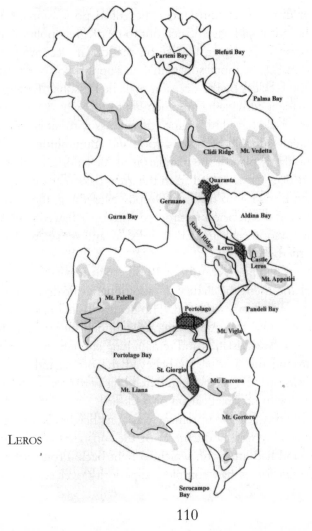

LEROS

16

THE BATTLE FOR LEROS

Perhaps under different circumstances the Allied possession of the Dodecanese Islands could have turned out to be of great political and strategic importance. However, to take on the job of occupying and defending the islands, without substantial air support for our forces, bordered on the reckless by the decision makers. Lessons of the past should have made a convincing argument as to just why such a dangerous mission would have little chance of success without air superiority, and adequate supplies of troops, food and ammunition.

It was a foolhardy plan by the mandarins in Alexandria, cosily cosseted in their offices, far removed from the great risks that were being run by the men thrown into the fray. Despite everything, they would have their way, and the decision to proceed with their flawed plan was made. The enemy soon challenged that decision, and yet again a harsh lesson was learned.

The Germans had taken control of Rhodes before we even set sail from Haifa, giving them the luxury of additional airfields to add to those that they had already captured. The nearest Allied base was in Cyprus, but it was said that Allied aircraft stationed there hadn't the range to fly to the Greek islands and remain long enough to do battle. Like others around me, I foolishly believed the propaganda at the time. All that was on offer to the men defending Leros was a morale-booting fly-past, with no practical aid or back-up.

At a time when Allied air supremacy was at its height elsewhere in the Mediterranean, we were at the mercy of the constant barrage from the Luftwaffe, and had little with which to fight back. From dawn to dusk, the German forces had complete superiority over sea and air, and could do exactly as they pleased. *The Long Road to Leros* by Marsland Gander, the *Daily Telegraph*'s special correspondent, and the only journalist who was actually on Leros during the battle, told how, while en route to Cairo to file his world-exclusive report, he stopped off in Cyprus, 250 miles from Leros. While there, he saw a squadron of USP38 Long Range Lightning Strikers aircraft on the ground, which, he said, could have been used more effectively in the battle for Leros. With this kind of support, an Allied strike against Rhodes would have deserved serious consideration. However, for the remaining two months of the Allied occupation of Leros, trapped by circumstances, we could do little but give of our best.

No permanent help could be expected from the Allied commander-in-chief, General Eisenhower, who refused to depart from the agreed plan for the war in Europe. When the idea of invading the Dodecanese was initially put to Roosevelt, he observed: 'Strategically, if we get the Aegean Islands, I ask myself, where do we go from there?' Clearly, the Americans would not agree to diverting support from the Italian front.

Orders came for the 2nd Battalion and others of 234 Brigade of the Royal Irish Fusiliers to defend Leros. With little hope of reinforcements, no air cover, insufficient equipment, and a force of infantry well below brigade strength, we were given a task that would have tested the mettle of an entire division. Leros was a natural fortress. Fortified as a naval base, its seaplane base had been completely destroyed by enemy aircraft well in advance of the German invasion, as part of the softening-up of the island.

With all the odds against us, we were sitting ducks, destined to become hostages to the superior enemy power in the eastern Mediterranean. German reconnaissance flights lost no time in gathering intelligence on the layout of our infantry defensive positions, heavy-gun emplacements and gun sites. Armed with this information, and aware of our lack of defensive firepower, they had a clear run to soften us up even further, and bombarded the tiny island almost two hundred times in five days.

For the following two weeks, the bombing of Leros continued relentlessly. By the fifth week, any hope of an end to the bombing disappeared. As if to emphasise their intent, the Germans threw swarm after swarm of Stuka 87 and 88 fighter-bombers at us, strafing and bombing incessantly.

With the fall of Kos on 4 October, the only British-occupied air-field had fallen into German hands. The naval base at Leros was now the sole British bastion in the northern Aegean, and the German fighters were giving it their undivided attention. If it was ever possible to sink an island, their saturation bombing should surely have done the trick.

We had little scope to move about on Leros, and except for those manning the ack-ack weapons and Bofors, most of our time was spent in the slit trenches. We were fortunate that our casualties were light, but the constant screeching dives of the fighter bombers was terrifying, and very demoralising. For some, it was Malta revisited, except that this time they couldn't even take shelter in the deep limestone rock.

For many, it was a bridge too far. The wailing of the air-raid sirens – there were more than four thousand bombing attacks on Malta and Leros during the war – and the decimation of everything around them, was enough to crush their already low spirit. Many of us were worried, not only about our hopeless position, but also about our shell-shocked comrades. Today, I suppose it would be called post-traumatic stress syndrome. It was pitiful to watch. On facing yet another incoming attack, they'd curl up shaking, unable to take any more, and there was nothing we could do to help them.

There was no pause in the aerial attacks, with more than a thousand sorties in six weeks, and we feared for the shell-shocked men's mental state, and the additional danger that their condition posed for us. We couldn't be sure that they could safely continue their duties, man guns or keep lookout. With no medical facilities or medicines available, our only option was to try to evacuate them from the front line.

There was always the worry that their sense of utter hopelessness would spread to the other men. This was yet another reason to remove them: morale was already low enough. Only a small number were evacuated, as others showed bravery above and beyond the call of duty.

17

BRAVERY BEYOND BELIEF

In the midst of all this carnage and battle fatigue, there were examples of sheer guts and bravery: men who, with no thought for themselves, gave their all for others. One in particular comes to mind. A close friend from home, Sergeant Doyle, the leader of the pioneer section and one of the early mine-disposal crew, gave no thought to his own safety when he saw a Greek woman stray into an anti-personnel minefield. One of the mines exploded, and she was very badly wounded. What was left of her legs was touching the tripwires of other unexploded mines. In her agony and shock, she was wriggling around, and it was only a matter of time before she triggered the other mines.

Sergeant Doyle spotted her. Far from backing away from the minefield, he kept going forward, crawling straight into it. As we watched in horror, there was little that we could do, either to stop him or to help the distraught woman. Any action could trigger a mine, making a bad situation worse. All the time, he kept talking across to her, trying to keep her calm, letting her know that help was on the way. She had nothing to be afraid of, he said, everything was going to be all right. His soothing voice constantly reassured her, even though she probably couldn't understand English, and was too shocked to realise what was happening. As he drew closer to her, he made safe the nearest mines, as he inched his way closer and closer to her mangled body. Finally, he succeeded in reaching her, and gently eased her back out of the minefield, to safety.

Doyle got up and got on with the job in hand, with no sense of his amazing bravery. Having seen to it that medical care was on the way, he matter-of-factly rejoined his platoon. I was happy to have these men at my side and was proud to serve with them. I never did find out if Doyle got a medal for his bravery. Often the bravest men weren't the ones that got the medals: we took them for granted. We split up immediately after this episode, and I never saw him again. I think of him often.

In the two months spent occupying and defending Leros, I never once saw a single British or American aircraft defending the island. With the exception of Dakotas dropping supplies prior to the invasion by the enemy, no Allied aircraft flew over Leros. The only British aircraft seen over the island from then on were Beaufighters on patrol, operating from a base hundreds of miles away. Low on fuel, they couldn't hang around to engage the enemy, and had to return to base. It seemed that we had been abandoned.

All of our support was withdrawn on 11 October, a month prior to the invasion by the Germans. The door had been left wide open: we were on our own. The Germans ensured that supplies and reinforcements for Leros never materialised. The British garrison, despite the courageous stand of the Durham Light Infantry, was no match for the Messerschmitts. The combined forces of Bofor gunners, Royal Air Force combatants, the Long Range Desert Group, the Greek SBS and other commandos could not beat off the German bombers.

The might of the German air, land and sea forces was thrown into the invasion of Kos, which had been occupied by the Allies for only two weeks. The Allied garrison, greatly outnumbered, weakened, and tired from their ordeal of twenty days' continuous warfare, were overcome in just twenty-four hours. The commando units did Trojan work, managing to get many of the Allied troops off the island before they were overrun.

After the fall of Kos, the number of aerial attacks against the embattled garrison on Leros increased. All buildings, installations and communications were completely destroyed. The Germans pounded the Italian six-inch coastal gunners, and German fighter pilots, with unflinching courage, plunged down one after the other, releasing their bombs in a thunderous roar. The Italian gunners remained defiant, but were powerless to stem this tide of destruction. With most of the guns now out of action, there were only four Bofors to meet the incoming attacks.

Emboldened by their own tenacity, the gunners sent tracer fire that seemed to streak from twenty different points of defence. I firmly believe that the courage of these Italian gunners was responsible for extending the survival period of the remaining manned Italian coastal batteries. As Ted Johnson writes in *The Island Prize*: 'It should be remembered that these Italians were being asked to fight against the German forces, who only two months previously had been their allies until the surrender of Italy on 3 September.'

I can offer no first-hand view of the Italian infantry, though much has been written about them. I can, however, speak for the Italian gunners who were operating close to our platoon's defensive position. I saw these men struggle valiantly, against heavy odds. The fact that Italy had surrendered unconditionally should have meant their disengagement from the war, full stop, yet they continued to give their all. The extension of German aerial activity after the fall of Kos could only mean one thing: Leros was not far behind. With our communications wrecked, and no means to put them right, we depended on Middle Eastern Intelligence to find out about German shipping movements between the islands. If the reports were accurate, it seemed that the enemy was engaged in a war of nerves. Coupled with the sustained attacks of the Luftwaffe, this meant that morale was put to the stiffest of tests. Relief came in the form of brittle humour, and a flood of obscenities directed at the German antagonists.

Around October, a rumour began to circulate that our only chance was evacuation. With German air supremacy and no moonless nights expected until late November, the chance of this becoming a reality was slim. Our only hope was to hold out against all odds. Our sole supply line of fishing caiques or nocturnal drops from submarines wouldn't be sufficient to meet the crisis. GHQ Middle East finally decided that Leros must be reinforced. Royal Navy surface craft, together with subs and caiques, were forced to run even greater risks to re-supply us with guns, stores and troops. Despite the crippling cost to ships and crews, they never flinched from the task, and did a wonderful job.

Finally, reinforcements began to arrive. On 18 October, B Company of the 2nd Royal West Kents was diverted from Samos, to join forces with the Royal Irish Fusiliers on Leros. We were grateful for small mercies. Dismantled guns arrived, but had to be manned by the already understrength infantry personnel. The garrison began to build up in dribs and drabs as the Faughs were reinforced by a further ninety men made up of mixed units. A battalion of the 4th Buffs, old friends of ours from Malta, arrived on 25 October, lucky to have made it.

They told us that, while they were on board the destroyer *Eclipse* the night before, calamity had struck. Ken Blake, from Hemel Hempstead, and my old pal Sergeant Andy Lennon told how, as they sailed through the Karabaka channel on 24 October 1943, en route to reinforce us on Leros, the *Eclipse* hit a mine. The explosion ripped through the boiler room, and a serious fire broke out, which spread to the ammunition stores. The destroyer broke in two, and sank within five minutes. Casualties were colossal: 374 men including seven army officers and 128 other ranks from A and HQ Company, the 'Buffs', lost their lives. The crew of the *Eclipse* was decimated, only sixty-four navy personnel survived. On board the *Eclipse* was Commodore Destroyers Levant, Captain Percy Todd. Ironically, he was making the trip to find out what was really happening in the Aegean, following complaints from his destroyer captains regarding the perceived futility of the whole operation. He never got to report on his mission.

Ken Blake, who described himself as 'one of the lucky survivors', was very badly burnt. After swimming around in the sea for almost six hours, he was eventually picked up by a motor launch sent out from Leros in search of survivors. Like many others, he was to suffer years of physical and mental pain.

On 5 November, we were reinforced by the 1st King's Own Regiment. As expected, the Royal Navy experienced heavy coastal attacks, and a further six destroyers, two subs and ten other warships were sunk, with a cruiser badly damaged. The loss of life was again substantial.

The enemy was closing in on Leros. A platoon from B Company of the Faughs, stationed on Stampalia, were withdrawn just in time to avoid the German attack.

On Levitia, an island within sight of Leros, forty-five members of the LRDGs – the Long Range Desert Group – were overcome by German forces. Kalimos, separated from Leros by only a half-mile stretch of water, was already in enemy hands, and every day we expected zero hour. Throughout the siege of Malta, we'd pushed hard and fast, doing a thousand and one jobs at a time. Now, it was much the same. Short on sleep and rations, alongside all our other duties we assisted the Madras sappers and miners in filling in craters on the roads. At the same time, we dug and blasted the rock to build gun sites for the extra Bofors that had arrived under cover of darkness, lashed to the hulls of submarines.

Like the majority of our battalion, I'd now spent almost six years abroad. Despite all my experiences to date, I still held out a faint hope that, somehow, we might be evacuated. That hope soon evaporated, however, when the visits from the Luftwaffe and FW190 ground-support fighter-bombers intensified even further. More modern than the Stukas, they were a clear indication that a German landing on Leros was imminent.

Despite all this, hope still dies hard. In an effort to boost morale, whispered messages came through that our efforts were somehow having an effect on the war effort, forcing the enemy to pull back units from other theatres, to the benefit of the Allied cause. 'Some f—kin' hope' was the general consensus. Judging by the frequency of the aerial bombardment even in the early days of our occupation of Leros, there was little sign that the Germans were weakening.

With no direct communication, and having to soldier in near-impossible odds, hope became the last bastion. As the enemy beat the s—t out of us, we put our reinforcements to the best possible use.

Our commanding officer, Lieutenant Colonel Maurice French, a very experienced soldier, reasoned that the most effective way we could defend and counter-attack was to push the invaders back into the sea. On 5 November, Brigadier General Tilney, the recently appointed fortress commander, arrived and immediately overruled French's plan, opting to defend the beaches. This was not, we believed, the way to go, but refusal to obey an order is a non-runner under any circumstances. Mickey French, as our CO was affectionately known, had the better plan. A more seasoned officer than Tilney, he had vast experience of defensive tactics in Malta, during the siege. His intimate knowledge of Leros, developed over the previous two months, meant that he knew the ground.

Tilney's plan involved spreading out the already depleted defence regiments in the hope that the Italian coastal guns would be able to pin down the invading forces, allowing us to counter-attack and push the enemy back from the beaches. As events unfolded, the Germans were not foolhardy enough to expose themselves to such obvious risks. Our CO argued that, by spreading our men so thinly along the coast, we would not be able to cope with the anticipated airborne parachute forces. As things turned out, he was right. Perhaps Tilney felt that the difficult terrain would make parachute landings impossible, but land they did.

The effect of these on the defenders of Leros was shattering: we watched helplessly as swarms of German paratroopers – the 'Fallschimjager' or 'hunters from the sky' – rained down on the island. After a month of relentless bombing, false alarms of landings, and the belief by our intelligence that the Germans were merely adopting a cat-and-mouse approach, designed to play on our tired nerves, the landings were finally about to happen. If the Germans were intent on driving us into a state of physical and mental exhaustion, they had succeeded in their aim. After weeks of being on full alert, sleeping sitting up in full webbing with our ammo pouches strapped around our waist, we were hungry and weary beyond belief.

All the time, the message was hammering at our subconscious: the f—kers were on their way. Once again, we steeled ourselves for what was to come. Despite our scepticism, the brigadier's new plan of defence came into effect on 6 November, six days before the Germans invaded. Weapons, stores and ammunition all had to be moved to new positions. Two-pounder anti-tank guns, boxes of grenades, VMG – Vickers machine guns – Bren guns and three-inch mortars had to be hauled over mountain terrain by already exhausted men. This was done in addition to the night fatigues of unloading precious cargo from subs and surface craft, as fast as was humanly possible.

The men worked like Trojans, knowing that Tilney was making a grave mistake. Our well-rehearsed plan of mounting a tight defence from secure positions was tossed aside. New orders from the brigadier resulted in a dispersed and understrength force being widely scattered across the island. For those of us who'd been on Leros since September, all our training and planning had been for nothing. Now, through the fragmentation of the various units, and the lack of communication, we were doing the job for the enemy: divide and conquer. My section of No. 9 Platoon was out of all contact with company and battalion HQ, and I'm sure the others were no better off.

18

THE GERMANS ARE COMING!

At 4 AM on 12 November, Sergeant Smudger Smyth told me to get my section to their battle positions: the German invasion fleet was on its way. After an instant of chaos, we were ready to do battle, with a clear view of the enemy craft from our position. Suddenly gunfire broke out, as the island's gun batteries pounded the detachments of the coastal raiders, the Brandenburgers Kustenjager Regiment. They were forced back to sea, out of range of the heavy stuff being flung at them. This brought a quick response from the Stukas, and as their aerial assaults silenced the big guns, the German assault troops made their second attempt to land. They approached the coastline arrow-fashion, moving diagonally toward Alinda bay, north of the Royal Irish Fusiliers' defensive position. The rest of the convoy was moving diagonally, towards the coastline of Pandeli bay, south of No. 9 Platoon's new position. The Italian coastal batteries and the British Bofors and twenty-five pounders all opened fire, sinking some of the landing craft. The noise was indescribable. Under the brigadier's orders, the beaches were to be the main focus of our attention. We had a reasonable sighting of the beaches, but when the Germans landed at the foot of the Appetici peninsula we had no view of them. This low landing point was on the seaward side of the hill, so when they first came ashore, no one knew how – or where – they'd succeeded in setting foot on the island.

Ted Johnson's *The Island Prize*, written some forty-nine years after the event, revealed how the Germans managed to land on Leros unseen. Johnson, formerly a lieutenant with C Company, played a major role in the battle for Leros. The enemy, with little interest in beach approaches, had made scramble landings, carrying full equipment and enough ammunition to last until the next day.

Scaling the north-east face of Mount Appetici with climbing ropes, the convoys were believed to be heading for Alinda bay, north of the positions held by the Faughs. In fact, they actually bypassed it, and made scramble landings at Grifu and Mount Clidi, the very places that Allied defenders believed to be unscalable.

The lack of communication in relaying information on the enemy's success allowed the Germans to establish themselves in these lightly defended areas. Subsequently the Buffs attacked but, with insufficient troops, and time having been lost, the Germans quickly repelled the Buffs' machine-gun attack with heavy mortar fire. The attack was halted, the little ground that had already been gained was lost, and the British lads were forced back.

High seas, cloudy skies and strong winds didn't deter the enemy from landing substantial reinforcements of paratroops, but as the day wore on, the Buffs, aided by other troops, retook Clidi, capturing one hundred and fifty prisoners, but suffering serious casualties in the process. The accurate bombing and persistent machine-gun attacks by German aircraft took their toll, and once again the hill was lost to enemy troops.

Appetici being out of view, the only indication to us that the Germans had landed was hearing the ferocious barrage of small-arms fire. We believed that the Italian infantry, in defence of their colleagues manning heavy-calibre coastal guns, had engaged the Brandenburg Regiment. Lieutenant Ted Johnson's platoon and the rest of C Company Royal Irish Fusiliers arrived on Appetici to counter-attack. Though slowed down by the activity of the dive bombers overhead, they prevented the capture of Castle Hill and Mount Appetici, but hadn't the manpower to push the enemy back into the sea.

Unable to see the enemy, and with a lot of hostile fire cracking around them, Lance-Sergeant John Caldwell was killed instantly. Sergeant O'Connell, badly wounded, died a short time later. The Brandenburgs, temporarily withdrawn to a safe position, were still high enough on the peninsula to direct their fire on the advancing Faughs, without presenting themselves as a target.

The action of Johnson's platoon and others of C Company in

recapturing the summit and two gun emplacements, before orders came to withdraw, was bravery of the highest order. They knew that the battle for Appetici was far from over. Four hours after the initial landings, A Company of the Faughs were still in position on the south side of Alinda bay. Due to our limiting position, my section was restricted to getting off some bursts of Vickers machine-gun fire at the enemy landing craft as they approached the coastline. We could see nothing of the Germans who'd landed at Appetici. Given no respite from the screaming Stuka dive-bombers, and the roar of exploding bombs, we could do little except take cover in the scrub and low trees.

At 10.45 AM, we were informed by Lieutenant Austin Ardill (later to be awarded a Military Cross for his gallantry) that the area was clear of the enemy. He had done a 'recce' and, on instructions from HQ, informed No. 9 Platoon's commander, 2nd Lieutenant Hillman, that we were to leave our foxholes and accompany him up to Leros Castle, to engage the enemy on the northern slopes.

Laden down with Bren guns and other gear, and under heavy air attack, we scrambled over five hundred feet of rocky terrain to the top of the hill, the climb made all the more difficult by the fact that we had to zigzag to avoid the dive-bombing Junkers 87s. The crashing explosions of the flaming bombs and the smell of cordite, as we moved upwards, was like Malta all over again. The large bomb crater that I saw halfway up the hill would have been a welcome temporary refuge in other circumstances, but now our priority was getting up that hill to the castle. One way or another, we knew that even temporary refuge would invite much more risk from the Stukas seeking targets than any attention our upward movement would attract.

We took cover behind any piece of rock or high mound, whenever the Stukas were flying sorties against nearby gun sites. My section made the five-hundred-foot climb in thirty minutes, without casualties. Although the enemy aircraft were concentrating on the large gun emplacements, we were encroaching on their general target area, and were fair game. Despite the lack of casualties, they managed to batter our eardrums and damage our morale. The terrifying screams of their dive-bombers and the roar of their cannon were an indispensable element in forcing home frustration, despair and apprehension when it came to the impossible task that lay ahead of us.

19

BRAVE DESERTERS AND DECENT MEN

Unfortunately, two members of my section, both veterans of Malta, succumbed to battle neurosis and deserted me on that hillside. They made for a bolt-hole somewhere near the town of Leros. They had survived almost three years of continuous siege, time and again showing the utmost courage and bravery during the siege of Malta, only to be met by the relentless bombing and strafing at the hands of the Luftwaffe on Leros. For more seven weeks, we had been pounded non-stop, and they had no more left to give. We watched over them as best we could.

Once inside the castle, we quickly set about getting our machine-guns and rifle positions sorted out. Satisfied with our defensive arrangements, Lieutenant Ardill left us, taking with him a fusilier, 'Beaver' Elliott, the battalion 'hard man'. Elliott had earlier been placed under close arrest under my care, prior to us leaving Palestine. He was awaiting trial on a serious breach of discipline, but with no place to confine him on Leros, I became his jailor. As we were under strength and in dire circumstances, I gradually let him drift into becoming a member of my section. Fully armed, he carried out his duties diligently, and only when a senior officer came into view did we quickly relieve him of his weapons. To this day, I don't know what became of him. Someone told me that he was decorated for 'distinguished conduct' in the course of a battle. Strangely enough, there were two members of our battalion named 'Beaver' Elliott. One of them was killed in action, but I never found out which one it was.

I can't recall the exact words that were exchanged between our platoon commander and me when I had to report the desertion of two of our men. One was a close friend of mine, and for this reason I undertook to search for them, in the faint hopes that the serious consequences of being charged with cowardice could be avoided. Our view of the Appetici peninsula was not good, except for the northern slopes. The edge of Leros town was also in our sights. Satisfied that the town was still clear of enemy troops, Jimmy Gollogher and I stripped off our heavy webbing and set off at 11.30 AM. I was carrying my 9mm Italian Beretta light machine-gun, while Jimmy had his Lee Enfield rifle. The Stukas were still making hostile incursions over Leros town, but we were confident that we could make the trip downhill without being sighted. We varied our approach, sometimes hunker-sliding on the rocky terrain, at other times making a quick dash between boulders.

All the time, we tried to think like a couple of 'bomb happies': where would they take refuge? Instinct would have told them that a rocky indentation might shield them from the bombing. A cave might fit their needs, but with an open front they would be too exposed and might possibly even be spotted by a trigger-happy sharpshooter. We were getting nowhere. As we were about to call off the search, Jimmy suddenly drew my attention to a house on the edge of Leros town, near where we'd taken cover. We could see steps going down to a storeroom or basement. Making plenty of noise as we approached it, calling out their names, we were met with a hearty response. The two 'boyos' were there.

Abandoned by a local family, the building was now no more than a shell. It was overrun by rats and stank of putrefaction. The men sat on the broken concrete, stripped of all their gear. They were disheveled, dirty and foul-smelling. It seemed as though this refuge – which they believed to be their only hope of survival – had enveloped them.

It was an awkward confrontation. Rather than feeling angry, I was more in sympathy with them. Here were two brave men, with whom I had shared fear and joy many times in the past. They had shown their mettle on many occasions, and no one who knew them could possibly call them cowards: but after three years of intense bombing in Malta, and more futile fighting on Leros, their nerve had finally gone.

Gollogher, a hard man, was completely intolerant of their actions. Unable to understand why they hadn't the guts or strong mentality that was the norm for him, he lost no time in branding them cowardly bastards. The men were oblivious what others thought of them, however. Neither of the two unfortunates was in any shape to withstand any more stress, whether from the enemy's unrelenting attack or our barracking; they'd had more than their share already.

We tried to explain that everyone felt fear in a war situation, and that we had no option but to get on with it for the sake of ourselves and others. This argument carried no weight with the shattered men. They were past caring. Threats and pleas to make them understand the gravity of what they'd done fell on deaf ears. I even threatened to shoot them, knowing full well that I couldn't bring myself to do it!

Jimmy was outraged at my compassion and had great difficulty in going along with my idea of reporting that we couldn't find them. Our problem now was to try and make it back so that I could take charge of my section. There was no sign of an enemy build-up in the area, yet the Stukas were still active south-east of where Jimmy and I had began our climb, back up to the castle. Small-arms fire and the occasional loud bang of heavy-calibre gunfire made us wonder whether the enemy had established a bridgehead, and were being engaged by our troops and the Italian guns.

Out of touch with any real information, we moved from boulder to boulder, hoping that we were being observed from the castle by the platoon sergeants, and not some enemy snipers. Finally, we made it back to the castle, taking a breather behind some broken walls, before reporting to 'Smudger' that the deserters were nowhere to be found. Before I could finish my explanation, I was interrupted by the excited shouts of one of our Bren gunners as he yelled: 'Enemy planes in sight!'

The sky west of our gunners' position was filled with Junker 52 troop-carrying planes flying in close formation. The German parachute regiments were on their way in. Flying low and slow across our front, as the crow flies, they were well within our range, and we had a good line of fire on them. Our anti-aircraft guns, situated on the mountain peaks, let go with a barrage of flak, all guns blazing, assisted in the barrage by tracer fire. As the planes came into range, the volume of fire increased dramatically, as all units engaged them. They were attacked on all sides, and the tracer ammo from the ack-ack and small-arms fire made for a devastating barrage, which penetrated the fuselages of the massive JU52s. As the attacks hit home, we could see the large aircraft sway, as plumes of smoke poured from them, and still they held their formation.

As they headed in the direction of Gurna bay, the ground fire against them intensified. In an effort to divert fire away from them, their ME110 escorts swept the hillsides with a menacing tirade of cannon fire. In situations like this, you ask yourself: 'Where's our f—kin' air support'? The same place it always was: somewhere else!

We were grateful for the protection offered by the castle, as the Messerschmitts had difficulty in scoring any direct hits. No casualties were reported as the German fighters broke off their strafing and linked up with the rest of their convoy, heading for the landing zone.

The enemy's airborne assault was directed at a piece of ground between Gurna and Alinda bay, an area unlikely to do the 'paras' any favours, littered as it was with rocks and boulders. Nonetheless, it was a good strategic area, chosen to divide the island's defence forces in two.

They came in at low altitude. Hundreds of parachutes were disgorged from the overhead aircraft, landing close to positions held by A Company of the Faughs, units of the Buffs, the West Kents and light anti-aircraft Bofor gun emplacements.

Once on the ground, they engaged in close-quarter battle with all units, with the Bofors depressing (raising/ lowering and rotating) to enhance the ground fire, while the commandos' firepower kept the Germans away from their containers. From the time the paras commenced their drop, they were well within range of our No. 9 Platoon, lodged in the castle. Meanwhile, left unattended by the enemy's fighter aircraft, we managed to get off a substantial number of bursts from our machine-guns. In situations like this, paras are helpless until they get to their containers and equip themselves with automatics and rifles. When they landed in that narrow inlet between bays, we lost sight of them, but all hell broke loose as all the other Allied units engaged them. Their casualties were estimated at sixty percent. Many drowned, others broke limbs on the rocky ground, and many more were killed in ground fire before they got a chance to leave their aircraft. Some were dragged over rocks and walls by their parachutes, their bodies smashed and broken, leaving them unable to release their chutes. More still fell foul of 'the roman candle', when their parachutes failed to open and they plunged to a rocky death or fell strewn across telephone lines.

More than five hundred sorties were made by the Luftwaffe on that first day of the landings, both on the coast and from the air, and the ferocity of the attacks was kept up for the duration of the campaign. The Allied defenders were in no position to consolidate their initial victory, under the barrage of dive-bombers, exploding bombs and bullets. Subjected to the close-range small-arms fire from the British commando units of Jellicoe's SBS, the Long Range Desert Group and the Greek Sacred Company, the *Fallschmirmajer* had difficulties in reaching their supply containers. Despite all this, the 1st Battalion of the 2nd German Parachute Regiment, supported by the Stukas, succeeded in establishing themselves in the narrow neck of ground between Gurna and Alinda bay.

Out of contact in our castle-top lair, we had no idea of the heavy casualties suffered by both sides until the following night. The worst hit was D Company – the Faughs. They had two platoon commanders killed and one wounded, with many other ranks also wounded. On the Appetici side of Castle Hill, the enemy took little time in seeking revenge for our having let loose on their invading paras. Pounding us for more than thirty minutes, they forced us to take cover away from the parapets. A couple of Brens, quickly mounted for anti-aircraft action, made little difference. The German pilots had won the day. We were lucky that we had no physical casualties, but the mental pressure was taking its toll.

Early on the evening of the thirteenth, a member of the Long Range Desert Group got through to us. This bald Londoner had tons of courage, and was a mine of information. He gave us a heavy haversack with about ten tins of McConachies stew, and was welcomed as a hero. Up to then, all we had left was a tin of hard biscuits. In the

The author, late 1940s

My father Thomas, who was a veteran of World War I and enlisted in the Defence Forces during the Emergency (1939–45)

My boyhood friend – and later best man – Bill Kavanagh (Sandra Mara's father), aged seventeen, in Palestine. We ran away together to join up.

Bill in the Paratroopers, in Malta

Gordon Wright,
a comrade of mine in the Faughs and the S

Walter Pancott at Omagh Depot, 1935

Andy Roy, aged nineteen

My brother Archie (centre) with fellow soldiers in North Africa, possibly in 1943, while
serving with the 7th Armoured Division

Sleeping quarters at Stalag VIIA, a transit camp for prisoners of war, Mooseburg, 1942
(Reproduced by permission of The Wartime Memories Projec[t]
from the Windsor Williams collection, submitted by his son Peter William[s])

My unit on the march in Malta. 'Wee' Davy Thompson is at the front of the column at the left of the photo.

The author (standing), with a broken jaw, next to Jock McBride from Ballymoney in County Antrim

Johnny King is in the centre, Tom McGee on the extreme right of the back row

Raymond Williams,
author of *The Road to Leros*

painting of the submarine *Trooper*, on which I served in 1943. The painting is inscribed
by one of the men who built her'. *Trooper* was lost later that year, with all sixty-three men
n board.

Leading seaman
Len Williams

Stoker Petty Officer Peter Adam of *Trooper*

Walter Pancott, Mat McGurk and Fusilier Mullan in Malta, 1938

'he three amigos': the author, Billy Brazil and Bill Kavanagh outside the Gresham Hotel
O'Connell Street, Dublin, after the war

The wedding of Bill Kavanagh and Mary Ellen (Helen) Harte, the author's cousin. The author (on the extreme left, seated) was Bill's best man.

Aunt Mary Ellen and her grandson Michael Pemberton

ith Palestinian leader Yasser Arafat in West Beirut, where Arafat was in hiding, *c.* 1985

eeting Ted Kennedy. Brian Lenihan in on the left, the author in the centre, and Jim 'Keeffe on the right

With Tom McGee (at left) at a reunion of the Faughs at Gough Barracks, Armagh, 1950s

The author and Maud on their wedding day.
Maud's sister Florrie is on the right.

...ith comrades on Leros, to mark the forty-fifth anniversary of the end of the campaign ...n the island. From left: Paddy Clare, Pipe Major Wilson, RSM Jock McGregor, the ...thor, 'Heelball' Kelly, Captain Thompson and Sergeant Andy Lennon.

...reunion of the 2nd Battalion of the Royal Irish Fusiliers at Armagh Barracks, 1952. All ...e men in the photograph were former prisoners of war. Standing, from left: 'Kid' Kil-...llon, Bobby Reden, Tom McGee, Ned FitzSimons, Johnny Nixon, Ballantyne, Forsythe, ...rgeant Craig, Danny 'Piccolo' Byrne and Christy Watts. The seated men include, at left, ...rgeant Nicky Pearson, Jerry Burke next to him, and the author on the extreme right.

The author with his wife Myra (at left), and Bill Kavanagh and his wife Helen (Mary Ellen Harte, the author's first cousin)

Members of the Irish Ex-Boxers Association, which was founded by Bill Kavanagh, the author and others to help former boxers who had fallen on hard times. Those pictured include, from left to right: Maud Harte, European champion Maxie McCullough, Nellie Kavanagh, Al McDermott, Eamonn Andrews (member and patron of the association), Willie Finnegan, the author, Bill Kavanagh and Grainne Andrews.

short time he was with us, he filled us in on what was happening on the island. I assumed that Lieutenant Ardill, knowing we had no food or water and no means of communication, had sent him to bridge the communications gap and bring us some grub.

The LRDG man promised to get word through about just how badly we needed communications links, but he could do nothing about the lack of water. The following morning, a couple of signallers, Derrymen Alex McBride and Tommy Lloyd, managed to bring a line into the castle. They'll never know how much that meant to morale. Sadly, the first news that came through to us in the days that followed was of the deaths of some of my closest friends, Polly McIlwaine, Sergeant John Caldwell, Sergeant Connell and 'Sab' McMaster among them. In the same period, the second-in-command of C Company, Lieutenant Hugh Gore-Booth, the son of an old aristocratic Sligo family with connections to Countess Markiewicz, was killed while leading a patrol in search of the enemy on Appetici peninsula.

My close pal and drinking buddy 'Gutrie' Kane was also killed. I mourned them all, as I thought of happier times. Around midnight on the thirteenth, the lack of water became a real problem. Dehydration was setting in rapidly, and everyone was suffering from severe thirst. We were very concerned about this situation, as it looked as though we were here for the long haul. Our 'bald eagle' had told us that a recce of Leros had shown it to be reasonably clear of enemy forces, so, with the approval of the platoon commander, I decided to risk the downward journey to seek out water, taking the large biscuit tin and a couple of empty bottles with me, in the hope of being able to fill them. Accompanied by Gordon Wright, we made the steep descent on our hunkers, moving quietly from boulder to boulder. We knew, through past experience, that there were water wells in the valleys, but there was no hope of reaching them. We'd have to try and reach the edge of Leros, to see if we could find water there.

As I was carrying the tin, I lost my footing on the rough ground and dropped it. The sound of it clattering and banging down the hillside ricocheted through the silence. We were sure that it could be heard throughout the whole Aegean. Doubts as to whether the area was as clear of Germans as had been reported meant that there was a need for greater vigilance. If the information was wrong, tracer bullets would soon be whizzing in our direction. The only response to the noise was three Verey lights – red and green flares sent up by the Germans to pinpoint our location – thankfully they were too far to the south-east to expose our position. We kept still, holding our breath as we waited another fifteen minutes before daring to make a move.

Our luck holding out, we made it to some houses on the edge of Leros, but found no running water. Eventually, on the lookout for anti-personnel mines, we found a burst main and followed it until it crossed some badly fractured ground by the roadside. The soil was damp, but there was no sign of water. We cleared the area, but still nothing more than a few squirts of untreated water appeared – even worse, it stank of creosote. Between the heat of Leros, and the diffi-ciult descent, we were now dangerously dehydrated; we cupped our hands and, very slowly, they half-filled with the dirty water. Slaking our terrible thirst with the contaminated water, we set about working out how we were going to manage to fill the containers. Taking turns at crouching over the squirting point and covering each other's back, it took us more than an hour to fill the tin two-thirds full. Filling the two water bottles took what seemed like an eternity, but we got there even-tually. The problem now was how we could carry a couple of gallons of water back up the rocky hill without being detected. With no han-dles to grip the weight on the tin, it wasn't going to be easy.

Slowly, we climbed, carrying, resting, carrying, resting, all the time losing small amounts of water, as it sloshed about in the open vessels. Two and a half hours later, we finally made it back to the castle. Corporal Bobby Peden, watching out for our approach, was the first to dip his mess tin into the container and get his fill. Watching the way he gulped it down, Sergeant 'Smudger' Smyth took charge, and doled out a small amount of the precious water to about twenty people. No one complained about the creosote taste, or the muddy colour, as they feverishly queued up to slake their thirst. They were so thirsty that they didn't care if the water had come from a nest of malaria-infected mos-quitoes. Gordon and I were very pleased with ourselves, although we were annoyed that the platoon commander didn't even bother to thank us for our efforts or the risks we had taken.

20

FRIENDLY FIRE AND LOUSY LEADERS

COST US LIVES AND LIBERTY

Into the early hours of 13 November, the German reinforcements came ashore, and supplies were dropped on enemy positions on Appetici. One of their fighters was hit by Bofors and anti-tank two-pounders, from A Company Royal Irish Fusiliers' position, on the southern slopes of Alinda bay. It was completely gutted before it could reach the shore. At 6.45 AM on the morning of the thirteenth, just hours after we had made it back with the water, a wave of JU52s arrived, with parachute-troop reinforcements and supplies. Once again, we caught them on the way in, just as they crossed the coastline. Level with No. 9 Platoon's machine-guns, together with a few other platoons of our battalion, they afforded us a very good shot, before their troop carriers managed to cross the coast.

The sheer power, speed and violence of the artillery and infantry that erupted on the enemy as they made their approach resulted in seven JU52 troop carriers being shot down. They sustained heavy casualties, but despite strong counter-attacks against the German paras with mortars and machine-guns, the Germans were not deflected from their purpose.

In fact, there were heavy casualties on both sides, with No. 9 Platoon of the Faughs still in position in the castle, engaging the enemy on the northern slopes of Appetici, while No. 7 and 8 Platoons had the harder task of close combat at the end of the island on Rachi Ridge, Merliviglia, where the Germans were making good use of snipers to pin down sections that were attempting to manoeuvre to advance positions on their flanks.

Three very close friends of mine, Sergeant George Mullett, Lance Corporal Tom Magee and Johnnie Justice from D Company, were pinned down by German marksmen as they tried to force the enemy to withdraw from their landing ground. Despite being attacked by small-arms fire, they continued to move forward, and reached a slit trench to take up a defensive position. Still presenting a threat to the German paras, a few snipers had them pinned down. In a different war situation, these sharpshooters would have been taken out by a rake of fire from tanks or stalking sections, who could get close enough to do the trick. But this was Leros, and there were no Allied tanks or stalking sections.

Pinned down by the enemy, and ducking the heavy return fire of their own troops to the rear, the three Dubs sat tight. After four hours, taking advantage of a strong counter-attack by their colleagues that distracted the enemy, they managed to break free. Tom Magee later remarked that, during those hours, they said prayers that they didn't realise they knew! All three were mentioned in dispatches.

Saturday the thirteenth of November, day two for us in the castle, was more of the same. With Stukas overhead and ME110s strafing the hillside, the enemy plan seemed designed to keep us on the fringe, leaving the way clear for the free movement of the German troops across the edge of Leros town, en route to the centre.

The Brandenburgers had attacked, and now occupied, Appetici summit, from where they were testing out the ground for further advances. The Faughs engaged them with small-arms fire, to slow down their forward movement, and their response came via aerial attacks, resulting in British casualties, with the Germans taking some prisoners before orders eventually came through to abandon the hillside. The Germans took over some houses on the outskirts of Leros town, and there was little we could do about it from our position, except for letting off an occasional burst of fire as they left cover, to move from house to house.

These temporary setbacks, inflicted by a handful of isolated British infantry, were not enough to deter the enemy from their strategic plan. They probably knew that we were short of food, water and supplies. We would be dealt with when the battle for the centre of Leros had advanced substantially. Meanwhile, with the Italian gun emplacements already taken out, their 'pillbox' defences charged and grenades lobbed in, the Stukas, ME115s and machine-guns kept us confined and isolated. The German plan to tighten their grip on the island had taken a substantial leap forward, but at a heavy cost. They suffered serious setbacks, and heavy casualties, and still had to break the back of British resistance.

For two days, a platoon of D Company Faughs held the Germano area, delaying the Germans and inflicting heavy casualties on them. The Faughs were unable to bring back their own casualties, the enemy keeping up a sustained attack as they withdrew.

The remaining three days of the battle for this small stretch of ground saw the British units make temporary gains. Though weakened in numbers, and disadvantaged by the lack of air support, they even managed to capture some Germans. But the enemy tactic of attempting to divide the island in two was beginning to pay off. The heavily reinforced units at Della Palma bay joined forces with their paras, launching attacks on a number of locations.

In response, all remaining infantry regiments co-ordinated attacks and counter-attacks on the heavily reinforced, and fresher, German troops. Backed up by the Bofors and ack-ack guns, the Allied soldiers moved towards the enemy positions. With an extensive barrage of mortar fire laid on by Corporal Williams, Sergeant Finlay and their crews, well over four hundred shells were hurled at enemy ground positions in just ten minutes. The barrels of the mortars became so warped from use that they were rendered useless.

This was the clearest indication yet to the enemy forces that the battle was far from over. In another section, forty German paras were taken prisoner, and the British managed to get many of their wounded back to regimental aid posts, some going directly to the Italian hospital at Portolago. Despite their substantial advantage in aircraft and other resources, the battles fought on Leros were some of the sternest tests faced by the German army in the eastern Mediterranean.

The Germans had planned their offensive of Leros thoroughly. Using a tough, tenacious force of paratroopers who'd seen action in Crete, Tunisia and Russia, they showed scant regard for their own safety or casualty rate. The Germans carried the fight to us, and fought for every stone and boulder. By now, the Faughs and other Allied regiments had been in the thick of the close-combat fighting, but the Germans were better organised.

Whenever their progress was interrupted, they used flares as signals to bring down the firepower of the Stukas, to tip the balance in their favour. The exhausted Allied defenders battled on, despite coming under heavy fire from a bombardment mistakenly laid on by our own Royal Navy.

Despite all of these problems, which included the constant disruption of our communications systems, the Allied units were still getting in good counter-attacks, and generally making life difficult for the enemy. Communications breakdowns were common throughout the battle. One night, in the course of a planned withdrawal from an attack on the enemy, the Royal Irish Fusiliers and other Allied units came under attack from friendly fire. Three British destroyers carrying out a bombardment of Alinda bay overshot the area held by their own side. Whether this was a miscalculation or a case of naval commanders having out-of-date information, who knows? Either way, the Faughs were forced to take shelter where they could. The Buffs suffered several casualties before their frantic signalling led to the bombardment being confined to German-held areas.

Our intelligence section stated that more than five hundred sorties were flown against us during our two-month occupation of the island. Many soldiers questioned the hierarchy and wanted to know why orders were issued that saw our own side drawn into an area that was being attacked by the navy. Did the backroom boys forget about the lads 'up front', or was it the lack of sleep and food that caused these dangerous decisions?

Our only solace was that the enemy were in the same boat. On two separate occasions, they sent up flares for Stuka support for their ground activity. The Stukas responded quickly, but the enemy pilots mistook the targets, and unleashed the bombs on their own men.

134

Realising their mistake, they regrouped, to wreak vengeance on the Allied targets, while allowing their ground forces to gain advantage, under cover of their fire. One such strike against the Faughs was not so successful. James Lucas, who served with the West Kents, described how a destructive onslaught of mortar and machine-gun fire was unleashed on the Brandenburgers at Appetici. The Faughs killed or wounded all of the German officers in that attack.

Our garrison, greatly reduced in numbers, and with a raggle-taggle intermingling of all the infantry divisions, was now receiving orders directly from HQ. Inevitably, this resulted in tragic mistakes being made. Number 12 platoon of C Company, the Royal Irish Fusiliers, were ordered by Fortress HQ to withdraw from Appetici and regroup at Meraviglia, their original position, which resulted in the pinned-down invaders being released, allowing them to regroup and fight more effectively against later counter-attacks. Our CO, Lieutenant Colonel French, was not told of this decision, and certainly would not have approved of it.

French drew up a plan to counter-attack the enemy, who by now were dominating the entire Appetici peninsula. The plan was that B and C Companies of his own regiment, the Faughs; HQ; and a Company of the 1st King's Own would enter Appetici on the night of 13/14 November. British destroyers were to bombard the area half an hour before we launched the attack, which was timed for zero two hundred hours.

For a number of reasons, the plan was not put into proper effect. In what later proved to be a false report, information suggested that the enemy was attacking Merliviglia in some force, from the direction of Rachi ridge, and it was believed that HQ was about to be attacked. Giving priority to this, the attacking force destined for Appetici was split up. One group was sent to defend HQ, the other, to continue with the planned attack on Appetici. Leading two understrength Companies onto the slopes of Appetici, French found that the promised bombardment hadn't materialised. His small force was caught short at first light, in an exposed position. The Germans took advantage of the situation, and inflicted severe casualties. Lieutenant

Colonel French was killed, still fighting, with a rifle to his shoulder. It was a sad blow to the Faughs and the King's Own.

The unfortunate circumstances that diverted the two companies from the fray was a matter of great regret to them. They dearly wanted to follow their gallant colonel into the attack, and they had great difficulty in understanding how their commanding officer was killed while leading troops of another regiment. The reasons why the Royal Irish Fusiliers were redirected remains a mystery that, to this day, has never been resolved.

I had served with Lieutenant Colonel French for more than six years, during the insurrection in Palestine, and in the siege of Malta. I also served with him in Syria, Transjordan, the Lebanon and Egypt. I was absolutely committed to his regiment, as were all those who had served with him. Here was a well-respected, honest and courageous man who knew no other way than to give his all. That his gallantry only merited a posthumous mention in dispatches filled all those who had fought with him, and who understood the nature of some of the toughest battles of the war, with disgust and disbelief.

*

At no time during daylight hours was the air clear of Stukas and Junker 88s. Sunday 14 November was no different. But this time, the already intense German air assault was stepped up considerably. The Italian ack-ack now having been wiped out, the German Luftwaffe put in a massive effort to rid themselves of the menacing British Bofors. Moving in a swarm, they overwhelmed the gun sights, leaving just three Bofors capable of firing. A destroyer made it through, to reinforce the overstretched Leros Brigade with two companies of the West Kents and their Battalion HQ, but the arrival of 1,300 German reinforcements, together with 88mm guns and a great deal of other equipment, meant that we would have a hell of a time defending our position. One company of the West Kents, supported by a mortar crew of the Royal Irish Fusiliers, was thrown into an attack on Rachi ridge, immediately after they had arrived to reinforce us. It was the same old story. With no reserves to hold the ground that had already been taken, they couldn't withstand the heavy German counter-attack, and had to withdraw, taking with them some of their severely wounded colleagues, including two company commanders.

Back at the castle, we were once again incommunicado, thanks to the Luftwaffe. Yet again, the 'bald eagle', the LRDG man, found his way back to us in the early hours of the morning, despite the Spandau guns that were trained on our position. As we talked, we could hear German voices, which carried across the silence beneath us. It was clear that some were situated low down on the castle hill.

Now into the fourth day defending the castle, we had had no food, with the exception of a few hard biscuits. Our visitor had little comfort to offer, having no rations except the two water bottles he carried, which afforded us temporary relief from thirst. His news on what was happening elsewhere seriously shook our already fragile morale. He had little hope for Leros, as the Germans outnumbered us on every front. As dusk settled on 14 November, the phone next to my Bren-gun position unexpectedly rang. The damaged line was breaking up, and I could barely make out what was being said, but the caller was anxious to be reassured that we still held our position, emphasising how vital it was. It was then that reality really struck home for me. A subsequent briefing of the section leaders by the platoon commander indicated that it looked as though the island would be lost and that evacuation was a very strong possibility.

21

DYING FOR A DRINK

Given our circumstances – we were besieged and isolated, without food or water, running low on ammunition, and with our communications shot to hell – we decided that Sergeant 'Smudger' Smyth and I should lead five men out of the castle. My small section would move out first, at 12.30 AM, with Smudger's group leaving an hour later. My section was to 'recce' the area at the bottom of the hill, in the hope of finding a safe route out, to allow us to link up with the rest of A Company, whose last known position was somewhere near Rachi ridge, south of Alinda bay.

As we descended in the almost-moonless night, we were enveloped in patches of heavy mist. An occasional break of light showed us the path ahead. We were moving down the same route where the Kustenjagers had recently been sighted, and engaged by us, from the castle parapets. Smudger's team was to try to make it to Portolago, in search of food, water and ammunition, to resupply the castle.

As I left the castle for the third time, two close friends of mine, 'Dobbie' Watson and Toddy, wished me luck – and boy did we need it. We had no idea where the German Spandaus were, nor any means of keeping track of each other's movements. We knew that we were on our own.

After making good ground, in the early hours of the morning the silence was broken by the sound of German voices. We were on open ground and exposed, and our immediate reaction was to look for any available cover and wait things out. We holed up in a bomb crater – provided by our friends in the Stukas. There was just enough room for the five of us to stretch out and 'earwig' for sounds of movement. With no one interested in committing suicide, we were careful not to raise our heads above the rim of the crater and provide a target for snipers. After what seemed an age, the Germans began moving to positions well to our left, giving us a chance to move out. We covered two hundred yards of dead ground out front of our position, hoping for a patch of moonlight to allow us assess the exact location and strength of the German forces – but no such luck.

We were forced to move further down the hillside, conscious that the enemy had probably dug in, and were dominating the approach. Any silhouettes showing up on open ground by the moonlight would surely invite enemy fire.

We crept along silently, waiting for the flares to go up at any moment, and expecting the hillside to be raked with bullets from the chattering Spandaus, or the rifle fire that would almost certainly catch us on dead ground. By now, we had passed the point of no return: with no more boulders or bomb craters to shelter us, it was s—t or bust. We stood up and ran, literally, for dear life.

We went to ground, and watched with baited breath as five flares went up. Our sighs of relief were audible, when we realised that the Bosche had misread the location of the noise. Not a single round of ammo was let loose at us.

We still didn't dare move a muscle. In fact, twenty minutes passed before I gingerly got up on one knee to have a quick look around. We needed to establish the location and strength of the Spandau enemy force that was firing the flares on our left flank. Minutes went by without us being able to do either. Suddenly Jimmy Gollogher thumped me excitedly. 'I can see the f—kers,' he said. 'They're sitting company-strength, or near enough to it.' Tucked in behind four-foot-high walls, the Germans were not presenting much of a target for rifle fire: all we could see was their helmets. We had to be sure of the position before we made a move.

To the far left of the hill was a badly damaged telephone pole leaning above a cluster of bushes. Moving on all fours, our five-man unit moved to take cover in the bushes. We managed to remain un-detected and got a good 'decko'. Expecting Jimmy's estimation to be on the high side, I was astonished to see a large group of fully equipped German troops, their rifles shouldered, less than 150 yards below us in the bushes. There was no sign of any automatic or fixed rifle sites, and their attention appeared to be directed at the castle. I assumed that they were a reserve force, sent to replace the one that had been engaged by our machine-guns earlier, and to hold the ground.

We had a dilemma. We'd discovered the location of the enemy troops, but we were massively outnumbered: a direct confrontation could only spell disaster for us. We resolved to move out. Moving on our hunkers down the hill in a diagonal line, we made for the edge of Leros. We remained out of view of the enemy, breaking cover only when we were within sprinting distance of a bombed-out building. As we made the sixty-yard dash, German guns raked the ground behind us, with the Spandaus' signature rapid firepower.

They say it's better to be born lucky than rich. Well, it was that day anyway. Lady Luck stayed with us, and we made it to the bombed-out building. With the Germans holding points dominating all routes, the possibility of us fulfilling our objective was becoming increasingly remote. Although we'd escaped the Spandau fire, the main group of Brandenburgs were now on their guard. Alerted by the stuttering gun-fire, they were watching their flanks closely.

It was now 4.30 AM – four hours since we'd left the castle. We'd had nothing to eat other than our ration of hard biscuits two days before, and, having had nothing to drink, and no sleep, for more than twenty-four hours, we were exhausted. With no Benzedrine to keep us awake, we were inevitably overcome by exhaustion, despite our best efforts to keep watch. I awoke before the other lads, and began to mull over our predicament. All our lines of advance had been sealed off, and there seemed to be no way out. Frustrated, I got annoyed with myself for not at least having had a go at picking off some of the Germans, but I took comfort from the fact that, although we were worn out, we were all still alive.

Within minutes of moving out, we heard heavy footsteps coming from a small building close by. Instinctively, we went to ground, as out in the open in broad daylight we were easy targets. Hopefully the noisy bastards would pass in front of our new position, giving us the element of surprise. We were very tense, assuming that a patrol had been sent out to find us after the Spandaus had opened up on us. It became eerily quiet. Twenty minutes passed, and there was still no activity. It was by now 6.45 AM and, true to form, the Stukas were passing overhead, en route to support their ground troops. Soon the German 110 fighters would be behind them, raking the hillside with bursts of fire, and making it impossible for us to retrace our route to the castle. Our dilemma was whether to proceed with our plan to attack the building, bringing down the inevitable Stuka attack. Despite the madness of it, we decided to charge towards an entrenched enemy, which was most probably armed to the teeth with mortars, grenades and machine-guns.

Almost immediately after we moved, we came under heavy fire, not from the building we were attempting to attack, but from a position three hundred yards to the right of us. The enemy firepower was hot and heavy, with rifle and automatic-weapon fire cascading around us. This fire was close, but thankfully not close enough: the poorly directed fire missed its targets. It appeared to be from an enemy patrol, which had been sent to recce its flanks. Our sightings were not ideal, but at least targets were presenting themselves, and we got off a few good volleys. Fortunately, this encounter distracted us from our main target, and forced us to go to ground before we got a chance to open fire on the building. To our amazement, a sudden burst of strong fire was unleashed on the enemy from an open position, close to the building occupied by German troops.

After fifteen minutes of combat, the Germans put distance between themselves and our support. Puzzled as to who had come to our aid, we took no chances and lay 'doggo' for twenty minutes, before venturing out to identify our saviours. Satisfied that the Germans had departed, I decided to risk calling out to the lads who had come to our aid. Their immediate response removed any lingering doubt, as my friends from Belfast's Ballymacarret, Sergeant 'Smudger' Smyth's group, always were noisy bastards.

To say that we were pleased to see them would be an understatement. Apparently, they too had left their blitzed-out refuge, well in advance of our attempt to 'go for it bald-headed' – no holds barred. Funnily enough, they'd had the same idea, and were awaiting their opportunity to strike at the enemy troops, when we had happened onto the scene. The question as to which of us would have carried the can for killing our own troops, if things hadn't panned out the way they did, doesn't bear thinking about. Thankfully, the hand of fate intervened in the most unlikely way – saved by the watchful eyes of a German patrol who'd fired on us first, stopping us from making a potentially disastrous mistake. The awfulness of what might have been was laughed away with jokes and slagging, 'Smudger' mockingly describing our awkward gallop, straight into his rifle sights, and teasing us as to whom he would have taken out first.

With no way out, all that was left was for Smudger's group to join up with us and head back towards the castle. Dawn had long passed, and the routine aerial and ground activity was well under way yet again. Although, operationally, we were not caught up in the midst of it, the terrifying combination of mortar, dive-bombing and automatic fire was none the less daunting.

Smudger had had some success in his objective. Laden down with heavy bandoliers of 303, some full water bottles, and some emergency rations, mainly hard dark chocolate, we slaked our terrible thirst on the untreated water, not caring where it had come from. The chocolate was so hard that it must have been designed by the enemy, to incapacitate anyone who was brave enough to try eating it.

I still couldn't get over the thought that Smudger's trigger-happy squaddies could have finished us off. Some loud mouth would still probably 'spin the bar', and tell how that Commando bloke, Johnnie Harte had dropped a clanger and attacked his own side!

Shaking off these negative thoughts, I listened to Smudger's opinion as to how best to get the gear, and ourselves, back to the castle. It was not going to be easy: we still had five hundred feet to climb, over difficult terrain, and with no way of knowing where the enemy was positioned.

Despite the crump of three-inch mortar bombs leaving the barrels, the screech of them in flight, the murderous sound of cannon fire coming from the Messerschmitts, and the intermittent sharp crack of rifle fire, we still believed that the battle for the island was not yet over. True to our training, we felt the compelling need to get the gear back to our lads. We tried as best as we could to plan our route back, taking into account the disastrous consequences of being ambushed or sniped at, or tripping anti-personnel mines.

We decided to split up, in the hope that at least one group would get through. Using the cover afforded by blitzed buildings, we made our way slowly, silently, back, ever watchful for any sign of the Germans.

The unit eventually made a successful entry onto the hill, and I began to believe that we could make it back. We crawled upwards in search of temporary cover, our progress spasmodically interrupted by the sound of small-arms fire. As we crawled higher up into a gully, there was a thunderous noise and we realised that the fire was coming directly from the parapets of the castle itself. It soon developed into a hectic exchange, judging by the rate of 303s raining down on the enemy, as they awaited an opportunity to advance up the hill. Being well positioned, we entered into the engagement. We'd lost contact with Smudger's group on the climb up, but they too joined in the attack, from a position to the right of us on the east flank. The enemy pulled back, sending up a red flare for aerial assistance. Almost imme-diately, two ME110s zoomed in and began raking the hillside with long bursts of cannon fire. 'This gully is a death trap!' roared Gollogher, over the noise. Nothing new in this bleedin' strafing game, but with no dried-up wadi to duck along, our best bet was to remain prone and avoid the heroics of testing our pea-shooters against the aerial artillery.

Initially, the enemy planes concentrated their attention on the cas-tle-wall area. Satisfied that the blokes in the castle had left their firing positions, they sprayed the rest of the rugged slopes for good meas-ure, enabling the German troops to regain their lost ground. Moving up the slopes, the Germans went to ground.

Gollogher, his morale temporarily restored, remarked: 'That f—kin' shallow gully saved our bacon against that strafing from the bastardin' Krauts.' For the next twenty-five minutes, the Germans con-tinued their aerobatic dives across the hill, scaring the s—t out of us, until even Gollogher – who, like me, hadn't been to church or chapel in many a year – began saying his prayers.

22

THE FINAL PUSH

There was now only two hundred yards of hilly ground separating us from the castle gates, and we decided to take the gamble of trying to get up there. Moving very quietly and cautiously, and hunching down, we faced the enemy position below as we went up the hill backwards, keeping the enemy in sight. Before we'd covered thirty feet of ground, a hail of bullets forced us to take cover.

We couldn't just lie there all day. With no other option, we spread out and took up better firing positions, hoping to surprise the Germans by opening fire on them. The plan was that, after a couple of minutes, every man for himself: we would cease firing, move out, and try to make ten or twenty yards upwards, before going to ground. This time, the Germans responded with Spandaus, blazing from an out-of-sight position. Ironically, it seemed that they were using the gun pits we'd hacked out of the rock face before the enemy landings. The rest of the Germans who'd earlier returned fire on our lads were now strangely silent.

We each made a few yards, only to be stopped short by the lightning zip of more bullets. Our latest move had given us much better cover, although it was not enough to stop the Spandaus from letting loose 1,300 rounds of ammo a minute, if we were brave or foolhardy enough to try to move out.

Laden down with our heavy gear, we were gasping for breath after the fifty-feet dash uphill. The s—t put crossways in me, I whispered to my dispersed group in a shaken voice, checking if they were all right. The last to reply, 'Brennan on the Moor', asked if I had any more bright ideas, adding: 'I suppose repatriation is out of the question, corporal?' When the nervous laughter had died down, I warned him not to roll and smoke any of the camel s—t he carried: 'Those f—kers already have murder on their mind. The last thing we need is for that stinking s—t to waft down to them. They'd really kill us then!' Jaysus help our sense of humour: you'd be forgiven for thinking that we were winning this battle, and that lying here was just a tactic, before we totally overwhelmed the German bleeders with our 'mighty mouse' firepower. For now, there was nothing else for it but to lie in wait, while I thought through our next move.

Gollogher helpfully suggested that it might not be such a bad idea to let Brennan light up. His logic was that it might fool the Germans into thinking that we had gas canisters, and then they would panic and retreat. 'No f—kin' fear of that' was Fusilier Ryan's retort. He added: 'You're not dealing with a crowd of lamebrains. Them Gerries are shrewd whores: they were forced to go to school under escort. Once they get a whiff of Brennan's foreign body, they'd send up flares and then destroy the whole f—kin' lot of us.'

I was still trying to find a way out of our predicament. We were obviously not a serious threat to the forward movement of the Germans. My only hope was that some of them had become less vigilant, and we could perhaps catch them off guard. Carrying the extra gear was slowing us down, as we tried to move upwards. We dumped most of the stuff, except for a few extra bandoliers of ammo, and agreed that, if we came under fire, the attempt to reach the castle would be put on hold. We moved individually, managing to move to the rear without losing much height. Closer to the ridge, we spread out and took up firing positions. The plan was to open up on where we thought the Spandaus were sited, and then make a quick bolt to the ridge, rolling over to reach better cover.

Confident that our movement had not been detected, we decided to have a rethink. We broke the silence with a quick volley of fire. The surprise element helped – but not for long. We had covered very little ground; more importantly, our situation worsened.

We had been deceived into thinking that the enemy were in position at the bottom of the hill. In the course of a previous engagement by No. 9 Platoon, they had been the only enemy troops on the hill; now, the firepower was coming from every direction.

Caught in the open, our advance upwards was abruptly halted. It was impossible to continue upwards. Our only hope was to lie still and wait, our hearts in our mouths, for the fighter planes to be called down on us. Incredibly, they never came. As we lay there, we had only one thought: somehow, we had to find a way off this f—kin' miserable hill.

I was at a loss to understand why Smudger's small group was not engaging the enemy. I could only assume that, being closer to the Germans, they had been either forced off the hill or wiped out. All sorts of scenarios went through my mind. Somehow, I couldn't help comparing our present 'no hope' state of affairs with my boxing bouts, with my fans yelling 'The crowd is with you, Johnnie' just when the other bleeder was knocking the lard out of me, and I was wishing I was a mere spectator. But like boxing, since you can't join the mob, you have to get on with the job in hand, do the best you can, and hope to survive the fight.

Now we were in a similar but much more deadly situation. Out of all communication, and with our eyes aching and sore from watching the bomb blasts and tracers, I complained loudly that I had a pain in my arse with the whole bastardin' shooting gallery. I was a grumpy, cantankerous oul' bollix, but I determined that, come what may, I'd find a way to extricate my little group from that hillside. I momentarily gave vent to my fury, stupidly getting to my feet and lashing out at our spent cartridges, scattering them in every direction. Quickly realising how dangerous and foolish I'd been, I quickly dropped back to the ground. Gollogher didn't hold back, as he unleashed a torrent of expletives at me, accusing me of gambling with his life. Mortified by the scurrilous though well-deserved abuse, I did the right thing and told him to f—k off.

Now that we understood each other, we got back to the business of survival. None of us were keen on being butchered by this blood-thirsty lot, but the idea of taking them on in close contact was suicidal. Our conversation was soon ended by the return of the Junker 87s, which were too close for comfort. We agreed to abandon the hill, and any further attempt to reach the castle. The battle for ground advantage was by now so close that any move would attract another foray against us. We had to stay concealed from the Germans below, and not cause the lads in the castle, now fighting the enemy on the seaward side, to be distracted by having to mount a rearguard action to save our bacon. Our last attempt to leave the hill had been foolhardy. This time, we would use less enthusiasm and more brainpower. So far, we'd been very lucky to survive three attacks. Someone up there was looking out for us.

The new plan involved Gollogher crawling face-down, fifty yards downhill, until he came within range of the German rifle positions. Resting for a couple of minutes, he'd fire one short burst at the enemy position with my beloved Beretta, before crawling backwards on his belly to take cover, rolling over and lying still.

The burst of Beretta fire was our signal to retreat, and crawl face-down to the nearest indentation. There, we waited fifteen minutes before linking up with Gollogher. On no account were we to open fire. Gollogher took the brunt of the return fire, as the tracer fire zipped around his position. His knees were cut to shreds, his face was scratched from keeping his head down under fire, and his khaki drill trousers had been ripped to bits by the rough ground, but he was still alive – as he made sure to let me know, with a barrage of expletives flung in liberal doses in my direction. He cursed me from a height, accusing me of 'duping' him into volunteering to act as the decoy, knowing full well that the Gerries were close enough to take him out. I was tempted to stir him up even further, by giving him a hard time, but, loving the lion-hearted f—ker, I held back on the sarcastic wit and thanked him for his courageous act, before giving the order to move out.

One of the known side effects of Gollogher's outbursts was his habit of going deaf, as was obvious from his continued expletives. 'Why the f—k did you not have the decency to thank me for volunteering?' he asked, as we all rolled around laughing.

Having got this far in comparative safety, we now headed on towards Portolago. We'd covered about a hundred yards on the sloping terrain when the enemy surprised us. The sudden 'crump crump' of mortar fire sent us diving to the ground. The riflemen, knowing that we were beyond their range, had called in the mortars, which could pinpoint the target and stop our progress. Fortunately, they had moved on us a little too late. Once again, 'Lady Luck' was travelling with us.

We had two casualties. Ryan suffered injuries from ricocheting shrapnel. He 'caught it' high up on the inside of his left thigh; the shrapnel almost took out, as he put it, 'the pride of Cavan'. Brennan, too, was hit by shrapnel, sustaining a tear to his left ankle. Again our luck prevailed: we stemmed the flow of blood. Casualties in tow, we moved out of range of the enemy fire. Keeping high up on the side of the hill, we found better cover, which allowed us to tend the wounded. Field dressings did little to stem the bleeding from the men's injuries – Ryan's khaki trousers were scorched and soaked in blood. After twenty minutes' rest, we continued our trek, with both lads making it under their own steam.

Early in the afternoon of 15 November, a cool breeze wafted in, briefly bolstering our morale, until we realised that with it came the distinct, foul smell of cordite and death. This sent a shudder through me: it brought to mind my many friends and colleagues, still lying where they'd fallen. The stench, combined with Brennan sneaking a few drags of his Turkish horses—t, made us want to retch.

Our priority now was to establish where the Germans were holed up: we had to assume that a rearguard had been left behind, on the ground below us. We waited for what seemed an interminable length of time, just listening. With no sight or sound of them, we pushed on towards the summit, surprised that our progress had not been impeded. We remained cautious, knowing that there were a dozen opportunities for the enemy to take us by surprise. Less than a hundred yards below, major battles had been raging the previous day; now, all was strangely quiet. It was hardly likely that we had been unobserved by the foe, yet we remained virtually unscathed.

As we made our descent to the verge of a forked road, we left the two injured lads to make the rest of the journey to the Italian hospital for medical treatment. The three remaining members of the unit headed towards the coast to rest up, and hopefully find something to eat and drink.

As we neared the coast, we concealed ourselves and kept watch. Immediately out front, in broad daylight, was a group of six civilians. Up to now, we'd believed that the civilians were hiding in the mountains, or had been evacuated to safer islands. Could they be Germans in disguise, or even the civilian collaborators we had heard about?

When we questioned them, they told us, in very broken English, that they were Italian soldiers. It seemed that they'd had enough, had dumped their uniforms and were on the run. Their story seemed plausible, given that their regiment had been stationed here since 1912, and many Italian soldiers had married Greek women. They would have little difficulty in passing themselves off as Greeks if they were challenged by the Germans. In their broken English, interspersed with Greek and Italian, and very animated body language, they made it clear that Tedici was swarming with heavily armed Germans, who were annilihating all before them. Having abandoned their uniforms, the men were making for safe havens, in the certain belief that the island was about to fall. Before we allowed them to move on, they told us about the fishermen's boats scattered along the bay. They advised us to get off the island and head for the Turkish coast, which was less than eighteen miles away. Then, free to go, they ran for dear life.

Safely back under cover, we considered the information the Italians had supplied. One way or another, we needed to get down to where the boats were tied up. At least we might get something to eat: if the boat was large enough, it might have a small cabin or even some stores. Although the thought of escape crossed our minds, the war was raging, and we couldn't abandon our No. 9 Platoon, trapped in the castle.

Moving along the inlets, we were careful not to run into anti-personnel mines. As we moved, we checked the inlets for small boats, but nothing we came across was seaworthy: they had either been strafed by enemy aircraft or had had their bottoms stoved in by German ground troops – they wouldn't get us across a puddle, never mind the open seas. Gollogher was outraged, and released a string of curses, calling the former Italian soldiers, now self-declared civilians, and all their antecedents, 'lying, cheating, rotten whores'. I jokingly asked him whether his anger meant that he really had intended to flee and forget his mates. That one backfired, as he harangued me to hell and back. Ray Williams, author of *The Long Road to Leros*, described how his group had had a similar idea of getting off the island. He reckoned that, as the sea was still warm after months of sun, and they were good swimmers and had a knowledge of the tides and currents, they could make the eighteen-mile journey to Turkey.

But the Germans had left nothing to chance, and had wrecked any boats that were within reach of us. Worse still, Ray witnessed a group of would-be escapers who were lucky enough to find a seaworthy craft and make a getaway to the open seas. They were caught in the searchlights sited on the headland, and the Germans immediately brought heavy-calibre tracer fire down on them. It tore the boat asunder. The occupants never stood a chance. With all hopes of escape gone, Ray and his group had no option but to come to terms with being taken prisoner.

Events subsequently proved the Italians right. The very next day, the island was surrendered to the Germans. The constant drone of enemy aircraft putting in thousands of sorties had taken its toll. Our rate of movement was suffering badly, and I couldn't get my red-eyed Faughs to step up their pace. My thoughts turned to Smudger and his small section. Were they still pinned down on the hill or, worse still, wiped out? I hoped and prayed that Smudger's resourcefulness would get them through. Somehow, we had to get back to help our lads inside the castle. If our luck continued to hold, we might find our gear, and make it back.

Checking that the coast was clear, we dragged our reluctant bodies once more into the breach. Moving north, we got close to Anchor, also known as Yeechia, at the southern end of Meraviglia. All our efforts to check for sounds of enemy movement were drowned out by the constant rat-tat-tat of machine-guns and the screeching of mortar shells. Moving in fits and starts, we eventually made it back to the castle hill.

Assuming that we were unobserved, we continued to creep forward without a shot being fired at us, lying 'doggo' from time to time. Spotting the targets, we quickly joined the exchanges. Unexpectedly, and for no apparent reason, the Germans disengaged. It crossed my mind that we should chance moving towards where our gear was stored, in the hope that we could then make it to the castle gates. With no fire coming at us, we became over-confident, and moved too quickly – only to be met by a hail of bullets, which forced us to return fire and go to ground.

Once again, the hill became silent as the Germans disengaged. We dared not move. What the hell was going on? We soon had the answer. In the silence of the late afternoon of 15 November 1943, a powerful force of enemy troops, backed up by heavy machine-guns and mortar fire, and supported by Stukas, attacked from every possible angle, swarming over the hillside around us. If the Stukas were designed to sink the morale of the lads on the parapet, it didn't work. This small band of men threw what little they had at the attacking Germans. With the din of battle all around us, we quickly joined in the attack.

The enemy troops advanced rapidly, in the face of our small-arms fire. Too late, it became obvious how we had got that cushy ride on to the hill: they had allowed us pass, in order to keep the element of surprise intact. With guns sited behind every rocky outcrop, they pushed upwards with huge momentum. Their advance became irresistible as they got into assault formation.

Moving in small groups, the Germans were spread out across the lower end of terrain, going to ground when they'd made good distance. Under cover of mortar fire, the first platoon began advancing upwards. Like legions of Roman centurions, on a given signal, and taking advantage of the firepower ahead of them, the back-up troops would launch themselves onto the lower hill and take up the positions vacated their colleagues. Thus the pattern continued, until they had at least two companies' strength in attacking positions. It was now clear that these were the troops we'd come across behind the four-foot walls near Leros town: they had been waiting for the order to lay siege to the castle.

As far as we knew, we were the only Faughs outside the castle: we assumed that Smudger's group had had it by now. My attention was suddenly drawn to rifle flashes directed at the advancing Germans from somewhere above us. I later learned that Smudger's small band had made it back to the hill and had given a good account of themselves. Amid the smoke and mortar-bomb fragments, and the dust and soil that was thrown up, it became difficult to see the Germans spread out on the upper hillside; suddenly, they rose as one, releasing firepower from hell as they made a final push. The firing from the castle could still be heard, but with their ammunition running low, it became very light. The Germans continued to surge forward.

We never made it back to get the ammunition, water or emergency rations we'd hidden away, but even if we had, it would have made little difference. We could have held the attackers off for no more than another twenty minutes at most, and the castle would still have fallen. The four of us were in grave danger, but as long as the castle held out, we had no choice but to help its defenders as best we could. We knew that as soon as the Germans got a clear view of us, we'd be wiped out.

I've often been asked: 'Were you scared to death?' It's funny, but the truth is that I wasn't. I had a persistent apprehension, but not once during those six long years of fighting did I even feel homesick. Having said that, things that had happened to me as a youngster came to my mind – sometimes at the oddest times. I recall how once, while taking cover, I doodled on the ground with a spent cartridge, recalling my brother Arthur, eating bread and dripping on the steps of our house in Hardwicke Street. At this time, Archie, as we called him, was serving in North Africa. There were times when the anxiety built up, but you kept it in check, unless of course you were one of the poor unfortunates who'd become bomb-happy. In later years, the pent-up stress and anger experienced by soldiers comes to the fore.

'You Are Now a Prisoner of War'

Prepared for the worst, a bullet fired from behind us sent us ducking for cover, as we quickly crawled away from our little hideaway. Our instantaneous reaction was: if there's one bullet, then there are probably a lot more to follow. This time we were wrong, though, and no more bullets came our way. In the midst of our crawl, a very loud voice, speaking in fluent English, hailed us: 'Irelander, there is no hope for you. Leave down your arms. The war is over for you. You are now a prisoner of war.' The single shot had been fired as a warning, before he called for our surrender.

As I looked behind me, I realised that the voice came from a man wearing the uniform of a German *hauptmann* (captain), who was standing in the middle of his platoon – still lying flat on the ground. In the chaos, they had managed to get behind and to the side of us, cutting us off from any further progress. With no chance to smash our rifles (or my Beretta) – a standard practice to deprive the enemy of additional fire-power – we dumped our guns on the ground. So on 15 November 1943, two months and two days after I'd arrived on the island, and less than a month before my twenty-third birthday, I was a prisoner of war. We had engaged the enemy in close combat six times over the last four days, and we had now become their prisoners. The captain's last words, before he ordered us to be moved on, were to tell us that the castle was about to surrender. I felt angry rather than depressed, but then the reality of the fact that we had been captured began to sink in – and it hurt.

As I despondently trudged along, my thoughts went back to the lads in the castle, and I thanked God for my luck, after five long years in combat. I had survived ambushes and engagements in Palestine in 1938, the siege of Malta, being depth-charged in a submarine, raids into enemy-occupied territory, three weeks patrolling the North African and Sicilian coasts on an MTB, and finally, all the fighting on Leros.

What happened next left me astonished as the German officer turned and ordered his men to stand up from the prone position they'd occupied. In what seemed like a choreographed movement, fifteen Italian soldiers and their German escorts rose to their feet as one. In aggressive tones, the Germans ordered the Italian POWs to pick up the heavy mortar parts and base plates. As disgusted as I was at having being captured, I couldn't help wondering how the f—k the Germans had managed to climb more than three hundred feet, to within about forty yards of our position, prisoners in tow, without our realising it. Were the Italian prisoners deliberately put out in front, where they were exposed to our fire, completely against Geneva Convention protocol? It certainly seemed that way.

The officer in charge treated us with respect, but kept the three of us well away from the Italian prisoners. The Italians, laden down with gear and obviously exhausted, were harangued and jostled by the German troops, who gave them no respite when they tried to draw breath. Some were forced to walk along the most precarious slopes, leaving them exposed to what small-arms fire was still coming from the parapets. Fortunately for them, the resistance from the castle had grown much weaker. Our safety was assured, as they moved us to the outside of the general advance positions. Bent over, and stumbling under the strain, the Italians were struggling to keep their feet, as they reached the scree close to the castle wall. The Germans halted them, and kept them standing, until the two companies had come together, ready to take the castle.

23

Taking the Castle

The Stench of Death and Destruction

After four days and nights of continuous harassment and isolation, outnumbered six to one, with a complete lack of aerial or ground support against heavy weaponry, and having endured two months of persistent bombing, the defenders of Leros Castle were finally overwhelmed. Making the final push forward, the Germans overran the castle. On taking it, they gave aid to the captured casualties, and the German officer openly praised No. 9 Platoon for their courageous and lengthy defence of their post. Hungry, thirsty and battle-weary (not to mention filthy, after weeks without a wash), we were marched back down the hill we'd just risked our lives climbing, to join the other POWs who were already in German custody. They split us into various groups: Smudger and one of his men were in a different group from me – so I had no chance of asking him what had happened the rest of his section. That was the last time I ever saw him. Even now, more than sixty years later, I don't know what became of him.

For the rest of us, what followed was a very harrowing experience. As we marched along somewhere in the vicinity of Appetici, the sight of dozens of Allied and German soldiers lying dead on the road and hillside was a stark reminder of the ferocity of the battle for Leros. At least I was still alive. Absolutely sick with my lot, weary and worn out, I was pressed into handling the mutilated corpses that were strewn along the way. I placed large stones over the ones with the more gruesome injuries, ensuring that their identification discs were in place, so that they could, hopefully, at least have a proper burial.

I had a sudden and desperate sense of guilt about being still alive. Surrounded by the acrid smell of cordite, and the whining screams of bombing that was all around us and the smoke that lingered in the air, we set to covering up the decaying, putrid bodies of those poor unfortunates. We could only do so much, as the Germans were anxious to move us on. Many of our comrades were left where they lay; I hoped that, somehow, someone would take care of them and ensure that they were buried before the hot sun took its toll.

I couldn't stem the swell of anger that erupted in me, as I saw the decimated bodies of some of these soldiers. I felt disbelief that anyone could suffer so much pain. Some of the bodies were scorched by mortar strafing and had burst open, the horror – impossible to forget. Others, it seemed, had died instantly. The cliché 'I'm glad he died quickly' came to mind – they were the lucky ones, which is more than can be said for the other poor f—kers. Each pallid face told its own story; each had given his all. After more than an hour of this grisly work, our German captors took us off the hilly graveyard, gave us water, and marched us to Portolago. As we marched, our path was constantly crossed by stretchers carrying the wounded. I couldn't get those images of death and destruction, or the awful stench of putrid bodies of comrades and foes alike, out of my mind. I never have, they're still with me today, more than sixty years later.

THE LIMITS OF ENDURANCE

It is difficult to say just how much hardship it takes to bring someone to the limits of their endurance. Despite the battering and hardships of those nine weeks spent fighting on Leros, the revulsion of the death scenes on the hills, the fear, deprivation, and sheer futility of it all, my will to survive was still strong. I had reluctantly accepted that the Allies' situation was deteriorating, and that any hope of pushing the Germans back was all but lost. The Germans, firmly entrenched and supported by the Luftwaffe, would settle for nothing less than the complete surrender of Leros. On the evening of 16 November 1943, the Germans took the last remaining bastion that was holding out against them: Brigadier Robert Tilney's headquarters. Tilney, armed only with a rifle, realised that the situation was hopeless, and surrendered the island to General Mueller's stronger forces.

The Earl of Jellicoe, himself a leading commando, and his fellow commandos made good their escape from Leros but continued to be a thorn in the side of the Germans on the other islands, mounting lightning raids designed to damage or take out military structures. In the course of their exploits, though, many lives were lost, including that of my good friend and leader from the Faughs and SBS missions, Charlie Clyne, then a captain.

On 17 November, the remainder of the British and Allied forces were rounded up and taken to Portolago. Those of us who had been captured two days previously searched for familiar faces in the new arrivals, all of us anxious to link up with our fellow Faughs. Dishevelled and despondent at the surrender, our gait showed all the weariness of battle fatigue, as we dragged ourselves through the rubble – all that was left of Portolago.

We were halted at a large war-torn building, the outside of which was to be our home for the next five days. Used to sleeping on the open ground, and with the weather still bright and warm, we sat down and talked about each other's experiences. Each of us had his own version of how a particular battle had been fought.

We still hadn't been given any food: the fact that we'd had nothing to eat for several days was starting to have an effect on our weary bodies. Sadness and apprehension was the general mood, not knowing what was to come. But the immediate problem, as well as our pressing need for food and water, was our overwhelming desire to wash away the smell of death, from the poor unfortunates we had had to cover up, that still clung, pall-like, to everything.

It was a pleasant and welcome surprise when both water – foul-smelling though it was – and food, in the form of slimy macaroni – which smelled even worse – eventually arrived. Slopped into tin cans and steel tobies, or helmets, it was the best meal we'd ever had!

I was lucky enough to meet up with some close buddies: QMS George Mullett, Walter Pancott, 'Wee' Davy Thompson, Bobby O'Neill, Andy Roy, Johnnie King, Tom Magee, Matt King, 'Pukie' Orr, 'Red Digger' Dawson and 'the Nazi' McCormack, so called because of his love of wearing high-peaked caps. Mullett, Thompson, (Walter) Pancott and O'Neill were still nursing wounds, and McGee and Andy Roy had persistent hacking coughs.

All around me were animated conversations, telling of a particular platoon or company: who'd been injured, who was MIA – missing in action – and who'd been killed. Sadly, many familiar faces were missing from our bunch: long-time friends of mine such as Gutrie Kane, 'Sab' McMaster, 'Beaver' Elliott and Polly McIlwaine. I unashamedly shed a few tears as I thought of our close friendships and memorable deeds. With the mention of colleagues who'd lost their lives, there was a lull in the conversation, and a sense of despondency came over us for a time – only to be replaced by more stories, about the good times we'd had, with our now-deceased pal, as tales of battles won and lost filled the long hours.

Even basic facilities were nonexistent on the Portolago roadside, and the resourceful amongst us used their helmets when nature called, tipping the contents down a nearby grating. With the temperature still in the high sixties, the smell from our helmets was rancid, but we still had to keep them attached to our haversacks. Each of us in the bustling throng of prisoners tried to distance himself from his neighbour's foul-smelling equipment.

Bad as the situation was outside, things became even worse when the Germans herded us into the building. Indoors, we had nowhere to dispose of the contents of the helmets. The heat, stench and sweat made for stomach-churning company. When the chance came to empty the helmets, it was a miracle that we made it outside without saturating each other, such was the race to get rid of the contents.

Soon the reality of our situation began to hit home, and we set about trying to find anything in the abandoned building that might come in useful. For my part, I found a discarded RAF greatcoat. As we'd had no British aircraft on the island, I wondered how it came to be here. While it was not much use in the present heat, the coat would be worth its weight in gold, come winter.

One of my mechanically minded buddy acquired a small spanner and some nuts and bolts – difficult to conceal during the frequent searches, but would undoubtedly be of use down the road. Tom

McGee, the Liberties boy from High Street in Dublin, slagged me on my good luck, telling all and sundry that if I fell into pig s—t, I'd still come up smelling of roses.

As yet, most of us had not been put to work – although Raymond Williams and a couple of others were pressed into loading German gunboats with coal. The Germans, who openly despised the Italians, quickly replaced Raymond and his crew with their former allies, and forced the Italians to finish the job.

My thoughts were with my fallen friends. Between us – Guthrie, Sab, Beaver, all of us 'wild men' – we endured hours of 'military discipline' together at the hands of Lackery Woods in the glasshouse, but it was all worth it: the fun we had! Polly McIlwaine was a fellow member of the regimental boxing team. Undefeated in five years, this wiry Belfast man from Sandy Row had no problem in moving up from flyweight to featherweight, and could still win his fight easily. Denied a wonderful future in the professional game, he left life as he had lived it. Moving his two-pounder anti-tank gun to a more exposed position, from where he could continue firing at the advancing troops, was just one fight too many, but he died trying. The ordinary German troops showed, by their attitude to us, that they had sympathy for our plight, but could do nothing. Their humane feelings towards us were appreciated, and, with no thoughts of hostility towards them, we bedded down for the night.

24

On the High Seas Again – Cattle Class

On 20 November, our fourth day in captivity, our German captors separated us from the Italians, and ushered us onto a German naval vessel, destined for God knows where. As we clambered up the steel ladders, young German sailors carried out a quick search of their prisoners. Concealed weapons were surrendered, found or confiscated. Some of us had managed to hold on to our haversacks, which proved a godsend while we were in transit as they kept what little belongings we had together. For my part, with the exception of the greatcoat, I had only what I stood up in: a battledress blouse over a khaki shirt, tropical trousers, and my long-range desert-group boots. I also had that very versatile steel helmet. Ray Williams, a 'cute hoor' from Cumbria, took the risk of concealing his army jackknife by hooking it onto the fly buttons of his trousers – at some inconvenience and at no little risk to his 'John Thomas'. The searcher having been deceived, Williams kept possession of the knife, which proved to be a very valuable asset in the days that followed.

After the searches had been finished, we were pushed up on deck, and were directed in sign language by a very dour-looking German to climb into the hold. Once he was satisfied that he could pack in no more unwashed, sweaty bodies, he closed the hatch, plunging us into darkness. The air turned blue with cursing and swearing, and elbows and arms flailed about as we tried to make some space for ourselves in the inky-black hold. It took some time for the mass of heaving humanity to adjust to the new surroundings. Things weren't helped by the whining of a couple of 'battle happies', moaning about their predicament, and the carnage that would come about if we were hit by a Royal Navy ship. The heat and stench below deck was claustrophobic, and prompted angry demands for fresh air. Suddenly, we felt the ship moving: with no idea where we were bound, speculation was rife. The general feeling was that we were heading for mainland Greece.

There was nothing to do but try to get some shut-eye. Short silences were interrupted by the sound of flowing urine. Like Niagara Falls, it gushed noisily all night long into the metal helmets. Not a word of anger was uttered at the ongoing noise as the general sigh of relief all round indicated our unity of purpose in emptying our bladders. Johnnie King, while claiming that he didn't want to be 'a s—t-stirrer', jocosely remarked that any alternative use of the helmets would only be allowed when we reached land again.

The terrible discomfort of the sapping heat and lack of air was added to by the nauseating smell of the urine emanating from the overflowing helmets. We urged one of the boys nearest the ladder to try to slide the hatch open. After some time, he managed to work a small opening, through which he shouted to the German guard. By means of body language, he convinced the guard that we were suffocating. The guard quickly returned with an officer, who slid the hatch back the full way and let five or six of us at a time come up on deck. Manoeuvring the pisspots up the ladder was tricky, but no one dropped their cargo, for fear of retribution from their fellow travellers. The fresh air was a godsend. Ignoring the guards' instructions to empty the contents at the bow, we quickly dumped our loads overboard. Greatly relieved to be out of the choking atmosphere and away from the terrible stench, we lost no time in taking in the fresh air: anything less would have been a 'mortaler' – a mortal sin.

We were obviously very reluctant to get back in the hold, but as we were being held at gunpoint we hadn't much say in the matter. We offered each other comfort with nods, winks and signs as we climbed back down the ladder. For the remainder of the journey, the hatch door was left open, enabling us to keep in contact with some of the lucky bastards who were sleeping on deck by shouting up to them.

The scene had again been set for the wag to make the most of the turbulent Aegean, sick stomachs and heavy hearts. But this time, he became the victim of his own threat; while offering solace to a friend, who had become so seasick that he was pleading for a peaceful death, the 'wag' happened to get in the line of fire, just as his friend parted company with the contents of his stomach. It was not a pretty sight.

Despite all our efforts pleading with the guards, no food came our way. The Germans did the best they could, but they simply had nothing to offer – except for buckets of lime juice, which they lowered down to us. I never fully understood the point of this, although on my return from escapades on board *Trooper*, the sailors at Medway had urged us to drink it to prevent scurvy. One sailor talked of its value in keeping 'the pecker' easy! Right now, though, survival took precedence over sex – not that there was any of the latter to be had. We happily gulped down the lime juice.

The cool night air brought relief to our weary bodies, but sleep escaped me. I spent the night watching and listening to the sailors as they went about their work. As daylight broke, restless bodies took a chance and climbed the ladder, out onto the deck. Some time elapsed before the cheery f—kers returned – still with no idea as to our whereabouts or destination. The guards didn't challenge them, and we took advantage of this, taking turns to have a leisurely twirl around the deck. The rest of the journey was a pushover, with the hatch open, and the invigorating sea air keeping us cool.

If things stayed like this, the steel helmet might even become redundant. One observant German sailor, seeing us perched precariously on the ladder, trying to pass our smelly chain of make-do potties from the hatch below, up the ladder, and across the deck, without spilling them, shouted '*Nein! Nein!*' and rushed away. He returned with a large drum, which he lowered into the hold but nobody wanted the new latrine close to them. The Germans made the decision for us.

From what the lads on deck told us, we believed that mainland Greece was our destination. Better still, we heard that they had managed to knock off some food from the Germans. This sparked off savage individualism, as six or seven men all scrambled to get a foot on the ladder. Discipline was quickly restored, and four of us were nominated to go up on deck and recce the situation. It was a scavenging mission.

When we got topside, we found that, sure enough, food had been pinched, but by the time we got to the scene of the crime, the party was over. All that was left was a grim-faced German sailor, standing over busted bags of sugar and lentils. He said nothing: his fixed bayonet did the talking for him. The culprits had been much quicker off the mark than us, and had already been there and done the job, before being chased back to the hold, under threat of a jab from a bayonet.

After twenty-four hours confined in the inhospitable hold, with more than a hundred other unwashed souls, inhaling the smell of sweat, urine and vomit, it came as a great relief to hear that we were nearing Piraeus, and would soon be ashore. By the time we hit the deck, the preparation and manoeuvring for docking was well under way. Even then, in 1943, the port was still busy and seemed to be chock-a-block with ships coming and going. We never saw the scenic islands we'd passed on the voyage, and to be honest, most of us didn't give a f—k. Some of our comrades who had been berthed on deck talked of the great beauty of the islands, but we were in no mood for a geography lesson. Our only interest was getting food and water – and finding out where we were heading.

25

THE MARCH TO ATHENS

Once we had docked, we were ordered up the gangway, where we were immediately surrounded by Germans, who set about forming us into ranks, five abreast. Greek civilians looked on as the German troops counted and re-counted us. Some of the lads started messing up the ranks, deliberately causing confusion and consternation amongst our captors before they finally gave us the OK to move off.

The civilians looking on must have thought we were a sorry-looking rabble. That was soon to change. Our regimental sergeant major, 'Ducksy' Traynor, trembling with emotion, issued us with a stern warning in his broad Belfast accent: 'You are still members of the British army and you should not behave as rabble. Those civilians are our allies, let them be proud of us.' With some difficulty, given the state of our health, we straightened up and struck out at a fast pace. When the pace slackened – as it was bound to do over the eight miles – we gave a stirring rendition of 'Roll out the barrel', which helped to cover up our feelings of discomfort and defeated the efforts of the German propaganda aimed at the many civilians who were lining our route. Ray Williams recalled how his group was shadowed by a German movie camera, mounted on a car. Every time the Germans spotted a couple of ranks straggling, they tried to get it on film. The Greeks shouted excitedly, warning them what the Germans were up to. The lads would immediately brace up and break into a run, raising two fingers, Churchill-style, to the camera. After several attempts to catch the stragglers, the Germans gave up, and settled for whatever footage they already had.

As we left Piraeus behind, the Germans began to lose their temper with our indomitable singing. Deep into the countryside, with no one around to see what was going on, they unshouldered their rifles and, sputtering with anger, pointed them aggressively at us. But it would take more than this to kill off our repertoire of songs. The increase in the numbers of Greek civilians lining our route told us that we were nearing Athens. Our feelings proved right, as we were marched along roads criss-crossed with tramlines. The civilians, at some risk to themselves, tried to slip us food or drachma, while the Germans drove up and down our lines on motorcycles, stopping every now and then to threaten the Greeks with drawn revolvers. We passed some beautiful buildings, no doubt steeped in history, but I have to admit that my appreciation was reserved for the first bit of grub that would, hopefully, pass my lips. That, and a little shut-eye, were my only ambitions right then. But that was still somewhere down the line.

*

It was December 1943, and Franklin Roosevelt, Winston Churchill and Joseph Stalin were meeting at the Tehran Conference – at the end of which they issued a joint statement which finished with the words: 'We came here with hope and determination. We leave here, friends in fact, in spirit and in purpose.' On the long march to Athens, we passed a huge poster, obviously the work of German propaganda. It showed Churchill and Roosevelt seated separately, and behind them stood a grinning Stalin, his teeth bared as he plunged a dagger into each man's back.

We must have looked a terrible sight as we dragged ourselves through the city centre. Our military gait having been lost, all we had to fall back on was our battered morale – and our sense of humour. Tom (Big Maggie) McGee told us not to worry too much about not being in the 'pink' of health; after all, as guests of 'Der Führer', we could look forward to snug, comfortable cages to hole up in. What with that, and three squares a day, washed down by a pint of plain, we'd soon be on the pig's back, he promised, with a knowing grin.

By the time dusk fell, we were ready to sleep in the gutter. We dragged our exhausted bodies through the rain-soaked centre of Athens, with heavy legs and heavier hearts. Nothing could stop the banter, though, particularly when we spotted an advert for Haffner's sausages (made in Dublin). We were halted outside big gates leading into a former Junkers aircraft-manufacturing hangar. We flopped down on the cold concrete floor, exhausted. After a few sips of stagnant water from a barrel we found inside the building, we promptly fell sound asleep. When I awoke, I realised that I'd fallen asleep on concrete saturated with oil and grease, which had seeped into my tongue and throat. I felt sick and, despite my unsated hunger, had no desire for food. I was grateful for one thing at least: my greatcoat had soaked up most of the oil. Blessed is he that purloins without malice, but with good forethought. That greatcoat was to be my saviour on many more occasions. Concerned that some sneak thief might acquire it as I slept, I decided that, rather than using it to lie on, I'd wear it at all times. It became my only solace at times, and we built up a partnership that always came up trumps when the chips were down.

I decided to try to find some of my buddies – not an easy task, in this Wembley-sized space. I nudged and elbowed my way through the throngs of men, all steadfastly clinging to their belongings. My joy at finding Johnnie King, Andy Roy, Danny Lannigan and Joe Kane was indescribable. We'd been split up after our capture and I wasn't sure if I'd see my friends again. Lannigan was a loveable rogue: if a stroke needed to be pulled, he was your man. Such were his powers of persuasion that he convinced senior officers that his grandmother had died on no fewer than ten different occasions. Danny, being experienced in these matters, advised us not to make a rush for the door when the Germans opened it. The only thing we could be sure of, he said, was that the first lads out be given some dirty job to do. He was dead right: the first men out were given the job of emptying the barrels of urine. That was before we discovered a slit trench, in the middle of the roadway, close to our building. We were amazed to see six of our blokes crouched down, their trousers around their ankles, using the slit latrine sited in full view of offices occupied by six female Greek staff. Sergeant Major Traynor complained bitterly to the Germans about it, but they refused to budge. Despite the dysentery that was rampant, we had no option but to continue to use the exposed latrine for the duration of our imprisonment. It was just one more degrading moment for us.

26

The Great Drachma Heist

Although we were under guard, we could move around the compound relatively freely. On a recce, we found a kiosk that was still in operation; it had been put in place by the Germans as a facility for the local workers to buy basic goods. Pushing our luck, we discovered that the owner was happy to barter. Having no drachmas and nothing to barter, we set off in search of some loot but found nothing. We found out, too late, that the kiosk man accepted any coinage. If only we'd known, we could have pooled the bits and pieces of Italian lire and Syrian piastras we had to buy some food.

Tired from our fruitless efforts, we dozed off for a bit in the hot sun, and were awoken by a loud, friendly voice, speaking to us in English. We were ordered to join a queue for a food ration. Like grey-hounds out of the trap, we needed no second invitation. Slowly, in groups of five, we snaked around our internment building, until we reached some large bins. We were like the Bisto kids as we inhaled the aroma of the hot macaroni. We held out our mess tins, steel helmets or any container we could lay our hands on, and a ladle of macaroni was doled out to each of us. Ravenous with hunger, we devoured it in seconds, hoping to get a second helping, but threatened by the mob behind and the persuasiveness of the guards' bayonets, we moved along sharply. My throat was on fire as the hot, lumpy macaroni tried to break through the thick grease and oil that was still lodged in my gullet.

Sated, I felt energetic enough to resume my hunt for loot, but the Germans had other ideas. They ordered us to assemble in rank order in front of some senior German officers. Stepping forward, their *oberst* (colonel), speaking in fluent English, began by describing us as Irish soldiers who had fought bravely for Britain's cause, and said that Germany had no quarrel with Ireland. At this point, Sergeant Major 'Ducksy' Traynor stepped forward. Identifying himself as the senior NCO, he told the colonel in his strongest Belfast accent to address us as *British* soldiers. Ducksy then walked among the ranks, reminding us all that, Irish or not, we were enlisted British soldiers.

Taken aback by this surprise interruption, the German officers had a whispered discussion. Accompanied by a couple of guards, two of the officers walked through our ranks and singled out some of the men, who were then taken away for 'questioning', during which they were given the 'opportunity' to go on radio to speak to the Greek people. Exactly what they were to speak about remained vague. Ducksy and Company Sergeant Major Tommy Dooley were among eight people taken away for interrogation. All refused to go on radio, or to enlighten the Germans as to why so many Irishmen had joined the British army to fight in the war. Sergeant Major Traynor took issue with this treatment, and reminded the Germans of our rights under the Geneva Convention. The matter ended there.

Our diet consisted of the macaroni, which, although lumpy, was welcome. The announcement that we were to get a ration of bread and margarine for each day we remained in Athens was music to our ears. As we joined the interminable queue at the distribution point, every fifth man was issued with a loaf of bread and a small amount of margarine. The onus was on him to dole this food out fairly. The fact that the bread was black and made from wood-pulp husks and rye, was bad enough; to be given the impossible task of slicing it into five equal shares, without the benefit of a knife, while under close scrutiny from four hungry soldiers, was a task for only the bravest.

Try as they might, even to the point of measuring each slice with a piece of twine, the poor bugger could never divide the bread well enough to please everyone. We were all grateful to get the food, even though it tasted absolutely brutal and had to be swallowed quickly, to kill the taste. The bread was also an excellent purgative – not exactly what the boys with dysentery needed! As we were badly in need of some decent food to supplement our meagre rations, it was imperative to beg, borrow or steal something we could exchange for cash.

Danny Lannigan and Joe Kane went rooting in small rooms off the main building, while I went with Johnnie King and Tom McGee, to look for any of our former drinking buddies, in the hope that they might have a few bob. Although they were nearly as badly off as we were, we managed to cobble together an array of different coins of small denominations, but it wasn't enough to persuade the Greek extortionist to part with even a small piece of bread. We were considering our options when we heard Danny's familiar whistle. Beckoning us to follow him, he unrolled a threadbare blanket, inside which he'd hidden a next-to-new suit of clothes. The suit was very big, and the blond-haired, six-foot-two Joe Kane suggested that he could make better use of it to escape. He was immediately savaged by wee Danny, who said: 'As it is, you look like a f—kin' Swede, albeit a hungry one. Dressed up in civvies, strolling the streets of Athens, you'd be a Gestapo man's dream.' Still haranguing him, he said: 'Have you lost the bit you have, you'd attract more attention than a brothel would clients.' Eventually realising that the big fellow was winding him up, wee Danny let loose a string of obscenities: 'F—k the lot of you, I'm on my way to the kiosk. When I persuade Al Capone to fill me up with goodies, yis can rot in hell before I part with a single crumb.'

Andy Roy and Davy Thompson reminded him that he'd need help to get past the German sentry. Danny, always pragmatic, was quick to accept this advice, and got Joe, Andy and Davy to distract the sentry by making silly requests for cigarettes. The more they asked, the angrier the sentry became. In the end, he lost his temper and pushed them back, away from his post, giving the fleet-footed Danny and myself time to make the short sprint from the sentry's box to the kiosk, which was like Aladdin's cave, after four days of bartering with the prisoners, many of whom had given up their own clothes for a small portion of bread.

Danny pushed his way into crowded kiosk, where 'Al' was on his own, and between bartering with those inside, and serving those Greeks outside, he was under pressure. Taking full advantage of the situation, Danny dropped the suit on the floor and whipped up a big bundle of drachma notes he'd spotted behind the counter. He scarpered out the door, beckoning me to join him. With nothing in our hands, the sentry let us pass. Once inside the barrier, the Belfast spiv left us all for dust; we found him settled in amongst a crowd of prisoners. He whispered to us to watch out for the searches that were sure to follow. Andy Roy reckoned that the kiosk crook would have to think hard before reporting what had happened to the Germans. With no love lost between the Germans and the Greeks, he'd get little sympathy, and heavy sanctions.

So we waited. In between exchanges, while the others kept watch, Danny counted his hoard. 'Ten thousand drachmas', he announced. We were over the moon: we thought we'd hit pay dirt. King and McGee, who'd been ploughing their own furrow without success, were delighted that they'd thrown in their lot with us. King wondered aloud how the extortionist in the kiosk had been so careless as to leave such a fortune lying around. We decided to wait and see what kind of reaction there was to the money being missing before making any further moves; it seemed that Andy was right – there was no sign of any searches being mounted. We found out that a Greek van driver had been doing his own bit of business, smuggling bread into the compound, and bartering for anything he could acquire. Danny wanted to test him with one of the drachma notes, when the time was right.

On day five of our imprisonment, we went through our usual routine. With nowhere to wash, we filled our multi-purpose helmets with water for shaving, and then almost cut our throats with a blade that was so old and rusty, it must have been used by the entire British army. We washed off the muck that clung to our boots with the leftover water, and threw the rest into the open latrine, before giving the helmet a rub with a dirty rag. A quick dash to the grub queue followed, where our food was ladled into the smelly but prized helmet. The helmet, apart from its other uses, had saved my bacon from shrapnel and bullets on more than one occasion, and had been awash with muck, dirt, blood and urine; it deserved to be well protected!

On day six, with no warning, Danny decided to start moving the stolen drachma into circulation. In the absence of any hue and cry, it was worth the risk of trying to buy bread from the Greek van man.

With nothing smaller, and no hope of getting any change elsewhere, we'd have to produce the thousand-drachma note. With the thought of some real bread, a mug of acorn coffee, and some decent macaroni, we were all willing to be the one to take the risk. Danny had checked out the system, and reckoned that Joe Kane, being the tallest, would have the best chance of getting through the milling crowd to the van. Half an hour passed, with no sign of the 'big fella' returning. The normally calm Danny was getting increasingly agitated, and was casting aspersions on the honesty and integrity of Big Joe, suggesting that Joe had gorged himself on a couple of loaves, and would undoubtedly return with some cock-and-bull story. He even wondered if the bastard had been serious about escaping.

I was sent out to do a recce. When I got to the van, I had to jostle my way through hoards of aggressive, arm-swinging squaddies, all forcing their way forward. Big Joe almost trampled over me, as he made his way back from the van. Empty handed, his khaki drill shirt ripped to shreds, his hair dishevelled and his face scratched, he gasped for breath. Joe's ever-present smile was gone. Alternating between groaning and nervous laughter, he tried to explain his lack of success, but he was so agitated that I couldn't make head or tail of what he was trying to say. Finally, he composed himself enough to tell me about the disaster that had befallen him. After a monumental struggle, Joe had made it to the van, where he had tried to barter for some bread. Waving his thousand-drachma note under the van driver's nose, he'd expected his hand to be snatched off by the greedy Greek. In broken English, the van driver disdainfully informed him that his offer for the bread fell short – by nineteen thousand drachma!

The shock of this realisation left him punch-drunk, and with the smart remarks and slagging from some of his fellow Faughs, he had to stop himself from lashing out. Thankfully, his sense of humour prevailed, and by the time we made it back to tell Danny and the others, he could see the funny side of it. Danny, however, was less than impressed. As we approached the group, empty-handed, he jumped up and demanded that we stop messing about and hand over the goods. The story gradually unfolded, and after great laughter, the gravity of the situation hit us all – all, that is, except for Andy Roy, who, preferring his fags to food any day, pleaded with us to split the money so that he could buy at least one cigarette. Wee Danny promised him the first packet of Gallaghers he could buy for a thousand drachma.

With no prospect of supplementing our scanty diet, we resigned ourselves to waiting for the next issue of 'garbage grub', as we called it. Although it was early December, the heat and brightness of the sun kept our spirits up. Our poor diet was aggravated by an inadequate supply of fresh water, and the state of our personal hygiene reached a new low. Our faces hacked about by decrepit blades, all we could do was hide the gashes with a growth of stubble. We looked like hardened tramps who'd been too long on the road. With nothing to occupy our time, boredom set in, relieved only by the ongoing ack-ack fire, and the clustering of black blobs of shrapnel in the sky, as we amused ourselves by trying to identify our own aircraft. As we watched the aerial displays, we were subjected to a blow-by-blow account from one 'win the war' squaddie, who told of his single-handed feats of bravery on the ramparts. Nothing could shut him up, and Danny, exasperated, finally asked him how many medals he'd won for being so brutal with the truth! Poor 'win the war' took the opportunity afforded by the gales of laughter that ensued, to slip silently away.

27

COFFIN TRAINS, AS PRISONERS HIT A NEW LOW

Word filtered through that we were to be moved on again. Where exactly we were headed was still a mystery, but the consensus was that anything would be better than this God-awful existence, with little or no food, and nothing to do all day. Davy beguiled us with tales of the wonderful food to be had at our next halting place. He was cut short by Johnnie King, who remarked that nothing could make macaroni taste like steak, onions and mash! Walter Pancott, alert as ever, reminded us that, whatever the Germans had in mind for us, it wasn't our well-being. Any real food coming the Germans' way would be strictly reserved for themselves.

Twelve days after we'd arrived in Athens, we were on the march again. Though unwashed and dishevelled, we did our best to form up as well-drilled units, singing as we moved through the streets. After half an hour, we arrived at a railway junction and were handed into the loving care of a sizeable welcoming committee of German guards accompanied by vicious-looking guard dogs. Once we were inside, they split us up into groups of forty or forty-five. I was separated from many of my fellow Faughs: Joe Kane and I had to part company with the rest of our syndicate. Each group, accompanied by guards on either side of us, moved across a maze of railway tracks until we came to a long line of goods wagons. The big sliding doors were pulled open, and we scrambled aboard the cattle trucks. Packed in like sardines, we had no room to stretch out. We arranged to take turns standing at the single makeshift window at each end of the wagon, the opening just large enough to prevent us from suffocating. The only other 'concession' afforded us was two make-do piss tins. For those suffering from dysentery, it was no laughing matter, and we suffered alongside them. Those with the strongest stomachs cleared the foul-smelling mess from the dirty straw floor as best they could, dumping it out through the opening, as the train lurched along.

It wasn't the only use of the thin layer of lice-ridden straw scattered on the floor. I watched as one desperate soul stooped down and picked up a piece of urine-soaked straw, rubbed it between the heels of his hands as only a hardened smoker could, and, pulling a filthy-looking cigarette paper from his battle-dress pocket, rolled it around the crushed straw and lit up. It was a pitiful sight to see him coughing and spluttering as he made vain attempts to prevent his precious 'smoke' from disintegrating.

Dysentery soon became the biggest problem on board, as we travelled without rest or respite through Greece and into Bulgaria, where it finally came to a halt. We heard the sound of chains and locks being removed, and finally the doors opened and a guard jumped aboard our wagon. With a wave of his automatic pistol, he ordered us to line up, around the walls of the wagon. We quickly fell in, expecting it to be a feeding stop. Instead, we were told to get out of the train and were steered across the snow-covered tracks to an open field, where a deep trench had been prepared. Expecting to be lined up and shot, we looked at the deep, snow-covered trench and saw what we thought was our last, icy resting spot. With great relief, we realised that they wanted us to use the trench as a toilet. We were happy to oblige. With an entire train-full of men in action, no doubt the Bulgarian farmers had enough fertiliser to last them a thousand years. Job done, we ploughed our way back through the deep, biting snow to the 'comfort' of the foul-smelling trucks.

For the next two hours, we lived in hope of getting some food, but it was not to be. Our misery was only added to when we came under fire from an air attack. Isolated in a siding and with no visible markings, we were target practice for Allied aircraft, which would naturally assume that we were an enemy supply train. When the air-raid sirens sounded the all-clear, we shunted into the station, where, finally, we were given soup and bread, which we devoured without tasting. Sidney Morrow, the worse for wear from dysentery, was now showing serious signs of decline, and had to be helped along the queue to get his food. After being carried back to the wagon, he took one sip of the soup and passed the rest to his buddy, before hanging his haversack on a nail, his uneaten bread stored inside, ready for when he was well enough to eat it.

We chugged out of Sofia, making several stops along the way. At each stop our engine was detached and used to back up enemy wagons, laden with military ordnance en route to the Balkans. During these manoeuvres, we sat for hours in the bitterly cold meat wagons, passing our time, miles from anywhere, reminiscing about the friends we'd left behind. As we crossed the border into Yugoslavia, we stopped again. This time there seemed to be no reason for the stop, and we had no way of attracting the attention of the guards, to let them know we needed help. Our buddy, Sidney Morrow, was in a very bad way. He was shivering and disorientated, and was lying across the legs of his friends. Badly in need of urgent medical attention, we were at a loss as to how to help him. We had been given a ration of food two days earlier, so we knew there was little chance of the doors being opened again for any other reason. The train rattled on, not stopping again until the following day. When it did, the clamour of voices from our wagon caught the attention of one young German guard: although none of us could speak German, the solder quickly got the message, left his comrades and ran for help. Within minutes, accompanied by two guards and a *hauptmann*, he unlocked the door and opened it wide.

The *hauptmann* jumped aboard and, speaking in English, told us to stand as far back as possible. The guards were on alert and watched us closely, keeping us covered with their machine-guns while one of them accompanied the *hauptmann* on board. Kneeling on the filthy straw, the German captain took Sidney's pulse and checked his eye movement. He ordered the sick man be hospitalised immediately. Within fifteen minutes, Sidney was stretchered out of the death wagon and into a field ambulance. As he was being lifted out, a friend of his, another larger-than-life character, shouted after him, begging for his forgiveness. We didn't understand what he meant.

As Sidney was being lifted off the train, someone took his haversack – his only possession – and was attempting to hand it down to him, when he noticed that the straps were open. On closer examination, we found that all of Sidney's precious bread rations were missing. No amount of accusations and finger-pointing could identify the culprits. Sidney's friend was a huge man – the tallest, heaviest man in our wagon. A good athlete, he was known for his enormous appetite. Although he was a gentle giant, he was always complaining about his hunger cramps, and the aches and pains in his legs. It annoyed the hell out of us: we were all in the same boat, after all.

On more than one occasion, while the train was in full flight, the big fella rushed to the barbed-wire opening to vomit. We couldn't understand how he could be so ill so often, as he had had so little to eat. This became a regular occurrence: more often than not he was dry-retching, in between bouts of sleeping. Nobody commented on it, as we talked about home and departed friends, and about our hope that, by now, Sidney was in a hospital bed somewhere. Talk of Sidney made the big man all the more agitated, until it finally dawned on us just what had happened: Sidney's 'best friend' had stolen his rations. As to whether it was the bad bread, or guilt about taking it, that had caused his sickness, who knows? At least now we could understand why he had begged for forgiveness, as Sidney was being carted away. I don't know if he ever forgave himself but I suspect that, like me, every minute of the fourteen days and nights of the journey to hell were indelibly marked on his mind. The reaction against him was swift and emotional, but gradually the outbursts lost their sting, as we left him to torment himself about what he had done.

28

RANDY GUARDS, STOLEN SALAMI
AND THREATS OF A FIRING SQUAD

The train rumbled on, its speed only increasing the power of the icy-cold wind that swept through our wagon. The following afternoon, the train pulled in to a siding about a mile from Belgrade's main train station, where we were again treated to a feed of watery macaroni. There was a delay in closing the doors after we'd been given our food ration, and, sensing that something was up, I positioned myself and Joe Kane in the doorway. There was a lot of movement between the ration store and our wagons, as our jailors went to and fro. We could see what looked like heavy coverings being placed between the adjoining railway lines, but we had no idea what they were for.

Minutes later, the German guards retrieved the covers and walked towards our wagon, calling out for teams of two men to go to the station to collect more rations. Like a flash, Joe and I were on the ground, ready to volunteer for this particular duty. After six men from our wagon had been sorted into three pairs, with one guard to a pair, we were issued with one large covering per team. In the dusk, we had assumed that they were heavy coverings, but they were just a few blankets.

The guards forced us to us walk in between the railway tracks, despite the cinder track offering a less difficult route, and we found it hard to negotiate the sleepers and large stones, and stumbled as we walked along. In the distance, we could hear the wagon doors being slammed shut, and then the sound of ground-to-air combat, reminding us of just how vulnerable we were. We walked on, with only the thought of purloining some extra rations keeping us going. The German guards appeared relaxed, and talked and laughed amongst themselves as they ushered us along the platform to a large storeroom-cum-canteen. They forced a path through a crowd of German military, who stood to one side as we were locked into a large room, with glass doors, three-quarters of the way along the platform. We were each given a small stool to sit on as we waited for instructions, and watched as 'Fritz', our guard, talked to the local workers for a few minutes before moving us to a smaller glass-panelled room. We could smell something cooking – the aroma wafted through the overhead grating – but whatever it was, it was nothing pleasant.

We could do nothing but wait. We watched through the glass as our escort directed his attentions – dishonourable, it seemed – towards a young Yugoslavian woman. We prayed that his hormones would get the better of him, and give us an opportunity to escape, but before our prayers could be answered, two *Feldwebers* (sergeants) suddenly entered the room, thwarting his efforts. Our guard, his face flushed, stood smartly to attention and saluted, as they got on with their business. As soon as they had departed, the guard again sought out the young woman. This time, to the outrage of her colleagues, he was even more daring, but the woman made no effort to discourage his advances. If things had gone much further, the entire Wermacht couldn't have stopped him from what he had in mind!

Realising what was going on, his fellow guards restrained him and warned him about fraternising, before moving him on. The guard reluctantly tidied himself up, as the young girl was harangued by her colleagues. Judging by the finger-wagging and the high-pitched voices, it was a fair guess that she was about to spend a long time in 'Coventry'. When the drama was over, we were moved to a big room, where the blankets were now spread out. Dozens of rolls of salami and loaves of bread had been placed on the blankets, which were then tied up in each corner, leaving a space for each arm to go through, haversack-style, ready for them to be hoisted onto our shoulders. The loaded blankets, ready for transit, were left under the watchful eye of the senior store man, while we were taken upstairs.

Our guard ordered the middle-aged woman working in the upstairs kitchen to give us something to eat, and she quickly ladled piping-hot macaroni into empty powdered-milk tins. It was much better than the watery stuff we'd got on the trains, and I gulped it down ravenously. I hadn't realised quite how hot it was, and in my haste I scalded myself badly, and my lips broke out in blisters. But I felt so warm inside, for the first time in a long while, that I didn't care.

The senior kitchen hand signalled to the guard that he had something for him, and the guard disappeared out of sight, behind some large boilers. The woman lost no time in refilling the milk tins, and again, I quickly gulped the food down, ignoring the pain of my scalded lips and tongue. The woman and I had a long conversation without uttering a word: the language barrier didn't prevent us from understanding each other. She saw in my eyes that I was very grateful, and she – if her stream of low, harsh-sounding ranting was anything to go by – was cursing the German occupiers of her homeland. As she made agitated gestures in the guard's general direction, the good lady gave us yet another helping of the precious macaroni. Despite my near-starvation, I had difficulty in swallowing this helping. My bloated stomach resisted all the way but, urged on by the good lady, I managed to force yet another helping past my stinging lips. There was no way I could have refused this determined woman, who was probably a partisan in her spare time. Before we had it finished, the guard arrived back on the scene, and took issue with our benefactor. As their voices rose, we worried that things might turn sour for our Angel of Mercy, but she had the last word, releasing a barrage of vitriol in his direction as he walked away.

Downstairs, the guard ordered us to load the blanket on to Big Joe Kane's shoulders, and we set off back to the train. I was hoping that the cold night air would cool my burning lips, and that my sore stomach would ease up, before it was my turn to carry the load. The cold and rain, coupled with the awkwardness of negotiating the sleepers, made the going difficult, and poor Joe swayed from side to side under the weight. When it was my turn, my knees buckled under the weight, and I staggered and stumbled. The guard was not happy, as he kept shining the torch in my eyes, blinding me and making me trip over a

179

broken sleeper and pitch forward. Soon it was Joe's turn to take the load again.

Working to a prearranged plan, it was down to me to steal the rations. As I got closer to Joe, I slipped my hand into the blanket and grabbed a roll of salami, which I stuffed into the inside pocket of my 'smother' (my RAF greatcoat). While the guard wasn't looking, I managed to extract a few more salamis, and I hid them away in the deep pockets of the coat. Feeling confident now, I made another dive into the blanket, whispering to Joe that we'd scored well, as we pulled up alongside the wagon. We were ordered to swing the blanket up onto the wagon, which was high up on the siding, and as Joe and I tried to get a good swing at it, the guard spotted a roll of salami that had been pushed upwards by my exertions and was now peeking out from the side pocket of my coat. He grabbed the salami and waved it excitedly, shouting to the other guards, who quickly surrounded me and separated me from Joe.

In the heavy rain, I was searched, until they found all six rolls of the spiced sausage. There was consternation amongst the guards, especially the one in charge of rations. I was alone, wet, cold and devastated – and surrounded by armed guards who were, to say the least, not feeling very friendly towards me. Joe was searched too, but after finding nothing on him, he was bundled into the wagon and the doors were slammed shut. On orders from a senior NCO, I was frogmarched all the way back to the station, with one guard in front and another behind. I feared the worst. My main worry was that I would be tried in a kangaroo court and I hated the thought of being separated from my fellow Faughs. Maybe they'd keep me in Yugoslavia, doing field punishment or hard labour. I could live with that, as long as I had some hope of linking up with my buddies again.

I was soon ushered onto the now-familiar railway platform, which was thronged with uniformed men, who cleared a way for the guards and their prisoner. I was taken back to the canteen, which was full of high-ranking soldiers, who made throat-slitting gestures at me. The noise level reached a fever pitch as I tried to explain we had been starving – making gestures by rubbing my stomach – but it made no difference. Although I felt badgered, I managed to keep my composure and faced them impudently.

The first one to speak directly to me was the NCO, who tried to reassure me, saying in English: 'There is no need for great worry. Your crime is not a serious one.' Whatever he said to the gathering in German, uncontrollable laughter broke out amongst the mob. Tapping me on the jaw, the NCO told me that they were just making fun of me. I could have hugged him with relief.

Angry with his wasted journey, one of the guards pushed me outside and along the railway track at double pace. The icy rain was seeping down my collar, and my tropical kit was so wet it clung to my skin. The fast pace upset my bloated stomach, and I regurgitated the macaroni. Combined with the oozing of my busted lip, it all conspired to make me feel really ill. My front-line guard, though pleasant in appearance, was the one cracking the whip. When his hard-faced partner took over, I expected the worst, but was pleasantly surprised when he slowed things down to a walking pace.

As we moved along, the night was wonderfully silent. It reminded me of many a lone walk I had taken through the Irish countryside, and I allowed my mind to wander. My thoughts were interrupted by the rush of a train carrying heavy artillery to the Balkans – it hurtled by so close to me, I had to jump out of its path to avoid being killed. One of the worst things about war is the uninvited loud noises that explode into your consciousness, always dragging you back to the present. Right now, my ambition soared to the dizzy heights of making it back to the lice-ridden wagon – and my mates. That was, if it was still there.

In the gloom, I could just spot the prison train ahead. Using up my last reserves of energy, I quickened the pace, sighing with relief as the wagon door slid open. I was helped aboard by the willing hands and was hardly inside when the doors were slammed shut, and the heavy chains locking us in were put in place. For the next hour, I entertained my buddies with an account of events, and gave vent to my indignation. In my absence, my couple of inches of space had been taken over, and I twisted and turned, trying to get room even to squat down. Forced to sit upright as the train rattled along, tormented by the lice working overtime, I eventually fell into an exhausted sleep, as we chugged along through the night.

The next morning, still somewhere in Yugoslavia, we came to a halt and were taken off the wagons and directed to some slit trenches. Perched like hens about to lay, we hovered over a long wooden support pole, our feet deeply embedded in snow, as the biting wind pierced our numb backsides. Most of the men were still riddled with dysentery, and it was spreading rapidly. It wasn't the most dignified time in my life. Our business done, the train pulled away, and we crossed a bridge over the romantic 'Blue Danube' we'd heard so much about: it appeared to be no more than a filthy green slime. Nonetheless, just then, I'd have given the little I had to hear my pal Johnnie King give a rendition of 'Call, Call, Vienna Mine'. I wondered what Johnnie was up to then.

The dysentery was having a punishing effect on us all. Even the most robust amongst us was in a debilitated state. Eleven days after setting off, we rolled into Budapest, where medical attention was given to the worst cases, and after two days without any food we got a small ration of skilly (soup). Although this was welcome, the heavily salted soup added to our dehydration and tortured my blistered lips. Our pleadings for water were ignored, the doors were slammed shut, and we were on the road again.

Twenty-four hours later we reached Austria, where we were finally given water. This came just in time, as by then we were desperate enough to recycle our urine – though God knows what state that was in. Utterly dejected, indifferent to day or night, I invoked the Man Above to bring this terrible journey to an end. No sooner had I finished my conversation with God than an air-raid siren went off. We were shunted into a siding, and prayed that the bombers would not hit our halting site, after all we'd been through. After we had been given the all-clear, our cattle wagons moved off, the wagons clanging against each other as the train picked up speed.

Two days later, we stopped yet again. Ordered out of the trucks, we were told that, finally, fourteen days after we had left Athens, we were at our journey's end. Despite our bedraggled state – we were filthy, lousy, sick and exhausted – we managed an enormous cheer. Word filtered out that we had reached Moosburg, some thirty-five kilometres north-east of Munich, more than 1,400 miles from Athens.

Escorted by German guards, we trundled along, shaking the louse-ridden bits of straw from what was left of our clothes as we went. After about three miles, we came to a barbed-wire enclosure. We had reached Stalag VIIA, a transit camp for POWs. Ushered through the huge gates, we got our first glimpse of the watchtowers spaced around the perimeter, and the many different nationalities in the camp, including French, Belgians, Americans, Yugoslavs, Serbs, Poles, Russians, British and Irish. It was immediately clear that the Russians, who made up the largest group, were being badly treated – they were so stick-thin and haggard they almost made the other prisoners look healthy.

Although the nationalities were segregated into different compounds, we ventured close to the Russian compound, and were surprised to find that the guards made no attempt to stop us. We were shocked at the Russians' emaciated state. The camp medical staff, who had lost no time in cleaning us up, showed little concern for the poor Russians. After de-lousing and a wonderful shower – despite the fact that it was mid-December and temperatures were well below freezing – we settled into the wooden huts, with their triple-decked, rough-timbered bunks. It was sheer luxury after the last few weeks. We hoped that this gunny-sacked shed would be a roof over our heads at least until Christmas.

After more than five years in a hot climate, still clad in what was left of our tropical kit – now just rags – the extreme cold hit us hard. The POWs' daily ration was one slice of black bread, two ounces of imitation margarine (a byproduct of the brown-coal industry), a bowl of nauseating skilly and a mug of acorn coffee. Not enough to nourish us, or even heat us up.

Too exhausted to bother about my surroundings, I didn't even notice the toing and froing to a particular hut until, one day, I checked it out for myself, and found that it was a barber's shop. Taking a chance, I wandered in and asked the barber, a French prisoner, if he would shave my head, to keep the lice at bay. He wanted to know if I had any cigarettes, soap, spam or bully beef as barter. I was taken aback: I had nothing to offer. As I left, disappointed, I noticed he had various goods on sale, including a large amount of cigarette papers, and realised that here was an opportunity. The sharp-practice shaver, like many other French prisoners of long standing, was enjoying a special right of immunity. I was sure that there was room in the racket for a man like myself. But how to get there was the question.

I shared my discovery with my pals, Wee Davy Thompson and Walter Pancott. Exchanges on the matter went from the ridiculous to the naive, as ideas from waylaying 'Frenchie' to forcible entry of the barber's bunk were trotted out. It was time to use a little initiative. The idea of having some of our smoking buddies come to our aid was vetoed. The heavy smokers amongst us were driven to distraction for a drag on a butt and, given their state of desperation, if they'd found out about the stash, they'd most likely beat 'Frenchie' if he got in their way – and this would bring down the wrath of the Germans on us all. We would have to shelve our plans for the time being. In the meantime, we were not too unhappy with our lot after the atrocious conditions in the cattle trucks. Here we could at least wash, shave, rinse out what passed for our clothes and even walk about, albeit under the watchful eyes of the heavily armed guards, accompanied by vicious-looking Alsatians.

After some time, we were each given a postcard to send home, to let our next of kin know that we were alive – if not well. This was a great relief for me, as I was concerned about my mother, no doubt worrying herself to death back in Dublin. Never a strong woman, she wouldn't be able for the shock of hearing that one of her brood was missing in action. I was worried that a telegram to my family saying I was missing in action would be too much for them to take. (My parents had already received a precautionary telegram – a standard practice – when I was on an SBS mission in early 1943, in case I didn't come back.) As a former British soldier and POW during World War I, my Da knew the score. He would try to reassure my mother – but she wasn't an easy woman to rein in, once the palpitations took over and the floodgates opened! Hopefully, the postcard would put an end to her worries. My parents had three sons serving in the war: I hoped and prayed my two brothers would make it safely through.

A few days after we'd given up our notion of parting the Frenchman from his worldly goods, the camp's senior officer arranged to issue one Canadian food parcel per man. We couldn't believe our luck! I enthusiastically ripped open my windfall, delighted to find that it contained a tin each of corned beef, spam and sardines, a packet of cream crackers, four ounces of coffee, some butter, powdered milk, a packet of sugar, raisins, a bar of soap, chicken extract, and a large bar of chocolate – enough to make a few decent meals. A special bonus for me, a non-smoker, was the packet of cigarettes: this was just the currency I needed to have my head shaved. Receiving this gift ranked alongside the time when, as a child, I had found a sum of money that was to elevate us from sleeping on the floor into new beds.

Thanking God, the Canadians and the Geneva Convention, I tucked into the goodies. I resisted the temptation to eat everything at once; instead, the contents of each box were pooled between three or four men, who put their trust in a designated person to eke it out over the coming weeks. With morale restored and our hunger sated, Christmas 1943 in Stalag VIII was streets ahead of the torture of the past few weeks.

There were other problems of a more basic nature at the camp. The camp, designed to hold ten thousand prisoners, was now housing many thousands more. The toilets inevitably became blocked, and the waste overflowed. The quick-thinking Ray Williams, who was never short of an idea when the chips were down, reckoned that we use the empty Red Cross boxes as makeshift toilets. Despite the cold, the nauseating smell from the overflowing toilets and the many make-do loos stacked up outside seemed to permeate our hut; worst of all, there was no chloride of lime available to neutralise the mess and kill the smell.

Even though we were infested with lice, we still found the idea of them marching up and down our bollocks, as we furiously fought for the space to tear at them, a source of great amusement. One wag claimed that the inside seams of his trousers – the largest breeding ground for lice in Europe, as he put it – was overstocked. He was determined to distinguish between the sexes of his inhabitants, so he could put French letters on the males of the species in an effort to halt production.

Despite everything, morale remained high, with optimistic predications that the worst was over: now we were finally in Germany and could avail of our rights under the Geneva Convention, which were not always afforded in the field.

29

POW No. 141686

The Move to Stalag XIA

On New Year's Eve 1943, twelve days after arriving at Stalag VIIA, our regimental sergeant major told us that the Germans were moving us out, to destinations unknown. Within three hours, we were split up and sent on our separate ways, marching in the bitter cold to the railway station, bound for God know's where. The piercing wind and heavy snow tormented me, and I couldn't shake off the numbing cold. I tried shadow-boxing, doubling up on the spot, and even 'training' with a skipping rope, but my vascular system was reluctant to work any harder. Blue from the cold, confused, and acting out of character, I was causing concern to my friends.

To add to my problems, some thieving swine had stolen my RAF greatcoat. Between thinking about my loss and the icy wind, with only my khaki rags left to keep me warm, my body had almost shut down. I was suffering from hypothermia and my mind wouldn't function: I couldn't think straight. I ranted and raved about the lily-livered bastard who'd stolen 'my coat'. 'Easy come, easy go, Johnnie', my level-headed mate Andy Roy volunteered. A trusted friend from the Sandy Row, he knew me better than anyone. With some gentle persuasion and his warning to 'Stop blathering, you silly bastard, you wouldn't know how to hate anyone. If you met the lousy whore in ten minutes' time, you'd probably ask if he was warm enough', I couldn't help but smile. I'd just have to get on with it: after all, most of the lads had only threadbare blankets around their shoulders.

What awaited us now was even more daunting, as we marched yet again towards the dreaded cattle wagons. Soon we would be aboard and the hunt for space would begin. All the delousing at Stalag VIIA would be for nothing, as once again we'd be back to scratching and searching for lice like chimpanzees in the zoo. Conditions were as we'd come to expect: a bitter wind whistling through the barbed wire opening, no sign of food or water, guaranteed infestation and stinking piddle pots. Back to normal, you might say!

To our surprise, our journey ended after just three days, on 2 January 1944. Unsteadily, we vacated our mobile doss-house and inhaled the cold, fresh air. Willingly, we obeyed our captors' orders to form up in fives, and moved off in complete darkness at a comfortable pace, marching through several small villages. En route, we learned that our next 'hotel' was to be Stalag XIA, in a place called Altengrabow, not to far from Magedeburg, in Bavaria.

As we approached the camp, we could just make out the searchlights from the guard towers as they criss-crossed in the night. As we went through the huge gates, we were hailed by the raggle-taggle odds and sods, who'd obviously had long service in this, our new residence. The ice dangled from the barbed wire on the compounds, as the multinational reception committee, thirsty for information, called out to us. Their eager search for a familiar face, or a regimental cap or tunic badge, brought no joy. A snarling *Feldweber* (sergeant) broke up our chit-chat, and marshalled us into groups of ten, pushing us towards an improvised washroom, where the delousing began again in earnest. After having shaved our heads, testicles and any other parts that they felt appropriate, we then washed in lukewarm water before having lashings of powdered insecticide poured onto our tackle, ready for inspection. A sullen-looking doctor poked at scrotums and surrounding areas with a long pencil-like object, his revulsion clearly visible. As if we needed reminding about how scruffy we were, the German *wehrmacht* laid it on thick, telling us that we needed a lesson in hygiene. He could at least have apologised for the bluntness of their razor blades. We were all too aware that it was vital to be clean, but his haranguing brought home to us the power that the guards now had over our lives.

This episode over and done with, we were despatched into the cold night air, bald as the day we were born, and limping into the night like multiple 'John Waynes'. The silence was broken only by the groaning and grunting as the stinging pain of the butchered areas of our bodies met the icy cold. The night of a thousand cuts! Photographed with a metal number plate hanging around our necks, like common criminals, our welcoming party came to an end.

As the searchlights weaved their way back and forth around the compounds, we were ushered into a large shed. It held nothing more than three tiered shelves, running horizontally on either side of the building, which had previously been a stable. Grateful to be issued with a small, threadbare blanket that had obviously seen service on the Russian front, I scrambled up to the top shelf, with Davy, Walter and Andy below me. Together with two hundred other souls, I bedded down in this damp, mouldy-smelling stable and thanked God that at least some of our little band had made it this far. Although exhausted, between the overcrowding, the musty damp, and the lack of any heat in sub-zero conditions, it was difficult to get any sleep.

As day two at Stalag XIA, Otto, a German corporal with a pronounced limp, entered our lives, making his presence well and truly felt. With his German bent for organisation and punctuality, he burst into our sleeping paddock at an ungodly hour, bellowing at us with a roar of 'Raus! Raus!' We were shocked at the velocity of his wake-up call, after a night with little sleep and aching limbs. Already dressed, I staggered about and managed to get my feet on the ground, stamping the ice-cold surface with my wooden clogs and flailed my arms around, in an effort to thaw out, as we stood to for the early-morning roll-call.

Standing there on parade, I was sure rigor mortis would set in, as I began touching my toes and limbering up; the rest of the lads followed suit, breaking ranks in the process. Otto almost blew a fuse, and his twelve-hundred-horsepower voice soon brought our shenanigans to an end. A quiet smile crossed Otto's face for an instant, before he allowed himself to laugh out loud at our antics and we were relieved to find that he wasn't such a bad bloke after all. He showed us uncommon politeness, and even managed to make jokes in his broken

English, as he hobbled through the ranks doing his headcount. Over the next twelve months, we got to know Otto a little better. We came to realise that he was a decent sort: an ordinary soldier who'd had his legs and part of his upper body shattered while fighting on the Russian front. Taken off active service, he had a relatively cushy number, and had no desire to be posted back into active service. Once our daily count was over, Otto's supervision was unobtrusive, and he reserved his distinctive early-morning wake-up call for when senior officers and NCOs were present. From time to time, we played little tricks on Otto, in the hope of provoking a blockbusting response. It worked the first time, but after that, he'd limp away with a smile on his face, leaving the word *schweinhund* hanging in the air.

Following the daily inspection, and satisfied with the tally, Otto and the *Feldwebel* (sergeant) would pass on the numbers to the camp commandant, and await orders to dismiss the prisoners. Finally, after forty-five minutes of standing in the snow, in what was left of our uniform, we were free to queue for our ration of acorn coffee, as the *Feldwebel* lectured us on our obligation to salute all German officers we came across. Stupidity on both sides led to some petty reprisals. Our blokes deliberately ignored the presence of the German officers, which led to our being assembled outside while the guards upended our bed spaces, searched our pockets and emptied the contents on the ground in front of us. Comically, before they had time to confiscate it, a lot of the stuff found its way back into our pockets. Not that there was much to confiscate; with no food parcels on the horizons, we had little of value.

Our 'man of confidence' (MOC) – a go-between who represented POWs in dealing with their captors, provided for under the terms of the Geneva Convention) – RSM Ducksy Traynor, supported by Sergeant Major Tommy Dooley, had a showdown with the camp commander, during which they objected to this collective-punishment routine. They were summarily dismissed by the commander, but they stood their ground. The senior German officer had them marched away to do seven days' solitary confinement, which he extended to ten days when they refused to apologise. There was little that we could do to help our pals. We had no food to offer them, but with the indulgence of the German sentry we managed brief conversations with them when they were exercising. They had little room to move but managed to throw their clothes over the wire, for washing. The troughs in the washroom had a cold water supply that regularly froze solid. The only solution to the problem was to burn bits of paper under the pipes to try to thaw it enough to wet the clothes, give them a quick rub and get them back over the wire to the boys.

We realised that we had little choice but to salute the German offi-cers, but we hadn't surrendered yet. We organised things so that three or four of us would deliberately walk across the path of the officers, forcing them to return our salute. This continued all day every day, almost wearing them out, until eventually it dawned on them what we were up to. They soon made themselves scarce, doing a speedy about-turn whenever they saw us approach, and the requirement to salute them soon petered out. So, despite the boys' ten days of solitary con-finement, we had the last laugh.

Inevitably, it wasn't long before our clothes became lice-ridden again. I regularly used a small candle to burn the seams of my trousers – if you could still call them trousers – in an effort at least to reduce the lice population. But despite my best efforts, the chasing-and-burning routine was here to stay.

The sleeping quarters were no joke. The hundreds of men were racked with coughs and other illnesses, making sleep virtually impos-sible. Top-tier dwelling was not all it was cracked up to be, especially if you were tall: I regularly hit my head on the roof beams. Between my own curses, and the litany of swear words directed at our German captors, we had some hilarious moments in that palace of infestation.

The more imaginative amongst us rigged up gadgets to brew tea, connecting the contraptions to the electricity wire to boil water. 'Top bunkers' would keep a sharp eye out, warning of the approach of any patrolling guard, trying to find out why the camp lights were flickering madly. A diversion was created, and the brewers' equipment was hid-den within seconds. The guards were convinced that we were hatch-ing an escape plot but, finding nothing amiss, the search was inevitably called off. Just as well it was only tea and not porter: we'd have wrecked the lighting system of the entire population of Altengrabow!

Other ingenious devices were cobbled together by members of the Royal Electrical and Mechanical Engineers – the REMES – aided and abetted by RAF personnel. They got to work making receiving devices, with bits and pieces of metal they found around the camp. Getting news of the Allied forces' advances was a great morale-booster, especially as, by that time, our daily rations were limited to a mug of acorn coffee, a loaf of bread between eight people – the previous 'divvie up' between five seemed like a luxury now – and added to by a small bowl of watery soup. We were so hungry that we actually appreciated this slop, and were extremely grateful when the occasional Canadian Red Cross parcel got through.

The middle of the stables was taken up with long trestle-like tables. At night, these were used as sleeping platforms, but during the day they played a major role in keeping boredom at bay, when they were the location of bridge schools, discussions on DIY, and even language courses. As time passed, prisoners became experts at their chosen subject: there was precious little else to do. The few words of several languages I learnt myself came in handy for doing business with French, Polish and Russian prisoners and, on occasion, even the Germans themselves. Somehow, we all managed to get our message across in the universal language of bartering!

With nothing to look forward to, other than the watery skilly, with the grease of some unidentified animal floating in it, and your ration of rye wood-pulp that passed for bread, hunger and boredom were constant companions. One day, while I was scouring the ground close to the barbed-wire fences that separated us from the other prisoners, the cold cutting through me, I started to shadow-box in an effort to keep myself warm. After about ten minutes, I heard a loud voice, in a language I didn't understand, coming from the French compound. I looked up and saw two POWs urging me to come over to the fence. Sensing an opportunity, I made a beeline for the wire, and was surprised when twelve French Red Cross biscuits were thrust into my hand. I knew to expect nothing for nothing, but I couldn't understand what the prisoners wanted. Frustrated, one of the men began to shadow-box, showing all the moves of a handy boxer. I realised what they were after – the biscuits were an incentive. I headed back to my own hut, looking for someone who could speak French, and an English chap offered his help.

The next day, at the same time, we went back to the fence, but there was no sign of my benefactors. Eventually, my bilingual friend located the French boys and got to the heart of the matter. The lads were organising boxing matches between the different nationalities, and were anxious to get the British and Irish involved. I was to act as a go-between and arrange bouts with the two self-appointed promoters. The interpreter said that, as prisoners of long duration, they had good connections through the French Red Cross, who had persuaded the German authorities to give them the use of a building to hold bouts. I was delighted to have something to do to fill the long hours, as I trawled our compound looking for possible contenders. My initial search yielded only two names: Charlie Smyth, a Londoner, who had boxed for the Royal Army Service Corp at lightweight, and Kilty O'Rourke, a Cavan man and former member of the Faughs boxing team. I was delighted to have the chance to box again, and Billy Meniece, my mentor from my fighting days in Malta, back in my corner again.

Within a week of our initial contact, the three of us were boxing inside the French compound. Kilty and myself lost on points over four rounds, while Charlie won easily, and delighted the international audience. The two French organisers also boxed on the bill, and were delighted with our showing. Cigarettes were both the entry fee and the prizes, and the French gave me some more Red Cross biscuits, to add to the purse of cigarettes. Although, as a non-smoker, I could have bartered the cigarettes for bread, on this occasion I shared them out between my friends Wee Davy, Walter and Andy, and kept the biscuits for myself. It had been a long time since they'd had a cigarette and they were ecstatic: the pleasure of dragging on a smoke eased their pain. To see their tense faces relax with every drag of the weed strengthened my resolve to remain a non-smoker.

The fight game was proving popular once again. When the French realised that we had no gloves for sparring, they loaned us theirs. Our Man of Confidence got permission for us to train in the wash-house, and eventually he even produced four sets of gloves. Unfortunately, when we were split up and sent to different POW camps, we lost some of our best scrappers. On the advice of Meniece and Charlie White – Charlie Smyth's corner man – we stalled the French for a while before agreeing to box again.

On our first outing, we had been out of condition, not having trained in a long time and, combined with our discrepancy in weight and poor diet, it had favoured our opponents, who were fitter and had ways of supplementing their diet. As a come-on, the French offered a higher purse of more biscuits and cigarettes: our resolve weakened and we agreed to box in their compound. This time it was down to me, Charlie Smyth and a chap from the West Kents, as Kilty O'Rourke had been injured. I was beaten once more, as was the guy from the West Kents, but the French had no one to match Smyth, who ran out a clear winner again. The Poles and Serbs raised the roof in support of him, passing us extra cigarettes in appreciation. I beat a hasty retreat with my ears ringing – and my ribs sore to the touch. On the way back to our compound, I risked approaching a German sentry and, in my best Dublin accent, asked '*Cigareten for brot?*' – translation 'Cigs for bread?' He urged me to wait and, in the fading light, I could see him bend over something. We did a quick swap, and I made a beeline for our hut with my precious bread.

I was still feeling battered after my fray. My opponent was so concerned about the state of my health after the fight that he risked crossing the wire into our compound, to see for himself how much damage he'd done. He apologised so profusely that I got tired of it, and almost told him, through my swollen tongue and split lips, to f—k off.

In March 1944, our fifth week in Stalag XIA, two wonderful events happened. A new intake of prisoners arrived from the Italian campaign, and the first issue of Canadian Red Cross parcels arrived. Searching the faces of the newcomers, I was delighted to find Billy Brazil, a friend from my juvenile boxing days at St Joseph's Club, in Dublin, in the thirties. Before he'd had time to settle in, I'd signed him up for the team. I was delighted when he introduced me to big Bill O'Connor, a very handy heavyweight, and his friend Jim Donnelly, another Dubliner. They were still suffering the effects of the arduous campaign in North Africa and Italy, and needed time to build up their strength. They became part of our boxing team, and over the following weeks' training, they came into their own, and were very hard to stay with – a real handful in the ring.

With Kilty back on form, we all linked up for our next outing and gave a great account of ourselves: all five of us won our bouts. Charlie Smyth now had a rival for popularity, as Brazil's extraordinary speed and skill became an immediate hit, with all the nationalities picking up the chant of 'Brazil! Brazil! Brazil!'; this became his pre-fight chant at subsequent outings. Unfortunately, the Germans decided to send the Irish prisoners to the newly set up Stalag 3A, which was to be a specifically Irish camp; when they failed to get our cooperation for this plan, it ended up being a multinational camp. Some of us, including me, claimed that we'd been born in Northern Ireland, so as to be able to stay with my northern friends, with whom I'd campaigned through thick and thin since 1937. Jim Donnelly, still very ill from the North African and Italian campaigns, ended up in the hospital and missed the transfer to Stalag 3A.

Over the next eleven months, I took part in seven contests, mainly against French and Belgian opponents. My penultimate bout against a Belgian fighter, held in the British compound in 1944, was not without some drama. A Belgian boxing veteran was both the referee and the sole judge. I had the better of my opponent over three rounds. As soon as he raised my opponent's hand as the winner, the Polish prisoners revolted, pelting him with stones, and even throwing a chair into the ring. Continuous booing followed from what was becoming an ugly crowd. Panicked, the Belgian sought advice from the French organiser, and then made towards me, to raise my hand, but was prevented from doing so by my corner man, who advised him to call it a draw. He then raised *both* our hands! But this didn't satisfy the crowd, and Otto had to step in and take control of the situation, dispersing the audience back to their compounds.

30

All Chiefs and No Indians

In accordance with the Geneva Convention, any prisoner holding a full rank from corporal upwards could not be forced to do work in a POW camp. Knowing that we were literally starving, the Germans tried to lure us into transferring to work camps, where extra food was available. On principle, we would do nothing to assist the German cause, or help them to release German workers for front-line activities in the armed forces. Despite our hunger, not a single man volunteered. The Germans decided that they would transfer a number of prisoners below the rank of corporal to the work camps. We weren't done yet. While we continued to hold out, prepared to live with our starvation diet and lousy conditions, the lads below the rank of corporal were taking to promoting themselves, by stitching an extra stripe on to what was left of their uniforms.

At roll-call the next morning, the commandant, moving through the ranks to take count, found it hard to believe that *all* his captured prisoners held full rank, and were therefore protected under the Geneva Convention. Otto, the giant German guard, found it hard to conceal his smile. As he moved through the ranks behind his commandant, he muttered in English: 'All bloody chiefs, no bloody Indians.'

The commandant, naturally furious, kept us on parade, in atrocious below-zero weather, for more than two hours, carrying out a full search of our huts. A further 'lightning strike' roll-call and search later that morning found nothing, despite his best efforts. Meanwhile, Davy was tormenting us with his descriptive reminiscence of the beautiful soda farls his wife baked for him back home. You could almost see the melting butter running down his chin as he washed the farls down with a cup of steaming-hot tea. He'd then produce a filthy rag to 'wipe the butter from his mouth', and lick each buttery finger, before lighting up a butt-end no bigger than a fingernail. Blowing the smoke upwards, he continued to drink his imaginary cup of tea. This became a regular occurrence, with Davy dining on a different meal each time. As he tore up a slice of bread to mop up the remnants of a portion of spare ribs, he'd break into song:

Ham and eggs may do old hags and other sort of gluttons
But when I go down to Gresham St and into Lizzie Huttons
I throw my kadie below the seat and yell for bacon cuttings.

All this talk of food made us even more conscious of our hunger, and yet another crazy idea broke through the laughter. While I was rec-ceing the cookhouse to relieve them of their spuds, I noticed a small window on the side wall of the kitchens. There was a big tree on the adjacent ground and, better still, the area was obscured from the searchlights. Accompanied by my partners-in-crime, I ventured forth to see what we could acquire.

The window, although easy enough to open, was narrow: we need-ed someone agile enough to twist their body like a contortionist. Our good pal George Mullett sprang to mind. As company quartermaster sergeant, George, a Dubliner, had a ton of guts, and, better still, he was very supple. He lost no time in checking out the job in hand and, satisfied that he would be able to make it through the window, we organised the job for the following night.

The plan was simple. George would get in through the window, fill a couple of Red Cross boxes with anything he could get his hands on, and pass the boxes out to me. I'd hand them on to Walter, for offload-ing into a sack we'd hidden behind the big tree, until the sack was full. Davy and Andy were posted as lookouts but it didn't go exactly as planned. It was another bitterly cold night, with an icy wind blowing. In the pitch-black darkness, Walter didn't see or hear any movement to cause him alarm, but when he returned from picking up one of the goodie boxes, he noticed a change in the weight of the sack, and quickly alerted me. By this time, George had been inside the cook-house for over twenty-five minutes, and we were happy that by now our sack should be well stocked. As a baffled Walter examined the sack again, he heard a slight movement nearby. His curiosity aroused, he picked out the outline of a dark shape, fifteen yards from the tree. Mystified, Walter reported that someone, possibly an off-duty German soldier, was stealing 'our' stolen goods from the sack.

I whispered to Walter to stop filling the sack, as I called Davy and Andy back from their lookout positions. The four of us went search-ing the area where Walter had spotted the silhouette. Fearing for his life, a huge Czech soldier, with no place to hide, emerged from the shadows, and in halting English nervously admitted his guilt, as he showed us the potatoes he'd taken from our sack. His long army over-coat had several huge pockets sewn inside, as well as the two standard pockets on the outside, all full of 'our' spuds. The coat dragged the ground: this, combined with his size, made him look like a monster. I had no idea how he expected to get back, over several high barbed-wire fences, to his compound. We gave him the benefit of the doubt. We felt sorry for him and, certain that the spuds were for consump-tion by himself and his friends, gave him enough to cover a couple of meals. He'd come upon our little initiative quite by accident, as he broke curfew to try and scavange anything lying around the com-pounds. We knew exactly how he felt, as we'd done the same many a time, and could see the funny side of it.

When George heard what had happened, he gave us an ultimatum: 'Get me out *now*!' He'd had no trouble wriggling in through the win-dow, but we didn't realise that there was a big drop on the inside, and with no one to give him a leg-up or anything that would support him, he was having real trouble getting out. Managing to reach the window, for the next fifteen minutes he wriggled, half in, half out, as we tried to manoeuvre him through the space. We grabbed at his threadbare clothes, trying not to rip them in our effort to haul him up. We start-ed to panic, as we were afraid that the noise would alert the guards. George was getting worn out, complaining that he was 'Like a sniper's dream: bang in the middle of a target shot.' He whispered angrily: 'Where the hell would you get a target that couldn't run, crawl or even slither out of range. Do *something*, I'm a f—king sitting duck here.' After what seemed like an age, George finally emerged, embarrassed, sore, and feeling sorry for himself – and questioning his own sanity in agreeing so readily to twist himself inside out for a few spuds – starving or not. But, George being George, he quickly put his anger behind him, and was ready to throw his lot in with us, whenever another opportunity came up.

Despite the ungodly hour, and his close call, George, though freezing cold and exhausted, insisted on us going into the wash-house for water to boil the precious spuds, such was his hunger. We could only agree: after all, he'd earned it. The trouble was, we had nothing to light the fire with, and this meant another trawl of the compound, breaking curfew and risking being spotted again in what would in all likelihood be a futile effort to find something with which to start the fire. The whole idea of cooking the spuds at that hour, with little chance of concealing the smoke and smell, not to mention the glow from the blower, was even crazier than breaking into the cookhouse. If we were caught, the Germans would put two and two together, discover that the spuds were missing, and set up a firing squad for us. In the event, we were so indebted to George that we agreed to go ahead. Fate thankfully intervened and prevented us from keeping our promise: we heard loud noises overhead, and realised that they were coming from Allied aircraft. In keeping with international practice, when air raids are anticipated, POW camps are lit up like Christmas trees. Trapped in a small open area, we went to ground, where the thieving Czech soldier had hidden out. Within minutes, the German guards were on the move, cutting off the route back to our hut. Our choices were stark. If we made a bolt for it, we'd likely get a bullet in the back. Alternatively, we could continue to lie low, in the hope that things would calm down and we could make good our escape. There was nothing for it but to doss down where we were and hope for the best, but in temperatures of minus nine or ten, we hoped and prayed that we wouldn't have to stay out there for too long.

About thirty or forty minutes later, the all-clear sounded, but it was still too risky for us to move right away. The ice was thick on the ground, and we were numb to the bone. The need to relieve ourselves became urgent, but the slightest sound or movement would give us away. We were almost at the point of crying with the need to go, but we were worried that the steam from four pools of urine, in sub-zero conditions, would be enough to rouse the attention of the guards. Nature won out, and we were relieved on two counts – the second being the fact that the guards were too occupied with other matters to notice the pall of steam rising beneath the searchlight. After some time, the coast became clear enough for us to make good our escape. Getting upright again was no mean feat; we were almost solid blocks of ice as we made our way back over the barbed-wire fences with our sack of spuds in tow. It proved well worth the ordeal: we were now assured of some food for the next couple of weeks, and the spuds were also a much-valued currency for barter.

31

Starvation Makes S—ts of Us All

Weeks passed, without any improvement in our rations, forcing many prisoners to steal from the potato pits where spuds were stored for winter. The spuds were destined to form part of our diet over the months ahead – if we lasted that long. The Germans spotted the prisoners and let off a few sharp bursts of machine-gun fire, putting an end to the escapade. The skilly soup was now as thin as water, and the prisoners were showing serious signs of malnutrition and starvation: most had swollen stomachs and sagging jaws, and were too weak to stand upright. If any more potatoes were knocked off, it would be impossible for us to survive. Quite apart from the guards' attitude to thieves, the other prisoners demanded that there be severe punishment for any prisoner found stealing. One Middle Eastern prisoner stole bread rations from his fellow POWs and was bodily dragged out by six prisoners, who had dumped him into a five-foot-deep rain-swollen s—t-house channel when Otto, firing his revolver in the air and roaring at the top of his voice as he limped towards them, managed to reach them just in time, before the man's entire body was immersed in the foul-smelling cesspit. The prisoner was escorted to the wash-house, and then to the Lazaretto (the camp hospital), for his own safety.

Dead Men Walking

The heavy rain had turned the ground into a mire. My heavy wooden clogs struck in the mud; I was almost too weak to pull them out, as I dragged myself back to my shelter. The stench from the cesspits hit my nostrils, making me retch. Never before nor since have I experienced such a God-awful stink.

Turning the corner, I heard grunts and groans coming from three Russian POWs. They were struggling to keep their feet in the muddy slime as they pulled a high-wheeled wagon over the toffee-like ground. The wagon was overflowing with the contents of the cesspit, which had been pumped out of it. The men looked exhausted and forlorn, their long, filthy coats hanging off their starved frames, and the bottoms of the coats dragging along the mud- and cess-stained ground. Their fur caps, worn on the Russian front, had seen better days, and offered little protection against the elements. Their precious mess tins were tied to their waists, or around their necks, with a piece of string. Despite all the horrors I'd witnessed in this terrible war, I was shocked by their plight. I was furious to think that they could be treated like dogs by the Germans because their government had not signed up to the Geneva Convention.

My gestures, an attempt at commiseration and support, were met by angry shouts from their German guard, who was well togged out in waterproof clothing. There was nothing I could do to help them. Drowned to the skin, I made my way back to what I now saw as the relative comfort of our prison hut. I later heard that the Russians looked on this job as a reasonably cushy one, given some of the other work they were expected to do!

The Russians had a reputation for being as tough as nails, and, when it came to their efforts to survive, were renowned for their daring. They wouldn't report the death of a comrade for a week or more, as the corpse would be dressed up and brought out, wedged between two men, for roll-call. The Germans were used to seeing 'sick' prisoners being supported by their comrades and, going quickly through a headcount, wouldn't notice the 'dead man walking'. This risky action ensured that they got the dead man's rations for an extra week or more. Desperate times prompted desperate measures.

The Russians perfected another ingenious scam. While standing in line for their rations, a few of them would have an empty sack tied to their back. They had stitched a wire hoop into the top of the sack to keep it open. Mess bowl in hand, and with a dirty rag up his sleeve, the man would push his bowl in and get his ladle of turnip soup. Moving back in the queue, he'd throw the contents of the mess tin over his back, into the sack. After a quick wipe of the bowl with the dirty rag, he'd move forward again in the queue, for another fill-up. The fact that the bottom of his trousers and the back of his overcoat were destroyed with the liquid pouring through the sack was a small price to pay for getting the extra food. Inevitably, the liquid trail gave some of them away, and earned them a few clouts of a rifle butt. Eventually, the Germans began to search them, confiscating the sacks before the prisoners reached the ration queue. This was a high-risk enterprise for such a small return, and was indicative of their extreme hunger.

For my part, there was nothing to do but to continue trawling the compound, in the hope of coming upon something useful. With darkness descending, and the cold and hunger taking their toll, each step in the biting wind felt like a dozen, as I tried to think of a way out of our dilemma. My thoughts were interrupted by loud exchanges between the guards and some soldiers driving trucks. Trying to avoid being picked up by the searchlights, I flattened myself against a brick wall to see what was going on. Not understanding German very well, I didn't get the whole picture, but I grasped that the lorries were heading for the cookhouse. I beat a hasty retreat back to my hut – or at least as quick as my leaden clogs and my frozen feet would allow. Climbing onto the top bunk, from where I had a clear view of the back of the cookhouse, I realised that, contrary to the Geneva Convention, there was a German garrison beside our camp and the Germans were stockpiling potatoes in pits.

I filled in the lads as to what was going on, and we began making plans. After roll-call the following morning, we began our reconnaissance, and discovered that, behind the cookhouse, and detached from the main prison camp, were five large ridges which were fenced off from the main camp. While the others kept a lookout, I confirmed that the ridges all held potatoes, which had been unloaded from the lorries the previous night. High above the wall of the cookhouse was a sentry box, manned by a German guard operating searchlights that covered this area. The garrison was separated from the camp by a wall which had one blind spot – next to the cookhouse – but the area was patrolled by sentries and their Alsation dogs. I checked the double strand of barbed wire and was satisfied that I could unravel it sufficiently to allow one man to gain entry to the potato pits and rebind the wire to avoid detection. The old SBS tricks always came in handy!

Myself, Andy Roy, Walter Pancott and Wee Davy Thompson put our heads together like military strategists planning a campaign, assessing the risks and trying to find ways of reducing them. No move could be made before we had established the pattern of the sentries on searchlight duties. Andy Roy, a light sleeper, volunteered to keep watch, even though he was desperately ill. For the next three nights, wrapped in a threadbare blanket, he kept the sentries under surveillance. He reported the pattern: a slow, methodical trawl back and forth with the searchlight, followed by a ten-minute break before the next trawl. We calculated that we could make the turnaround in ten minutes. The dog handler was another matter, though: Andy said that his visits to the pit were erratic. The only positive aspect was that, once we were inside the pit, its high sloping sides would hide us from the patrolling sentry – provided that the wind was in the right direction, and the dogs didn't pick up our scent.

On the fourth night, we put the plan into action. At around 2 am, heading for the cookhouse, we crept across the compound in complete darkness, the black of the night interrupted now and then by the piercing searchlight, sweeping the area, as we quickly got up close and personal with the nearest dark wall. I managed to unravel the wire enough to allow entry to the area where the potato pits were located. Gripping the empty sack, I crawled, belly down, for twenty-five yards, to where the pot of gold was buried. Lying parallel to the long sloping pits, I began clawing at the loose soil with my right hand. I could feel the precious spuds and, as I began to tug at them, I could hear a long, low rumbling. In pulling at the spuds, I'd caused a run in the pit, and the soil started to cave into the narrow gullies.

My heart pounding, and my imagination running riot, I was sure that the noise could be heard reverberating around the camp. Holding my breath, I waited for the searchlight to pick me out. As soon as that happened, I'd probably be savaged by the guard dogs. After several minutes without any reaction from the guards, my nerves settled. In pain, my hands frozen, I pulled two or three spuds at a time, while trying to keep my head below the top of the ridge. The sack was half full when I got Davy's warning to move out. Gently patting the soil back into position, so as not to alert the guards that it had been disturbed, I gingerly made my way back with the booty.

PEED OFF

Andy and Walter's timing was dead-on. Right on cue, Davy closed the wire just after I passed through it. His timing perfectly executed, we made our getaway seconds before the patrolling sentry arrived back. I was filthy dirty and covered in potato muck, but my biggest problem was the numbness in my hands, which were frozen solid. In desperation, I peed on them and massaged them vigorously to get the circulation going, while Davy gently twisted my frozen ears. Andy wrapped his threadbare blanket around me, and I walked about to get the blood flowing, before going back to our shelved doss-house. For the following five nights, we went back to the potato patch; alternating with Walter, we took turns going into the lion's den. Now much wiser and better togged out, with our ears and hands covered, the icy grip of the cold wasn't so bad. It was worth it to be able to supplement our diet, and have something to barter with the other nationalities.

Our rations had been reduced to a small loaf between six people, a pat of margarine, a cup of acorn coffee and some watery skilly: in short, not enough to feed a cat. My heart went out to the Trojan Andy, who coughed incessantly. Holding up as best he could, he fumbled in his pockets for his little tin box of loose tobacco, which he had collected from butt-ends.

Sharing the leftovers with Davy, who always seemed to have filthy-looking cigarette papers for a roll-up, the lads managed to get enough tobacco for a few drags. Letting their imagination run wild, they spoke in glowing terms of the virtues of good-quality tobacco. For my part, my self-delusions stretched as far as a dinner of roast lamb, roast potatoes, peas and Bisto gravy. Mmmmm!

After a few more days' potato-raiding, and afraid that the pits would collapse, we were forced to take even greater risks, moving to other pits nearer the patrolling sentry and the searchlight. We didn't do this for too long, though, as Andy was worried that 'even the cutest hens lay out'. He stressed that enough was enough, and insisted that we'd be better off without the spuds than dead men. The operation was called off: we had enough left for us to barter for another week.

32

THE RUSSIAN CHOCOLATE CON

When our spuds ran out, we were thrown back on the camp's starvation diet, and had no fights on offer from the French quarter. The only thing going for us was an improvement in the weather. As spring came and the ground thawed, we sat in the wintry sunshine daydreaming. One day, someone came up with the idea of fermenting barley. (How he acquired this idea is anyone's guess!) The finished product was easier to eat with a spoon than to drink but the effect was intoxicating, and we could genuinely claim to have both drunk and eaten well that day. The ingenuity of the brewer in rigging up the gear and connecting it to the bared electricity wire far exceeded the quality of the product, but we weren't complaining.

Many other hare-brained ideas were dreamt up as we sat in the sunshine. One suggestion, passed on to me 'in confidence' by a New Zealander known to all as Kiwi, was that it was time I 'got something from the Ruskies'. I was puzzled as to what he meant, but my confusion turned to enthusiasm when this top-notch barterer outlined his plan. He produced a piece of wood covered in silver paper, the same size as the bars of chocolate in the Canadian Red Cross parcels. Placing it in a well-preserved chocolate wrapper, he assured me that it would pass off as the real McCoy. I was torn between the devil in me, and my sneaking regard for the Russians. My head was saying 'no', but the 'yes' signals from my stomach were stronger.

Andy Roy was delighted with the idea, and began stuffing my haversack with paper, to give the impression that the food parcels had been restored. He promised that I'd be the only Catholic to get the freedom of the Sandy Row, if I agreed to go through with it. I was under a barrage from the syndicate to have a go – particularly from Andy, who would trade his share of the food for a cigarette any day. I was concerned on another front too. If the con trick worked, it might end my future bartering of genuine goods.

Weighing the pros and cons, I came to the conclusion that the possibility of seeing a food parcel again was remote, and decided to go for it. The hard-done-by Russians had a number of spivs, who managed to squeeze their way into the bartering racket while working outside the camps. Perhaps I could con one of these hard-nosed traders. I began watching the searchlights, for my opportunity to get over the wire unseen.

I worked my way over the French, Polish and Yugoslavian compounds, and it was pitch black by the time I made it to the Russian fence, where a lot of Serbs were having their nightly chat with the Russians. I showed off the 'chocolate' while saying '*Chleb*' – meaning 'Bread': a young Russian quickly shoved a loaf through the wire, and the exchange was made. My heart was racing, and I ran as fast as I could, to clear the Yugoslav compound before the Russian found out that he'd been conned. Discovering that his chocolate wasn't chocolate, the infuriated Russian alerted his fellow prisoners to the con.

Amid roars of laughter and threats to my person by the Serbs, the Russian's roars rang through the night. I couldn't understand what he was saying, but I knew he wasn't a happy man. With diplomatic relations at their lowest, I beat a hasty retreat, before his shouting alerted the German sentries. Back at the hut, the boys devoured the bread, while I tried to get some shut-eye, the nagging guilt of pulling a fast one on a fellow prisoner keeping me from sleeping. I tried to ease my conscience by remembering that he was a shady character who made a killing outside the camp, but it didn't help, as I lay there feeling sorry about what I'd done. I consoled myself with the fact that, with no more food parcels expected, I would probably never run into him again.

Five weeks later, some food parcels unexpectedly arrived in the British compound. I had mixed feelings: I was jumping for joy on the one hand, and dreading the inevitable encounter with the Russian on the other. I resolved to confine my trade to other nationalities, and steer well away from the Russians. Off I went with my first lot of goodies. Trade was brisk, and contact with the Russians wasn't necessary. My second and third ventures were equally successful, and with just two or three items left to trade, I confidently ventured out a fourth time, offering the goods to the French, Belgian, Polish and Yugoslavs. This time, though, there were no takers, as they had nothing to barter.

There was nothing for it but to push my luck with the Russians, and I doubled back to tell the syndicate my predicament. If I could get by without being recognised, it might work. Davy suggested that I brazenly deny being the con artist, while Walter said that we should send the Kiwi, as the con had been his idea. As it was getting dark, I decided to give it a go. Wearing glasses and a borrowed woolly hat, I headed for the Russian fence. I was edgy as I joined in the bartering, but after having had success trading soap and spam, my confidence grew. I had just one tin of bully beef left. Displaying it boldly, I asked for bread in return. Immediately a young Russian came forward, pushing a loaf through to me, and I parted with the bully beef.

As I walked away, pleased with myself that I'd finished the job, I heard roars of laughter coming from the Russian compound. Taking a closer look at my parcel, I realised that it contained not the bread I'd expected, but a rock! I could do nothing but laugh: it was payback time. I smiled at the Russian and said 'Tit for tat' as I gave him the thumbs-up. If nothing else, it helped to ease my still-nagging conscience.

POLES APART

If we thought the poor Russians were hard done by, the Poles weren't far behind. It had been raining for hours, and the camp was a quagmire, as we watched the Germans erect a makeshift tent, on the sea of mud that had been the sports pitch. We looked on as more than two hundred and fifty distressed, dirty and cold Polish civilians, including children, were herded into the tent, prisoners of the Reich. Some were emaciated, and all were soaked to the skin as they queued on weary legs for a ladle of skilly. On their second day, the rain stopped and they drifted towards our fence in search of a friendly face. Few could speak

English, but those that could told their compatriots of our serious concern for them.

The Poles told us about the ghettos in Warsaw, from where they'd been snatched. After being taken prisoner, they had no idea where they were. Though we hadn't a lot ourselves, we felt compassion for their plight. When a few Red Cross parcels came through, most of us shared our food with these poor wretches. Unfortunately, man's inhumanity to man is ever present, and a very small minority of British POWs exploited them, by trading food in return for their jewellery, or treasured keepsakes, which they'd hidden from the Germans, at risk to their very lives.

It was only long after the Poles departure that we learned the true extent of their hardships and bravery. They were part of an exceptionally heroic brethren that had stood up to, and frequently outwitted, the cruel SS. For this, they were now paying a terrible price. At that time, in late 1944, we, as POWs, were in complete ignorance of the extent of the cruelty and massive destruction of life that was being meted out to the Jewish people.

33

Dog Days

Queuing for our ration of skilly, we speculated as to what kind of animal might have been added to it, to give it some substance. Of late, there had been a greasy layer of animal fat floating on top of the slime. No one had ever seen the beast, but the gamblers amongst us ventured all sorts of opinions, from dogs to rats. No one really cared what animal it was, as long as there was some nourishment in it.

The bell ringing for skilly sent us racing into battle for position in the long, slow queue. Funny things enter your mind when you are cold and irritable, and the food line is moving at a snail's pace. In times like this, Davy, from Newtownards Road in Belfast, was your only man to move along with. He brought humour to any situation, and was sure to lift the mood.

On this occasion, Davy recalled a notice that our 'Man of Confidence', RSM 'Ducksy' Traynor, a stern but witty man, had put on the door of Stalag XIA. The sign said: 'Regimental Sergeant Traynor wishes to thank any prisoner who fed the wee Jack Russell. No doubt the prisoners who subsequently stole and ate the dog would also like to pass on their thanks.' The laughs and guffaws echoed around, as it passed down the queue, reminding those who'd been there, and giving a bit of humour to those who hadn't.

We started to reminisce about other funny moments in Stalag XIA. Sandy Row's Andy Roy recalled when a mutual friend called 'Heelball' – he of the borrowed-uniform fame – trying to get a vantage point to watch a football match, had perched himself on a roof covering the cesspit. Despite being a POW, he still managed to keep himself spick and span – or at least as well as could be managed. No sooner was he positioned on his perch than the rotten wood gave way, pitching him into the overflowing cesspit. Heelball lost many friends over the next few days: no matter how many times he tried to clean himself up, the smell just wouldn't go away!

With more and more funny stories being recalled, the time on the food line seemed to disappear, and even those humourless and normally bad-tempered POWs began to enjoy the craic, and even join in. Witty Walter Pancott from Omagh gave a blow-by-blow account of what had happened to a large number of Russian prisoners in Stalag XIA. Thin, haggard and having had no food during their long journey across Soviet territory, en route to the German prison camp, a few thousand of them had massed together in an angry mood on the sports field. They had no right of protection under the Geneva Convention, nor did they get any Red Cross aid. Starving and out of control, they charged at the German guards, forcing them off the field, and then rushed the fence, trying to smash it down. The panicked guards began firing shots over their heads, to no effect. One guard was so scared that he threw his Alsatian guard dog over the fence to attack the men, giving him time to make his escape. In sarcastic wit, Walter shouted to the guards: 'One dog is no use, it'd take a few hundred of them to feed these starving creatures.' Watching through the fence, we were abruptly rushed away at gunpoint, so we didn't see how the scene finally played out, or how the milling Russians reacted to the presence of the dog. All we knew was that, after a brief spell of growling and barking, the dog disappeared, and was never returned to its handler. It seemed that Walter's angry witticism was prophetic: no doubt the dog was the best – and only – meal some of the Russians had had in a very long time.

Finally, we made it to the top of the soup line, but as usual, after drinking our ladle of turnip soup, we were still hungry. We decided to get our MOC, Ducksy, to put pressure on the Germans to give us more Red Cross parcels. Ducksy went to the camp commandant, armed with the message that things could turn very nasty if there was any further deterioration in our health, and the Red Cross parcels which we knew had been sent to us were not released. We had no joy: the commandant claimed that the train stations had been heavily bombed, and the Red Cross parcels had been destroyed. Questioned as to how the Candians were still getting regular parcels, he said that the German authorities gave preferential treatment to Canadians as their government treated German POWs better than other nations.

Ducksy was not to be beaten, however. He badgered the commandant on a daily basis, until eventually, two weeks later, after more than two months in the camp, we were finally given a few food parcels. We thought all our birthdays has come together as we tore open the parcels and found coffee, blended tea, real butter, spam and bully beef – and a few fags thrown in for good measure. We couldn't have been happier, and eked the precious parcels out for a full two weeks, when we reverted to the camp diet.

To keep the peace, the Germans decided to issue potato peelings and turnip ends, to supplement our diet. After being told that we'd have to queue up for these rations, we put our haversacks in position at 6 AM, even thought they weren't dishing out the 'food' until 10.30. Everyone was on trust not to interfere with the bags, so no one lost their place in the queue. This system worked for a while, but the slivers of potato skins weren't enough to keep us from starvation. It wasn't long before even the potato skins became thin on the ground, and, motivated by hunger and fear, people started to jump the queue, and punches were thrown in an effort to sort out the messers.

On one occasion, when an RAF sergeant jumped a few places, to the disadvantage of another RAF sergeant, things became very bitter. There was an exchange of blows that had them rolling around in the mud, knocking six bells out of each other. Despite the mêlée, no one risked losing their place to break up the fight. The thought struck me that these boys would probably end up as commissioned officers, or wing commanders, flying RAF planes, yet here they were showing basic instincts no better than the common rabble. (Unlike other arms of the military services, promotion was ongoing for some RAF personnel, even while they were serving as POWs.) Wee Davy, seeing the humour in everything, remarked that they weren't much good as boxers: they had more chance of catching pneumonia, with their flailing arms fanning the breeze, than doing damage to each other. I'd had enough, and, with no guard in sight, I attempted to break them up; the fact that they were exhausted helped me in my task. It was an ugly scene, but with starvation, the freezing German weather, and dysentery and other illnesses, things had got to them.

Despite the paucity of the peelings, the queuing system had to be persisted with, as it gave a little extra for us to add to our small loaf of bread. Davy and Walter used their undiscovered penknives, which they had hidden from the guards, to good effect, getting the most from the hard turnip top before boiling it up with the potato peelings. The hot, watery waste vegetable 'soup' was very welcome, and helped ease the pain of the lads' wounds, which were still giving them trouble. Between Davy's thigh wound, Walter's shrapnel, my dysentery, and Andy's persistent cough – and no medical care – we were a right mess. Davy, up to his usual mimicry, finished off this exotic meal with his imaginary Havana cigar, while Andy moaned that, if we only had a few tea leaves, he could use them as tobacco.

Dependent on crumbs from our captors, man's animal nature often comes to the fore. On one occasion, the German cook, doling out the scraps, suddenly realised that he hadn't enough for everyone in the queue. Uncertain about what to do, he wasn't about to tell a long line of hungry men his dilemma. His solution was to throw what he had left on the ground, and let them scrabble for it. What resulted was a free-for-all on the dirty wet ground. Men of all ranks and ages, one of whom had served at Passchendaele in World War I, shamelessly scrambled in pursuit of scraps, bereft of reason, punching and shoving their friends and comrades out of their way, for something which, in other circumstances, would be fed to pigs. Of all the things that I saw people do in order to survive, that scene has always stayed with me, indelibly etched on my memory.

34

Kitless and Witless

The daily drudgery and search for food went on as normal in the camp. Finding something to eat was always on the agenda. As the days turned into months, we were always trying to come up with some new and ingenious scheme to outwit our captors. As Christmas 1944 approached, with temperatures well below freezing and food rations substantially cut back, rumours abounded that we were to be moved yet again, to another prison camp.

One of the few breaks from the routine in the camp was to be sent into the woodland under armed escort, to dig up tree roots for fuel. (With no fuel whatsoever, our stoves had not been on for more than seven weeks, despite the bitterly cold weather.) A few men from each hut took turns doing this job, which was a grim test of endurance, but still a distraction from our terrible situation. On one such occasion, I was part of the digging party. We pulled a high-wheeled wagon for more than two miles, in glacial iciness, and, after a short rest, set about digging out the deeply embedded tree roots. With the German appetite for organisation, we were quickly allocated specific trees, some more than two hundred years old. Despite using crowbars as levers, it was virtually impossible to shift the roots, which were deeply embedded in the frozen ground.

With noses running, the snot freezing onto our faces, and our eyes watering from the blistering wind, we weren't getting any warmer, despite our hard work. One smart-arse cynic from another group kept slagging us, telling us we hadn't got 'the right knack'. Davy, by now at the end of his already short tether, followed through with one of his smart remarks, retorting 'Nor the left one either' – which touched a nerve for the hapless slagger, who was nicknamed 'Kitless' due to the fact that he had parted company with his personal cannon balls in the Italian campaign. Taking umbrage at Davy's quick comeback, he lunged forward, knocking Davy off balance. You couldn't exactly say that a fight broke out: as both men were so tired and weak, more damage could have been done by a woodpecker, despite their pulling at each other. As the tussle was going nowhere, we decided to let them at it, and not interfere. Eventually the guards got fed up, and threatened Davy and Kitless with the butt-end of their rifles, if they didn't cut it out and get back to work.

When work resumed, it became obvious that our group was not up to scratch. With no experience of this kind of work, and little idea about how to pivot the levers to uproot the trees, we were worn out, and had little to show for our efforts. The other group was uprooting three trees to each one of ours. Kitless continued to slag us off about our paltry efforts, but we got the last laugh. At the end of the day, when the wood was doled out, the *feldweber* (sergeant) issued equal amounts of firewood to each group. Kitless was fit to be tied. His veins bulging, he did his best to intimidate the German NCO into yielding to his demands, but the German was in no mood for his behaviour, and left Kitless in no doubt about what would befall him if he continued with his ranting.

Later on, Davy made amends for his smart remark in the woods. Knowing that Kitless was listed for repatriation due to his injuries, he apologised and wished him good luck. There was no malice in his jibe, just the usual back-and-forth banter that was part and parcel of our existence. Back at the compound, the old fireplace was soon roaring, and as soon as the crackling noise of the fire took hold, there was a rush to get close to the heat. In fact, the area became so overcrowded that those of us at the back got little more than the psychological effect of hearing the sparks crackling. After lengthy and bitter exchanges between the 'haves' and the 'have nots', it looked like trouble was brewing.

The mood suddenly changed when Ducksy Traynor burst onto the scene and announced the arrival of food parcels. He was surrounded by a rabble, bombarding him with questions: how many parcels, how would they be divided, who was going to supervise the distribution and, most important of all, when would we get them? Sidestepping those questions, he admonished us with the reminder that we were all trained soldiers, and that he expected controlled behaviour when the final decision on the allotment of the parcels had been made. After his departure, there was no mad rush to return to the fire. Someone had realised that the heat was all going upwards rather than outwards – which soon discouraged us from jockeying for position. Still, we liked the cosy feeling given off by the flickering flame, so we kept it going until the wood ran out.

Christmas 1944 arrived. We got some food parcels, and the Kiwis, with little resources, organised a few good shows to keep us entertained. When the news came through that a young Jewish British soldier, taken away by the SS some weeks previously, had been returned to the camp in reasonable health, we had real cause to celebrate. It made that Christmas, my seventh away from home, AOK.

35

No Escape from Stalag 357

In late December 1944, we were ordered to assemble for an unscheduled search and roll-call. Rumours abounded that some prisoners were to be moved from Stalag XIA. Our fears proved well founded when Hauptmann Mench eventually confirmed the move, but he refused to tell us when we were going, or where we were headed, despite many requests from our 'Man of Confidence'.

At the beginning of January 1945, we were marched to the communal showers for delousing. With five men to one shower at a time, we jostled and elbowed our way close enough to the shower to allow a trickle of water to dampen our bodies before the dreaded call of 'Raus! Raus!' signalled the end of the drips.

With remarkable skill, we managed to wet our bodies and rub on the last of the almost-useless soap from the Red Cross parcels, in an effort to attack the dirt and grime, now layers deep, that had built up on us. Before we had time to wash it off, some villainous German turned the water off. This defied logic: the filth we had trudged more than a mile to dislodge was being carried back with us to the camp. Reduced to rubbing off the dried-on soap with a rough towel, we trudged back to camp in heavy snow and a foul mood, scratching our dry, itchy, soap-encrusted skin as we marched.

Back at Stalag XIA, every door, bed and table edge was used to alleviate the itch, before a couple of heroes stripped off and headed for the open washroom, to splash themselves with icy water. The next phase of delousing called for all our bodily hair to be hacked off with blunt and near-rusty blades. We placed great emphasis on the area around the crotch, where a brigade-strength of lice, watertight and

217

under no threat from the dribble of water, had taken up permanent residence.

After fewer than usual inspections and confiscations, and a minimal amount of harassment, we assumed that the camp commandant wasn't worried that we had anything useful, in the event of an escape attempt. The guards were more conciliatory towards us, their laid-back approach arousing our suspicion. Was German confidence of victory slipping away, or were we being lured into a false sense of security? Whatever it was, we were sure of one thing: we would be on our way yet again, in the freezing German winter, taking with us our trench foot, diarrhoea, abscesses and starvation, en route to God knows where. Under escort, we marched along railway sidings to the lice-ridden mobile doss-houses. We were no sooner aboard than we were attacked by the advancing army of wagon lice, undoing our recent delousing yet again.

We were back to long stopovers, without the doors being opened for food, water or fresh air, or to empty the toilet buckets – to the distress of the mortified dysentery sufferers. In the small hours of the second day of our journey, the train came to a halt and the doors opened, to a blizzard. Ordered outside, we were marched at gunpoint to a field that was deeply covered in snow, unsure what our captors had in mind for us. Was this the end of the road? Were we to end our days in this frozen field somewhere in Germany? To our great relief, we saw the slit trenches that awaited our 'outpourings'. With indecent haste, forty-five arses at a time deposited their load.

Back in the wagons, we were told that a ration of bread, water and macaroni would be issued to us after we'd ferried twelve wagonloads of faeces to the slit trenches. Not exactly the starter we'd have liked! Waiting in line for our food, I managed to catnap in more comfort than could be found on the wagons.

Once the rations had been issued, and the heads had been counted, we were under way again. Rumours of the progress of the Allies led some to believe that perhaps more favourable conditions awaited us: personally, I was more cynical. Eventually we arrived at our new quarters, Stalag 357. Apparently there were two POW camps called 357, one in the Ukraine, close to the Polish border, and ours, situated in Oerbke, near Bremen, which contained prisoners from thirteen nations, including the United States, Ireland, South Africa, Australia, Canada and Britain. Once again, after we had been medically examined and deloused, we were marched to wooden buildings, which housed triple-decked bunks covered with gunny sacks. Each building initially housed around one hundred and fifty men, but the number soon grew, with hundreds of men sleeping on the ground.

At six the following morning, a reception committee of goons came into our huts, yelling our favourite tune, '*Raus! Raus!*' as they banged on our beds, telling us to get outside for roll-call. This was followed by head counts and recounts; we stood in the snow for more than an hour before they let us queue up for a mug of acorn coffee. Now ready for the so-called documentation check, we got in line, unimpressed by the platoon of Brownshirts, revolvers, daggers and Nazi badges on display, as they marched outside, singing '*Wir fahren gegen England!*', loosely translated as 'We're on our way to England!' This didn't bother us because, unknown to the Germans, we'd heard through an RAF officer called Dean, who operated 'the Canary', a secret radio receiver, that the Allies were making great ground.

The document check was a farce, aimed at demonstrating the guards' power over us. Satisfied that our documents and POW tags were in order, we were lectured on the strict rules for Stalag 357's ten thousand prisoners. We soon got the measure of this awful place, as we walked the endless barren compounds. Everywhere you looked you saw near-skeletons, walking aimlessly, in search of any distraction. Hopefully, we would not descend to this level of misery.

Over the weeks and months, we scavenged the compound looking for scraps of vegetable waste. It was a free-for-all scramble on the filthy ground, by men of all ranks and ages, in pursuit of what wasn't fit for pigs. On many occasions, we complained about the threadbare, lice-ridden palliasses we had to sleep on. The Germans ignored us. We refused to turn out for *appel* – roll-call – and in response they tore out our bedding and piled it high outside the huts, where it remained, in all weather, for weeks. The ice and snow killed off the lice outside, but the bolshie little bastards, still residing in the huts, moved to the warmer quarters of our bodies. Ducksy eventually won the day by getting a guarantee that, provided we turned out for roll-call on two successive days, new palliasses would be issued. That's exactly what happened.

The biting German cold never seemed to leave us. Outside, we kept moving around in an effort to get warm, but the howling wind made this impossible. Davy Thompson drew our attention to the thin smoke drifting upwards from some huts in the distance. It took us fifteen minutes to make our way across to investigate, and we were pleasantly surprised by what we found. Three Canadians were on their knees, brewing coffee. It seemed that the Canadians were still getting Red Cross parcels, at a time when no other nationalities were so fortunate. They looked a lot healthier than us miserable lot, but they made no effort to share anything with us. But for the brass neck of Walter, who unashamedly said that they wouldn't miss a couple of spoons of coffee to share between us, we'd have been left looking on. Hesitantly, one of the Canadians half filled two improvised drinking vessels, to share between the five of us. It was like manna from heaven. The Canadians apologetically reminded us that, difficult as it was, for obvious reasons they had no option but to discourage the pleas of other POWs. We understood, but we still couldn't come to terms with why they were getting preferential treatment with food parcels, when other people were dropping dead from starvation.

We resolved to organise a rota of prisoners to put more pressure – if this was possible – on our 'Man of Confidence', to try to force the German commandant's hand, but after six weeks of constant demands, the commandant was still giving priority to the Canadians. Eventually, after two months, we were issued with one Red Cross parcel between two prisoners. All our birthdays came together, as we tasted spam and bully beef, and sipped real coffee for the first time in a very long time. These were to be the last Red Cross parcels we'd see until Liberation. With our 'Canary' still singing happy tunes, we were just hanging in there, trying to stay alive, until the Allies reached us. Seeing our renewed spirit, and guessing that something was afoot, the guards increased the searches and roll-calls, many carried out at ungodly hours, and became increasingly frustrated and aggressive when no escape plan was uncovered.

February was a bleak month, with no news coming through from our 'Canary'. In March, we heard the news that the US First Army had crossed the Rhine: we were certain that our release could not be far off. We occupied ourselves with trying to stick bits and pieces of maps together, working out strategies and guestimating when our liberators would arrive. Unfortunately, we were to endure several more months of very bad conditions before we would see freedom. The German authorities decided to move as many prisoners as possible to another POW camp. No one knew why, but we speculated that they didn't want the Allied forces to see the conditions under which we were being held, which were in breach of the Geneva Convention. For our part, we were worried that our liberation would be delayed further by this move.

We weren't wrong. In April 1945, more than a thousand of us were marched out of Stalag 357, destination unknown. We were sick and weak, but in fairness the guards didn't force the pace, but spread out on either side of our column at twenty-five-yard intervals, with a couple of motorbike outriders moving back and forth. After five hours on the move, with a short break for a ration of bread and water, we were back on the road. One of our outriders went ahead to commandeer barns where we could shelter for the night, but first we had another three or four hours' walk ahead of us.

Before being marched out of Stalag 357, we'd had more good news from the Canary, and I'd made up my mind to escape, as God knows what they were planning for us. It was dangerous – I had no plan, map or rations, or even the faintest idea where I was headed – but I decided to take my chances.

As we were marching, Davy Thompson and Bobby O'Neill saw me deep in thought, and kept tabs on me. I didn't want to involve them in my recklessness, but they knew me too well, and stuck close by, as the order to march on was given. Fifteen minutes out, I spotted my opportunity, and as we passed a deep ditch which offered some cover, I indicated to Bobby that I was about to do a bunk. I dropped into the trench and lay prone on the damp brambles. Within minutes, Bobby and Davy joined me, fifteen yards apart. Satisfied that the tail end of the march was out of sight, Davy jokingly asked about my master plan, as we rolled around laughing.

Not wanting to be found in open ground, we decided to find some cover. Moving out on all fours for about sixty yards, we spotted a small shed: the pile of logs stacked outside meant that the woodland couldn't be far away. Fifteen minutes later, we found it. We tried to shelter from the wind and rain, and get some sleep in the forest. After an hour's rest, we trawled in search of food and cover, but without luck. We were all in a bad way, between dysentery, hunger and diarrhoea, and making little progress. Davy literally covered our arses, keeping a lookout as we did our business. Suddenly, Davy raised his voice in warning. Too late, we looked around and saw a German *wehrmacht*, his rifle sights fixed on our bare behinds. The German yelled '*Aufhören! Aufstehen!*' ('Stop! Get up!') With the dysentery in charge, I stayed where I was, unable to obey his command. The German was soon joined by the rest of his section, shouting in angry chorus, as Davy tried to explain my affliction. Having finally finished my business – literally caught with my trousers down – I struggled to pull up my battledress and came face to face with the German sergeant and seven of his stooges. Meekly, we obeyed their instructions, and marched for twenty minutes to waiting army lorries, prisoners once more.

At the rate the Germans were putting distance between themselves and Stalag 357, it seemed that we were right, and liberation for the camp was close at hand. Although we were probably destined for a longer wait for freedom, I didn't regret trying to escape: nothing ventured, nothing gained. In other circumstances, had we been more sound of wind and limb, we might have made it.

We were surprised when, some hours later, we drove through the gates of Stalag 357. The guards seemed laid back and well disposed towards us, taking me to the camp doctor, who diagnosed a variety of problems, for which he had no medication. He dug up a concoction of white stuff, and detained me in his makeshift Lazaretto, giving me a cup of ersatz coffee, and a ration of rye bread and potato soup, before discharging me the following day. In the days that followed, the rations were sauerkraut and shredded cabbage fermented in brine – disastrous for my troubled stomach. Starving, I struggled to eat it, with disastrous side effects, and was soon back to the doctor, who could do nothing for me.

At this stage of my POW days, still on the prowl for anything useful, I came across a couple of drunken sods roaring and shouting, unconcerned about the guards close by. Next day, aided and abetted by the usual boys – Walter, Andy Roy, Wee Davy and Bobby O'Neill – we kept watch and saw the men from the day before, now sober and correct, approaching a hut. Chancing our arm, we followed them in, just as two well-oiled revellers were leaving. We immediately got the whiff of rum from them, but were stopped in our tracks by a POW, who was acting as bouncer. He denied that there was any drink to be had, and he was backed up by his mates, despite the evidence of left-over scraps of barley and rice grains clearly visible on the table. In other circumstances we'd have argued the toss but, outnumbered by a large number of hostile prisoners, we chose not to have a go. Juiceless and fruitless, we slithered away.

Soon, circumstances changed for the better. The guards, realising that the Allies would soon arrive mob-handed, became inordinately obliging, and handed out fruit, rice and rum essence, creating a plethora of would-be distillers. All that was left was to drink it: we were king for the day, and f—k the begrudgers. Those afflicted with the usual diseases had their enthusiasm dampened as they staggered towards the latrines, coming to a halt a hundred yards short of the place. Eventually, the gratings in front of the huts became the new loos for dozens of performers. The effect was so awful that our liberators would need to arrive in respirators. The supply of gargle dried up, but the pong remained for a further week. It became so bad that the Germans relented and gave us disinfectant, and power hoses to wash down our sleeping quarters.

Within days, the German security presence became almost non-existent: a clear indication that the Allies were closing in. Many of the lower-ranking Germans disappeared, and we were sorely tempted to do the same, but senior NCOs warned against it. Within two hours, testing the water, Walter, Andy, Digger Dawson and myself, joined by a few others, advanced on the large gate and walked free. Subsequently, an advance guard of British troops manning tanks arrived at the camp. The name of the unit escaped me, but I later learned that they were the recce troops of the 8th Irish Hussars, to whom I will be eternally grateful.

Hungry and weary, and waiting for the main body of troops to arrive, we descended on the nearest village. Together with POWs of all nationalities, we moved towards the huge doors of a warehouse, and forced them open. It was like Aladdin's cave, as we set about plundering the spoils. The booty was encased in large wooden boxes, the contents described in German. We managed to wrestle one case outside, using large rocks to break it open. Diving in, we pulled out some packaged material, only to discover that we had stolen a case of concentrated sugar – which was used to keep up the energy of battle-worn front-line soldiers, but was no good to us. Cursing our bad luck, we were passed by a number of Russian soldiers on their way to the warehouse. We abandoned the sugar and joined forces with them, competing for loot with everyone else. With the next case, luck favoured us, as it turned out to be a crate of meat. We secured two large seven-pound tins and battled through the throng, resisting all attempts to relieve us of our loot, as the starving men tried to wrestle it from us – only for us to run straight into the arms of the advancing British Redcaps. Four pistol shots echoed in our ears as, standing at strategic points alongside the advancing Allies, they put an end to the looting. Firing more shots, they yelled to the looters to withdraw. This had the desired result among the British POWs, but in the mayhem that followed, those of us who were close to the side gate managed to get out with our spoils.

Having made good our escape, we moved to a green verge and, with difficulty, prised open one of the large tins. We devoured the meat with dirty hands, not caring that it tasted gamey and very salty, leaving us with an immediate thirst. As we gorged ourselves, vast numbers of Russian POWs passed by, struggling to carry their booty, completely ignoring the Redcaps. Our good wishes went with them: we hoped that their plunder consisted of something more than concentrated sugar. After having been treated so abysmally by the Germans, this was their day.

As we headed back to Stalag 357, a fellow POW told us that he'd seen a German soldier's autocycle hidden in the woods near our camp.

Andy Roy, an expert on motorbikes, led the search. On finding the bike, an Italian Guzzi, he realised that one of the guards had left it full of fuel, ready for his escape. Andy started it up, and with me on the back, he took off, not knowing where we were headed. We were soon stopped by a young British officer, standing beside an open-hatched tank, who told us to turn back. Unknown to us, we had been heading towards Bremen, where a battle was still raging. Doing a U-turn back towards the camp, Andy took time out to give me a short course on riding the bike. With me driving and Andy as a nervous pillion passenger, we headed for the village. Andy several times expected to meet his maker, as I mounted paths and wobbled around, such was my lack of skill on the machine.

I pulled into the side entrance of a house outside the village, in the hope of getting something to eat, and we cautiously knocked at the door. An elderly man, still in his German uniform, opened the door and apprehensively let us in. Inside were a couple of women and some teenagers, who stood motionless, distressed at the presence of foreign soldiers in their midst. With everyone talking, and no one understanding, Andy's innate Christianity came to the fore. Putting his arm around the German soldier, he invited them to take a photograph, as they shook hands. A lot of gibberish followed, but no camera appeared. Andy moved around the room, shaking everyone's hand, and, using sign language and gestures, we offered to leave the house. Satisfied that our purpose was honourable, the German soldier asked us to be seated. They were aware that POWs were roaming the village, and were afraid of reprisals from the Russians in particular. We reassured them that British forces were occupying the village, and advised the elderly soldier to change into civilian clothes for his own safety. He immediately offered us the chance to wash and clean up, and gave us boiled eggs, fresh bread and coffee. Andy's actions had saved the day. Taking leave of this kindly peasant family, the lady apologised for the poor quality of the soap we'd used, and sent us on our way with more eggs and tomatoes: sheer luxury.

If Andy was worried about the perils of the ride out, the return journey was even worse, as I mounted paths, scattered chickens and drove through straggling POWs, often accelerating instead of braking.

We made it back in one piece. Back at the camp, we managed to scavenge a bar of soap that had been left from the Red Cross parcels. We went back to the village and gave it to the old lady, who was overjoyed at our gift.

Despite all the activity of Allied troops in the area, it was to be a few weeks before arrangements were in place to evacuate all ten thousand men from the camp. When my time came, I can't remember a lot about it, except that I was taken in a lorry to an airfield, and flown back to the UK. It was only after my release, at the end of World War II, that I found out that our POW camp was less than twenty miles from the notorious Belsen, where many thousands of poor souls met a horrific end at the hands of the SS.

36

FREE AT LAST, AND I CAN'T REMEMBER A THING!

It's strange that details of the moment for which we'd hoped and prayed for so long still completely elude me. I have absolutely no recollection of how we got to the German airfield, where it was, or anything about it. Perhaps my ill health and weakened state had something to do with it. I remember an advance guard of British troops manning tanks arriving at the camp. I also remember, during a stopover in Belgium, being met by the Red Cross, who offered me a trip to visit Brussels for a couple of hours: being too ill and past caring, I declined.

Landing somewhere in Blighty, I took my first steps on English soil after an absence of almost eight years. Transported in lorries to a large lawn, where lines of marquees had been set up, we were given a wonderful welcome by the Red Cross, who constantly thanked us for our efforts and the sacrifices we had made in the war. These remarkable people were the essence of everything that is decent: without their food parcels, I, and many others, would surely have died in those prisoner-of-war camps. After being stripped, washed and fumigated, and medically examined and questioned, we were issued with new battledress uniforms and gently ushered into one of the marquees, which was laid out with a lavish array of fine delicacies and hot food. Depending on your state of health, which was monitored by the watchful eyes of the Red Cross personnel, you were left to eat as much as you wanted, before it was time for the hospital cases to leave.

I was taken by ambulance to Cambridge Hospital in Aldershot, where the kindly matron and her staff from the Queen Alexander Nursing Service made a great fuss of me. After being allocated a bed, I was visited by a couple of consultants and their medical staff. With my preliminary examination over, I was free to get some shut-eye. Despite sleeping tablets, clean fresh sheets, a thick, well-sprung mattress, and soft pillows (none of which I'd had for years), I still couldn't get to sleep. Even though I was exhausted, I was worried that my dysentery would destroy the bed. Eventually I settled down, to be gently awakened by a cool, soft hand, to clean and pleasant surroundings that were so far removed from those of a prison camp that I thought I was dreaming. It was quite a contrast to sleeping on loose planks, and waking to the shouts of the German guards, the noise of the guard dogs barking and snarling, and the clogs thumping on the concrete floor as we rushed out to the icy compound for roll-call.

I was slow to adapt to the comforts of the hospital, after almost two years as a POW, but after a few weeks I began to leave my previous existence behind me. After a battery of medical tests and examinations, I was diagnosed with eye damage, malnutrition, anaemia, severe haemorrhoids, dysentery, abdominal problems and a few other complaints.

Realising that it had been eight years since I'd seen any of my family in Dublin, the Red Cross offered to bring my parents over to see me, and to put them up in local accommodation until I was well enough to be discharged. Grateful as I was for this wonderful offer, and as much as I wanted to see them again, I had no option but to decline. The last thing I wanted to do was upset my mother, who would have been overcome to see my emaciated body: her strapping son now only skin and bone, and with all my illnesses to boot. My father, on the other hand, a veteran of World War I and a former POW himself, would have taken things in his stride, probably having suffered even worse in his time. A few days later, my spirits were greatly lifted when my two brothers, Archie and Tom, dressed in the uniform of their respective artillery units, arrived at my bedside. It was an emotionally charged reunion. I was at a low ebb, and when I saw my two brothers for the first time in eight years my heart raced and, despite my best efforts, I shed a tear. Archie and my eldest brother Tom had had a tough time in the war, and Archie was recovering from wounds he'd received on D-Day plus 2 – but we were all alive. It was hard to find the words to talk: the lump in my throat almost choked me. It was only much later that Archie told me how shocked they had been when they first saw me: I was just a skeleton. I hadn't realised how bad I looked; by that time I had become used to seeing it.

With ongoing tests and medical examinations, I was pulled, poked and prodded on a daily basis. A sigmoid scope revealed that I needed immediate treatment for a serious stomach infection. In those days before penicillin, the only treatment for this condition was a daily enema, which contained a small amount of arsenic. The object was to retain the injected water for as long as possible. This was difficult, embarrassing and uncomfortable – to the point that, when I saw a nurse approach my bed, I began to ask: 'Friend or enema?' After some time on this treatment, I had the luxury of having my bed pushed out onto the sunny balcony for a couple of hours each day.

Two weeks after his first visit, my brother Archie made a return visit, and remarked on my increase in weight. Maybe he was just trying to make me feel better, but it certainly worked – as did the good food, great treatment, and daily visits from the Red Cross. In great form, I donned my newly issued greatcoat to hide my hospital 'blues', and went AWOL with Archie for a few pints.

I greedily gulped a good mouthful of a creamy pint of Guinness: it tasted wonderful, even better than I remembered. It had been so long since I'd had a drink that a few mouthfuls of the wonderful black velvet elixir were enough to get me drunk. We weren't out long as, acting on good advice from a Redcap, Archie soon steered me back to hospital, slightly the worse for wear. After admonishing me for my silly action, the nursing staff smiled benevolently, and no one gave me away to the matron.

The hospital was like a home from home for me, and I was nourished both mentally and physically. I enjoyed the banter with the other patients. One person in particular comes to mind. His bed was within earshot of the night nurses' station, where they had their nightly cup of tea and a chat. This good-humoured cockney, himself a tea addict, could overhear snatches of their conversation, as he persecuted them for yet another cup of tea at some unearthly hour. Fed up with his constant demands, the nurses ignored his pleas and stopped making him his middle-of-the-night brews. Devastated, he set about devising a scheme to get his longed-for cuppa. He attracted the interest of one nurse, telling her that he was an expert at reading tea leaves. The bluff didn't work initially, until one night, when things had quietened down for the nurses, and their curiosity about the insomniac's alleged psychic ability got the better of them.

Eventually, one nurse approached the soothsayer, who agreed to tell her fortune and was immediately rewarded with a mug of hot tea. Nurse No. 1 sat beside his bed and, finishing her own tea, hesitantly handed over her empty cup and asked him to read the leaves for her. Examining the leaves closely, he was able to tell the young nurse some things about herself that were known to only a few people. Very impressed with his powers, she excitedly went off to tell her friends. One by one, they turned up at his bedside to have their tea leaves read, each time bringing him a cup of tea.

The game was up, however, when the charlatan fortune-teller became too bold, and gave one nurse a spot-on description of 'her' boyfriend. They suddenly realised he'd been eavesdropping on their nightly conversations, and had picked up bits and pieces of information along the way. The nurse on the receiving end of the reading realised that he was actually talking about her friend's boyfriend. Keeping her composure, she let him dig his grave even deeper. By now he almost believed his abilities himself, but he was stymied when she asked him to explain the different shapes formed by the tea leaves, and what they meant. Unable to deliver a convincing answer, he faked an urgent need for the toilet. As he ran for cover, he could hear the laughter of the nurses, echoed by that of the patients, as we were filled in on the man's antics. Concerned at the length of time the chancer was in the toilet, a nurse went in search of him. Pushing open the bathroom door, she laughingly told him that a mug of tea was waiting for him. Unperturbed, the cockney lad emerged and gulped down his cuppa. For nights after that, he was plagued with comical requests to read the leaves of every patient on the ward. The nurses, by then feeling sorry for him, never failed to bring him extra mugs of tea, so either way he won the game.

After another month in hospital, I was in great form. My weight had increased, and for the first time in a very long while I felt mentally alert. All I wanted now was to get home to Dublin. I was given a leave-pass for an indefinite period, due to the decimation of the 2nd Battalion Royal Irish Fusiliers, and was ordered to await a call-up to a holding battalion.

With the chance to go home and visit my parents after eight years away, this indefinite pass was great news. Before heading home, I spent a week in Ealing with my brother Tom and his wife Kathleen, from Tourmakeady in County Mayo, and they and their Mayo friends spared no effort in entertaining me. The suntan I'd acquired after almost six years in the Middle East, which had been lost in the POW camps, had now been restored after my sunbathing on the hospital balcony, and I was in reasonable health. I felt more like a well-heeled tourist than someone who had recently been released from a POW camp. At the end of the week, Tom and Kathleen saw me off, as I headed for the mailboat to Dun Laoghaire, and home. I was as happy as a sandboy.

37

The Boys Are Back in Town

On the long journey back to Ireland, I tried to imagine my parents faces – whether they had changed much – and wondered what had happened while I was away. I couldn't wait to get back home: a far cry from the young lad who thought he'd never get away from Dublin!

As I disembarked from the ship at Dun Laoghaire, my parents, accompanied by my numerous siblings, aunts, uncles and cousins, were out in force to meet me, all of them in tears. After the hugs and kisses, we all boarded the train to Westland Row for the journey home. They couldn't believe that I was really back – large as life – especially as they had twice been notified that I was missing in action. With lots of laughter, good craic and reassurance, the tears soon dried up, all except for the 'Maasie', whose floods of tears rivalled Niagara Falls any day.

Aunt Mary Ellen, who had supported me through my rowdy teenage years, was there once again, to act as a guiding hand. Three days after I landed, she arrived down to my parents' house and invited me to a party she'd organised. She'd arranged for all and sundry who were close to me to celebrate my safe return home. Without a second's thought, the offer of a good hooley was quickly accepted. It was a roaring success, with as many of my family and friends as would squeeze into her place turning up for the party. The porter flowed, and the food, made by Mary Ellen, a wonderful cook, was outstanding. The party took off at a blistering rate, and went on for a couple of days.

I couldn't help thinking about how long it had been since I'd been in such close contact with so many attractive women. My cousins

Mary Ellen (Helen) Harte and her sister Rose, who had been children when I'd seen them last, were now beautiful young women. Cautiously testing the ground with the other young women present, Aunt Mary Ellen made a timely intervention, introducing me to a well-mannered, beautiful blonde. To my great embarrassment, she said: 'Johnnie, meet your future wife.' Aunt Mary Ellen was serious, but I took it to be the mood of the moment. I'm sure the then-eighteen-year-old Maud Murray, the girl who was under threat of being lumbered with a world-ly-wise twenty-four-year-old soldier, was embarrassed beyond belief.

Once we had been left alone, I was captivated by Maud's charm, modesty and good looks. I was even more impressed that, when she was asked to sing, Maud sang arias from various operas, and had the voice of an angel. She seemed too perfect to be true. I was in complete awe, and for some reason felt as though I'd known her all my life. Out of the blue, I was immediately proud of her, and wanted to protect her. Maud agreed to go out with me a few nights later, and I could hardly wait for our first official date. We went to the Carlton Cinema in O'Connell Street. Don't ask me what film we saw: I only had eyes for Maud.

My extended leave of absence lasted three months; every moment was savoured and put to good use. For the first time in my life, aged almost twenty-five, I supped porter with my da and five brothers. Da, who had three sons who were veterans of World War II, and I had plenty to talk about, and we exchanged stories of our wartime experiences. Christy, who never soldiered, and Richie, the youngest, still in his teens, tolerated our speculations about how many Germans had been killed in the wars. Jimmy, my eldest brother, listened, barely able to keep his republican views in check. He was passionate about Ireland and couldn't understand how three of his brothers could have joined the British army. For the most part, though, it was good-humoured slagging and banter, and he bore no malice towards us.

Da was overjoyed to have me keep him company at his ring-throwing competitions, which were common in Dublin pubs at the time. This was big-league stuff, involving serious gambling, and you could hear a pin drop as each contestant pitched. Despite my interest in these contests, I tried to spend time with my mother, to make up for all the worry I had caused her by failing to write home, even when I could have done so.

I linked up with my boyhood friends Bill Kavanagh and Billy Brazil – my sparring partner in Stalag IIA – and other buddies who were on indefinite leave. We spent many a good hour in Doran's pub on Marlborough Street, with Ned Fitzsimons, Johnnie King, Tom Magee and Christy McGuirk joining us on many occasions, and my old sparring partner John 'Spike' McCormack also dropping in for a chat from time to time.

I'd last seen Spike in 1938. By 1945, he was the reigning professional middleweight champion of Ireland. He was in serious training to defend his title and was on the dry, but he stayed around the pub and joined in the craic. There was no shortage of drink at those get-togethers, as most of us qualified to benefit from a British army ruling that awarded one extra day's pay for every month spent overseas during the war. With six full years to our credit, it was just a matter of going to the nearest Post Office, completing a form and, within days, the money would arrive, ready for collection.

I was still unsure whether I wanted to go back to the army, so in the meantime, though still serving as a regular NCO, I put my name down for a job in Guinness, the home of the black stuff. On a trip to the Metropole in Dublin, after just six or seven weeks going out with Maud, I proposed to her – knowing that I would be recalled to the army at any moment. I thought that keeping my job options open was a good move. I was lucky enough to be offered a job with 'Uncle Arthur' – the Guinness brewery – and, with mixed feelings, decided to leave my military career behind as soon as I could get demobbed.

Meanwhile, while wandering around Dublin, taking in the sights and sounds of my home town – a town which I hardly recognised, after having been away from it for so long – I paid a visit to the Carlton Cinema in O'Connell Street. While watching one of the newsreels, I saw the harrowing evidence of the atrocities that had been committed in the German concentration camps. I was filled with anger and disgust. The graphic scenes of death and human misery had burrowed deep into my subconscious. I kept thinking of the poor, haggard Russian soldiers and Polish civilians in Stalag XIA. I hoped that, by some administrative error, they had escaped the barbarity I could see being played out on the cinema screen. As I watched the incredible suffering of the poor wretches that day in the Carlton Cinema, their terror-stricken faces and protrubing ribs, my thoughts went back to the Polish prisoners and the few predatory soldiers who had taken advantage of their plight. Shocked and sickened, I walked out of the cinema without waiting to see the film. In a calmer moment, I trusted that the message of the mass slaughter of Jewish people and others would alert world leaders to similar threats of the cruel exercise of power in the future.

38

ORDERS FROM THE CAPTAIN

Orders came through for me to report for a posting to a holding battalion at Barnsley in Yorkshire. After three months of free rein, I was back in military surroundings, again subjected to supervision.

I was pleasantly surprised to find that Johnnie King, Ned Fitzsimons and Tom Magee had all been assigned to the same unit as me. Bob Harris, a real hard man from Belfast, who'd also served with us, had been recalled a few weeks earlier. We all joined forces as war veterans, thrown in among young soldiers who were unknown to us. The RSM put us to the test, to see if we could fit in and match the strength and stamina of the younger soldiers, by having us race over a mile of ground, in full battledress. In the past, we'd have taken this in our stride, but now we staggered and stumbled at walking pace. Gasping for breath, and bent over, we were well outside the required time, as we fell over the finish line.

The RSM had seen enough, and took an 'out of sight, out of mind' attitude to us, blessing his luck that we were just transitory soldiers. Being given jobs that took us outside of barracks meant that we didn't have to pound the barrack square or cow-tow to the senior NCOs. We were given the 'important' task of collecting coal from the local colliery, in thirty-hundredweight batches. We were conscientious enough about this task for the first three days, but by the fourth day we'd had enough: this was not what we'd joined the army for. On my third or fourth trip with my thirty-hundredweight load, I was joined by Bob Harris. Taking a break for refreshment, we bumped into 'the usual suspects' in the local working men's club, where, over a few drinks, they'd struck a deal with a committee member to supply the club with coal. The bargain having been struck, the coal delivered and the monies received, we stayed a couple more hours at the bar before heading back to barracks. When we arrived back, very drunk, close to lights-out, our fatigues filthy from the coal, and the lorry empty, we were met by two NCOs and the provost sergeant, who lost no time in having us discard our dirty fatigues, scrub down and change into uniform. We were then marched to a cell in the guardroom.

If a charge was laid that night, none of us heard it. Strangely, there was no mention of a charge the following morning either, as we were addressed by the provost sergeant, while we were still very hung-over. After we had been fed, watered and spruced up, we waited to be called before the company commander to be charged with conduct prejudicial to good order and military discipline – the theft of War Department Property. No doubt due to the gravity of the offence, we'd be remanded to appear before the Commanding Officer of the Unit. Kept in suspense, and close to s—tting ourselves, as the realisation of what we had done broke through our drunken haze, it was almost midday before the RSM marched into the guardroom. In hostile tones, he gave us the lecture of our lives, threatening us with everything short of a death sentence.

We hung around impatiently, waiting to hear our fate. Late that afternoon, the RSM made another appearance. Breaking the rule of never speaking until you're spoken to, I, being the highest-ranked amongst us, made our apologies: in truth, it was not too far from grovelling. Responding in a surprisingly conciliatory tone, the RSM remarked on how stupid we'd been. Referring to our past experiences, and our excellent war service, he pointed out that we had put our future army life in jeopardy, then stopped and shook his head in disbelief. With still no mention as to what charges were being laid against us, and with none of us foolish enough to ask, he turned to the provost sergeant and told him to have us ready when he returned, which would be within the hour.

Most of us were convinced that a trip to the CO's office was on the cards, but Bob felt that the will to punish us just wasn't there. He believed that they didn't want the bother of the paperwork, or the need to answer to superior officers, when they could simply transfer us elsewhere. Bob's instincts proved right: an hour later, the RSM informed us that we were being released without charge, and transferred to another holding battalion. McGee, Fitzsimons and King went one way, and I went another, to a different battalion.

39

THE GREAT ESCAPE

I was sent to Newcastle-under-Lyme, near Stoke-on-Trent, to yet another holding battalion. Reporting to the quartermaster sergeant, I found myself in the office of an old friend, and fellow war-veteran, Taffy Morse, who'd served with me in the 2nd Battalion of the Faughs. He greeted me like a long-lost brother: I knew that, if I stayed in the army, I would be well treated in his unit.

I was still undecided as to whether to take release to the regular army reserves or to continue with my army career. Either way, with Taffy doing the paperwork, the outcome would be OK. With the exception of my quartermaster pal, the only other Faugh amongst the hundreds of soldiers at Newcastle was Fusilier Mooney – he of the drinking spree at the Governor's Palace in Malta. Hale and hearty, he was determined to serve out the maximum twenty-one years in the army, until his retirement. We all had a few jars together, but apart from that it was very boring, as there was little to do.

Taffy, aware that I had itchy feet, gave me the job of picking up a young deserter who had been detained by the military section of Scotland Yard. The lad had served less than a month before going AWOL, and had been on the run for more than a year. I had the option of choosing an escort to accompany me. I thought of Mooney but quickly dismissed the idea, as with Mooney on board, neither prisoner nor escort would have made it back to barracks within a week, due to his fondness for a jar. I yielded to the plea of an ambitious, young, skinny Londoner, known as Lanky, who was known to be conscientious. On arrival at Euston Station in London, I arranged a carriage for our return journey. Accompanied by the lanky Londoner, I presented my papers at Scotland Yard and signed for the release of the prisoner into my custody. At the handover, I handcuffed him to Lanky, and waited for our taxi. In generous mood, I yielded to the prisoner's request to make a quick visit to his mother, to say goodbye to her. Following the brief visit, we headed for the train. With plenty of time before departure, I treated us all to pork pies, char and wads (tea and buns) – something neither Lanky nor myself had seen in a long time. Having eaten the pies I'd bought him, the prisoner complained that he was still hungry, despite also having eaten in his mother's house. Reluctantly, I ordered him another helping. By the time we had been served, the place was thronged with soldiers milling around, jockeying for position to get served quickly, before their train arrived.

When the train finally pulled in, it was already packed tight, and we tripped over kit bags, haversacks and hoards of soldiers, all blocking the passageways en route to our carriage. I covered the prisoner's handcuffs with my greatcoat, and offered some of them a seat in our carriage. We settled in for the journey, and I was just dozing off when I was nudged urgently by the prisoner, claiming that he needed to go to the toilet. I knew that we were in for a right trek through the seething masses, and the inevitable long queue for the toilet, but I couldn't take a chance that he was trying it on.

I gave strict instructions to Lanky, and sent him off to beat a path to the toilet, with the prisoner firmly handcuffed to him. Under no circumstances was he to undo the handcuffs until the toilet door was open and he had shoved the prisoner safely inside. Lanky was to remain alert, and as soon as the prisoner made to reopen the door, he was to re-cuff him, before letting him out. With great difficulty, Lanky managed to get him to the toilet door, where he released the cuff on his own arm. With lightening speed, the prisoner smashed the metal handcuff on his wrist into Lanky's face, and after a brief struggle he sent Lanky sprawling over the kitbags and sleeping bodies in the corridor. The prisoner locked himself in the toilet, smashed the window, and pulled the emergency cord. As soon as the train slowed down, and before Lanky could do anything about it, the prisoner made good his escape through the toilet window.

With a near-tearful escort in tow, I jumped onto the track as the train came to a halt, more in hope than out of any real belief that we would be able to catch up with him. Hopefully he'd injured himself jumping from the train before it came to a halt, but no such luck: the bird had flown.

Back aboard the train, I explained the dilemma to our fellow soldiers, in the knowledge that experienced men who make mistakes lose no time in limiting the damage. Outlining my case, I laid it on thick, and asked them to put themselves in my position. I filled them in on my active service, and what I stood to lose over a fleeing deserter. By the time I was finished, they were ready to help, and several witnesses volunteered to make statements against the prisoner, which would help to cover my ass so that I didn't get the blame. I settled for four witnesses. The charge I laid was that the deserter had stolen War Department property – to wit a pair of handcuffs. With regard to the assault and battery of his escort, I charged that Lanky had become unconscious for a few minutes and had needed first aid from a Royal Army Medical Corps man and how, despite a spirited chase, the prisoner had got away. I neglected to mention the fact that I was still dozing in the carriage when the prisoner went to the toilet. Had he thrown a punch at me, I would have knocked the lard out of the cockney wide boy.

Back at the holding battalion, Taffy Morse read my report, which included the name, rank and number of my four witnesses. With a knowing grin, he said that it would make a good yarn when I was eighty: how right he was in that. Over a few jars, Taffy told me that the pursuit of the deserter was low on his priority list – which was just as well for me. My stripes were still intact, the young escort was in no serious trouble, and my testimonial still read 'exemplary'. No matter how tedious things became in Newcastle, from then on I kept my head down and did not volunteer for more exciting duties. I needed scrapes like that like a hole in the head.

40

WEDDING BELLS AND ARMY BRIDES

To say it was love at first sign may seem romantic foolishness, but that's exactly what it was. With the date set for my wedding, Taffy arranged a leave pass for me and wished me luck, and off I went to Dublin, to marry the girl of my dreams. Within six months of my welcome-home party, we were married in Berkeley Road Church, close to the Mater Hospital in Dublin, on 25 November 1945. Maud's sister Florrie was bridesmaid, and my childhood friend and fellow soldier Bill Kavanagh was my best man. Bill later married my first cousin, Helen (Mary Ellen) Harte, having met her at my welcome-home party: once again, Aunt Mary Ellen did the honours as matchmaker. Aunt Mary Ellen, who was responsible for all such events in the family, also organised our wedding reception, and relatives from both sides pitched in to help. It was a great hooley, and lasted for two days, with no shortage of food or drink. A blind eye was turned to a number of gatecrashers, all of whom were known to us: they just wanted a few free drinks and a sample of my aunt's legendary cooking, which included a magnificent three-tiered wedding cake. On 9 December, to the sound of good wishes from all, we climbed the gangway of a ship bound for Liverpool. Unlike when I smuggled aboard as a penniless sixteen-year-old, this time, being a man of means, I paid the fare!

Maud went to live with my sister and her husband in Liverpool, while I reported back to barracks at Newcastle, pleasantly surprised to find that Taffy had arranged a cushy number for me. As I was a seasoned soldier (and all of twenty-five), assisted by a young sergeant I took charge of the drill and weapons training for the young soldiers who were waiting to be posted.

A very understanding Taffy arranged weekend passes, so that I could spend time with my new bride, until the time inevitably came for me to be posted elsewhere, this time to Cirencester, Gloustershire, in the heart of the Cotswolds.

To this day, I still find it difficult to understand the purpose of the posting. The duties of this small, tightly knit group seemed very remote from that of an infantry holding battalion. Loosely organised, and apparently self-governing, it was located in American-style 'Elephant' shelters – so called because of their resemblence to the high, wide, rounded back of an elephant – with very comfortable barrack rooms that provided relaxation and sleeping areas. It took me a while to get used to the easygoing atmosphere that prevailed: there were no demands to get on parade at the double. Another difference was that we were now soldiering alongside the WRAC – the Women's Royal Army Corps, a highly efficient bunch of ladies who were very helpful in briefing you on your duties. In my case, an Irish girl from Waterford called O'Shea helped me in sorting the substantial amount of post and documents that was coming my way, ensuring that no one missed a deadline and that no posting was 'mislaid' – something with which I was all too familiar, as it changed the course of my war and my time in the SBS.

They were a good crowd in Cirencester, and twelve or fifteen of us would often go down to the local boozer, half a mile from the camp, for a few jars and a bit of craic. On one such trip, the worse for wear, we took a firkin of beer from outside the storehouse and rolled it all the way back to camp. The Waterford lass was mortified, but the rest were on for a party. The fact that we managed to get the bulky cask back to the Elephant shelters, unchallenged by any sentries, is a clear indication of just how relaxed things were at Cirencester. Our problem was how to hide eight gallons of ale while at the same time making it readily accessible. We found the ideal location, in a shelter that had once been used for church services, and set up the 'bar'. A Scottish lad managed to get a tap from the canteen and set it up, ready for the party. Over the next couple of days, we all visited the 'sheebeen' until the well ran dry. The problem now was how to dispose of the empty cask. The solution was right under our noses: I found the cask a resting place behind the NAFFI canteen, with the other 'empties'. This was a case of hiding a tree in the woods. The lovely O'Shea stopped reprimanding us and got back on speaking terms with me. Although nothing was heard from the publican, who hadn't even missed the cask, the canteen manageress kept asking about the extra barrel, wondering aloud how it had got there. I enjoyed my time with that group of people in Cirencester, but I'd made my decision: it was time for me to move on to Wolverhampton, where I would await my release from the regular army.

Part of the demob process involved an agency assessment for job suitability – something the British army still does to this day. I listened intently as a man in front of me was interviewed by a clerk, to assess his job potential. Seeing that he'd been employed as a miner prior to the war, the clerk delightedly told him that he'd have no problem getting him his old job back, down the mines. I'll never forget the man's reaction. In angry tones, he shouted: 'If Aneurin Bevan* wants coal, he can f—king dig it himself.'

---

* Aneurin (Nye) Bevin, who was British Labour Minister in 1945, was the son of a coal miner, and was himself a miner until his health forced him to quit.

41

End Game

A New Beginning

The shrewd judgement by my aunt led to an exceptionally happy and enduring marriage to Maud: the marriage lasted for thirty-two and a half years, until her untimely death from cancer in 1977. The loss of my constant companion was more shattering than living under the threat of any bomb or bullet. Emptiness offers no cover, nor grief respite. For more than three years, torn as I was with unremitting grief, my only solution was to drown my sorrow, until one day I finally, and reluctantly, released Maud into God's hands.

Gradually, one day at a time, like a recovering alcoholic, I came to terms with her death, without ever forgetting her. Our marriage was blessed with two children: a daughter Marie, a doctor, and a son Thomas, who is in the printing business. I was doubly blessed in later years to find love for a second time in the form of a wonderful lady, Myra, who agreed to take me on, and become my wife. We have been very happily married for almost twenty-five years. After the war, I took a job with Guinness, the world-famous brewery in Dublin, where I was a union representative for twenty-seven years. I was elected to the Seanad in 1973, and was re-elected six times, serving there until I retired in 1993. I continue to be active in numerous organisations, and serve on several committees.

I am currently assistant treasurer of the Society of Former Irish Parliamentarians and was a founding member of the Guinness Workers Employment Fund, a precursor to the current Guinness Enterprise Centre, where, incidentally, my publishers are based. I was also vice-president of the Irish Ex-Boxers Association, and am honorary life president of the Guinness Pensioners Association and vice-chairman of the Jim Larkin Credit Union, based in Dublin's Liberty Hall. I continue to enjoy relative good health and have never lost my taste for travel and adventure – although nowadays it is more likely to be a holiday in the sun, or perhaps a gentle cruise – a far cry from the nightmare journeys on our prison ships.

I'm often asked, given what I know now – about the hardships, the wanton death and destruction of friend and foe, the prison camps, and all that went with it – whether I would do it all again. My answer is always the same: as long as there are people of the calibre of Hitler suppressing people, if it was within my capacity, I would have no hesitation in making a full commitment to ensuring people's freedom, whatever the outcome for my personal safety.

COMRADES

INSIDE THE WAR OF INDEPENDENCE

ANNIE RYAN

'an extremely worthy companion volume to the excellent *Witnesses: Inside the Easter Rising*'

Metro

'an interesting addition to the study of the period'

Verbal

'It is gripping warts-and-all stuff and deserves a wide audience and certainly adds to our understanding of this vital part of Irish history'

Books Ireland

Hardback €25 | ISBN 978–1–905483–22–8
Paperback €14.99 | ISBN 978–1–905483–14–3

Available from all good bookshops and from www.LibertiesPress.com

WITNESSES

INSIDE THE EASTER RISING

ANNIE RYAN

'an entertaining book that gives us an insight into the way some of the ordinary people involved in the Easter Rising recalled that experience forty years later. Their voices come through with a lively immediacy that is very attractive.'

History Ireland

'A remarkable new book'

Irish Independent

€13.99 | ISBN 978–0–9545335–5–7

Available from all good bookshops and from www.LibertiesPress.com

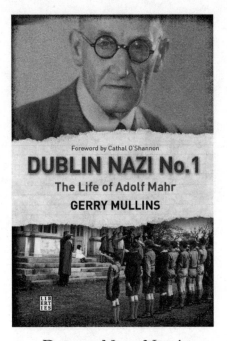

DUBLIN NAZI NO. 1

THE LIFE OF ADOLF MAHR

GERRY MULLINS

'Gerry Mullins is admirably even handed through this fascinating biography of Mahr'

The Dubliner Magazine

'an edifying, wholly absorbing account which traces the tragic consequences when unquestioning patriotism surmounts reality'

Metro

'Intriguing'

Sunday Tribune

Hardback €25 | ISBN 978–1–905483–19–8
Paperback €16.99 | ISBN 978–1–905483–20–4

Available from all good bookshops and from www.LibertiesPress.com

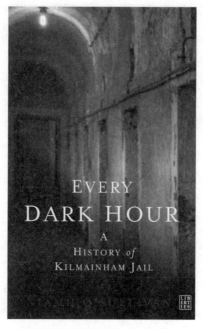

EVERY DARK HOUR

A HISTORY OF KILMAINHAM JAIL

NIAMH O'SULLIVAN

'O'Sullivan writes with enthusiasm and commitment in telling the story of the prison from its early days to its restoration as a museum'

Books Ireland

'recommended'

Irish Times

€14.99 | ISBN 978–1–905483–21–1

Available from all good bookshops and from www.LibertiesPress.com

DUBLIN 1660–1860

THE SHAPING OF A CITY

MAURICE CRAIG

'rightly regarded as a classic . . . a most readable and entertaining political and social account of the city's growth . . . obligatory – and pleasurable – reading for anyone who wants to know Dublin'

Books Ireland

'As a readable and scholarly summary and a sensitive commentary upon "buildings and other artefacts" the book is without rival in its subject'

Times Literary Supplement

'A pleasure to read'

Sunday Tribune

€13.99 | ISBN 978–905483–11–2

Available from all good bookshops and from www.LibertiesPress.com

BOOKS ON POLITICS FROM LIBERTIES PRESS

Causes for Concern

Irish Politics, Culture and Society

Michael D. Higgins

'ultimately, this book provides a timely overview of Ireland's transition to the third millennium'

Irish Book Review

'A fine collection'

Verbal

'a brilliant compilation . . . a wonderful, absorbing book'

Western Writers' Centre website

Hardback €25 | ISBN 978–1–905483–09–9
Paperback €16.99 | ISBN 978–1–905483–29–7

Available from all good bookshops and from www.LibertiesPress.com

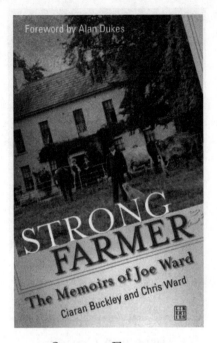

STRONG FARMER

THE MEMOIRS OF JOE WARD

CIARAN BUCKLEY AND CHRIS WARD

€14.99 | ISBN 978–1–905483–24–2

Available from all good bookshops and from www.LibertiesPress.com